ODYSSEY
OF
EXILE

ODYSSEY
OF
EXILE

JEWISH WOMEN
FLEE
THE NAZIS
FOR BRAZIL

EDITED WITH
INTRODUCTIONS BY
KATHERINE MORRIS

WAYNE STATE UNIVERSITY PRESS
DETROIT

Copyright © 1996 by Katherine Morris.
Published by Wayne State University Press,
Detroit, Michigan 48201. All rights are reserved.
"Ostracism and Exile," "Life in Brazil," "One Day in Miami,"
and all photos within these chapters are from
"Escape, Hope, and Disillusionment,"
© 1992 by Renée-Marie Croose Parry. Used with permission.
No part of this book may be reproduced without formal permission.

99 98 97 96   5 4 3 2 1

Library of Congress Cataloging-in-Publication Data
Odyssey of exile : Jewish women flee the Nazis for Brazil / edited
with introductions by Katherine Morris.
p.   cm.
Includes bibliographical references and index.
ISBN 0–8143–2562–9 (alk. paper). — ISBN 0–8143–2563–7 (pbk. : alk. paper)
1. Jews, German—Brazil—Biography. 2. Refugees, Jewish—Brazil—Biography.
3. Jewish women—Brazil—Biography. 4. Germany—Ethnic relations. 5. Jewish
women—Brazil—Social conditions. 6. Holocaust, Jewish (1939–1945)—Personal
narratives. 7. Brazil—Ethnic relations. I. Morris, Katherine, 1950–
F2659.J503   1966   95–39736

Olga Benario's "Letter from Ravensbrück" is from Fernando Morais'
Olga, translated by Ellen Watson, Grove Press, 1990.
Reprinted by permission of Grove/Atlantic, Inc.
and Peter Halban Publishers.

For my parents,
Vesta
and
Kenton Morris

CONTENTS

■

CONTENTS

ACKNOWLEDGMENTS

Odyssey of Exile: Jewish Women Flee the Nazis for Brazil was made possible by research grants from the Social Science Research Council, the Leo Baeck Institute, the German Academic Exchange Service (*Deutscher Akademischer Austauschdienst*), the Memorial Foundation for Jewish Culture, and the University of North Carolina at Greensboro. I would also like to thank the *Instituto Cultural Judaico Marc Chagall* in Porto Alegre, Brazil, for their warm collegial guidance and support, especially Sandra Lemchen Moscovich and Marlene Kulkes.

I had the good fortune to meet many extraordinary women in Brazil and in the United States who contributed to this volume: Käte Kaphan, Hertha Spier, Eva Hirschberg, Trudi Landau, Alice Brill Czapski, Renée-Marie Croose Parry, and Annelise Strauss. Especially hospitable in São Paulo were Eva Reichmann, Trudi and Jean Landau, Eva Hirschberg, and Bella Herson and her daughter; in Rolândia, Mathilde Maier, Nikolaus Schauff, Inge Rosenthal, and Käte Kaphan; in Rio de Janeiro, Elisabeth Eckardt and her family; and in Terra Nova, Dorothea Wiedemann.

Rabbi Alejandro Lilienthal, Rabbi Henry Sobel, and the late Rabbi Fritz Pinkuss welcomed me with their congenial hospitality in Porto Alegre and São Paulo.

A special note of thanks is due to Andreas Lixl-Purcell for his advice and enthusiasm. I would like to thank Karl Schleunes for his encouragement and the many letters written on my behalf. Kenneth and Renée-Marie Croose Parry enlightened me with their constructive comments and insightful suggestions, particularly at the final stages of the project. Andrew Bulgin provided good humor and invaluable assistance, and I am indebted to Matthew Kaplan for three of the translations.

INTRODUCTION
—■—

Why a book about German-Jewish women who fled to Brazil to escape Nazi persecution? Although the experiences of those émigrés who sought refuge in North America are well documented, and though much has been written about politicians, scientists, and writers who lived in exile, little has been published about less prominent refugees. More specifically, few books have described the private experiences of women, how they coped with the difficulties of exile, and how they rebuilt their lives.

I wanted to investigate how women fared in a third-world country, an "exotic" land, and probably not their first choice for a new home. Life in Brazil in the 1930s and 1940s, with its patriarchal culture, its unstable economy, and its tropical climate, could be described as an adventure, at best. The ability to make the most of setbacks and tragedies was the outstanding characteristic of women immigrants to Brazil. It was necessary for their survival. The contributors of this book were educated women from the German and Polish middle class who had enjoyed certain privileges and freedoms before the Nazis came to power. They escaped to save their lives, and confronted the challenges of a different culture and language.

European women in Brazil faced problems that were exacerbated by social and political factors, in particular by the all-pervasive sexism. The unique political climate in Brazil created difficulties that would not have existed in countries such as the United States or Canada. Exile in Brazil was highly dangerous for women like Olga Benario, the Communist activist who was killed in a concentration camp after being forcibly deported to Nazi Germany by the Vargas dictatorship.[1]

Why is the public so fascinated with war memoirs fifty years after the event? And, more to the point, why is there such interest in the war from a *woman's point of view?* Wartime experiences highlight the qualities of personal sacrifice and communal effort that have grown rare in today's society. As we question the history written by men about men, there is a great need to complete the picture by exploring the experiences of women.

This collection offers a rare glimpse into the personal histories of some women refugees who lived through this cruel era. The authors include in their recollections the small and seemingly unimportant details of daily life—rendering their narratives more universal, and more memorable. Although women have always held a significant place in the history of German Jewry, their contributions, until recently, lacked recognition.[2] Many cultural historians are now focusing on gender in literature and history, and on how extraordinary events affected ordinary people. The devastation of World War II shaped the lives of all who suffered under Hitler's

World-wide reception of German Jewish refugees, 1933–38, from *Atlas of the Holocaust.* Courtesy of Martin Gilbert.

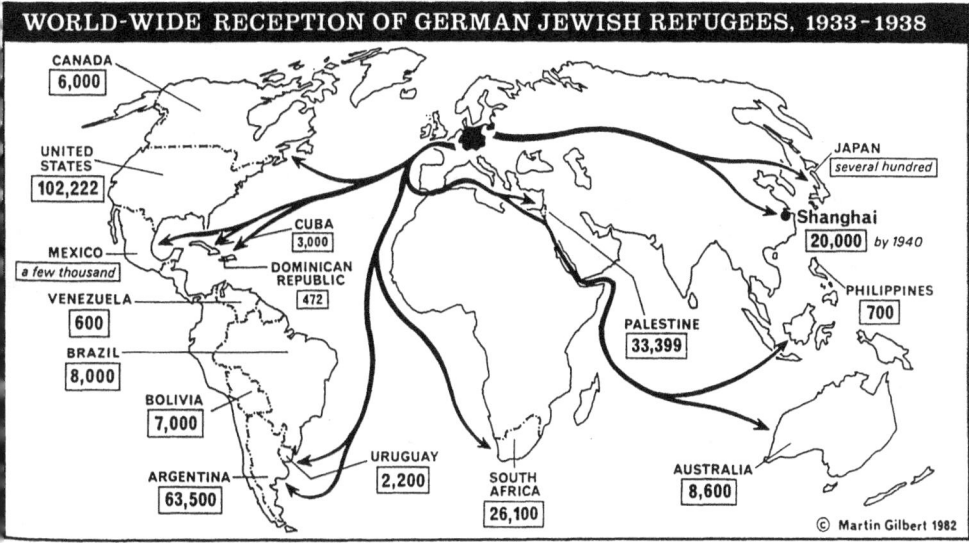

WORLD-WIDE RECEPTION OF GERMAN JEWISH REFUGEES, 1933-1938

persecution, but men and women were not affected in the same way. Women's experience of culture is different—and radical historical change tends to dramatize this disparity.

Recent theory on autobiography analyzes the unique way women write about their lives. Some critical frameworks are useful in examining particular aspects of autobiography, such as identity, experience, and textuality.[3] For example, how does the author express her identity, how is she related to the others in her text, and how does she distinguish herself from them? Usually writers define themselves in relation to other family members, (whether they are parents, siblings, or spouses). For Alice Brill Czapski, an adolescent at the time of emigration, her mother becomes crucial to her fate. Annelise Strauss has strong emotional bonds to her surrogate family in the United States. Usually there is more than one "self"—the author and the protagonist: the adult author writes of the girl or younger woman who experienced the Third Reich.

Do these writers view themselves as exemplary individuals or as average women? Unlike the more traditional autobiographies that usually focus on famous men, these autobiographies do not boast authority. Most women understate their actions and reactions to political circumstances beyond their control—they see themselves as citizens and victims. Although they consider themselves typical, they realize that their experiences are unique. This paradox of seeing their lives as both singular and representative, or this need to distinguish themselves from others while simultaneously identifying with them, "is the most pervasive characteristic of female autobiography."[4] The fascinating portrayals of National Socialist Germany and emigration stem from this inner conflict—of feeling needed and being ostracized. Circumstances forced them to abandon a familiar, more predictable existence, and face the unknown.

The past is a collection of experiences, and in order to write about their lives these women chose pivotal events that shaped their destiny. The selective nature of memory influences how these authors view their past in the present. In other words, their experiences have become their manuscript through a process of selection and omission. Their lives have become art. The craft of writing approximates but never fully recaptures the past. Autobiography has been called "an interpretation of life that invests the past and the 'self' with coherence and meaning that may not have been evident before the act of writing itself."[5]

Women shape their past by articulating their experiences, thus preserving the meaning of what they endured. This is more evident with formal autobiographies such as Renée-Marie Croose Parry's, who is at present still working on the story of her life. In her contributions, we see the author articulating the meaning of her past through sensitive analysis and description, and by omission and juxtaposition. Her young self is defined through the erudition and commentary of the mature woman. In describing her youth in Nazi Germany and in exile, she notes: "I was living primordially, with my five senses."[6]

The women in this anthology provide multiple perspectives, creating a mosaic composed of four distinct categories: persecution and exile, the concentration camps, transfer to Brazil, and restitution. What is unique about the way these women write? It is their individual portrayal of an often unthinkable existence in the 1930s and 1940s. They use the genre of autobiography, although not all did so consciously when recording their experiences. For example, Käte Kaphan tells the story of her young daughter who was in school during the Third Reich; Eva Hirschberg relates how she succeeded in freeing her husband from the concentration camp of Sachsenhausen; while Hertha Spier condenses the six years endured in Hitler's death camps into just a few pages. In the act of writing they have created poignant narratives that provide new visions of women's lives when cast into extraordinary circumstances—and not what women's lives "should be."[7] Indeed, the memoirs reveal no conventional romantic plot, nor do the authors refrain from expressing their anger or powerlessness.

Some of the women wrote their autobiographies for their children. They wanted to preserve their family histories, especially since many of their loved ones were killed during the war. In describing their experiences they structure and give deeper meaning to the past.

Alice Brill Czapski chose to write her narrative from the perspective of two personas: that of a mature woman, and that of a young girl. Though she composed her memoir in 1991, she also quoted from a diary that she had written in 1933. Annelise Strauss wrote about her experience as a mature woman, describing events in her youth that were to shape her entire life. Strauss was one of the many women who came to Brazil while the government was still encouraging immigration. She recalls talking to Oswaldo Aranha, the Brazilian ambassador to the United States, in Washington D.C.

in 1937: "I felt greatly encouraged when he said how welcome immigrants were, especially those of different educational and cultural backgrounds who had knowledge of several foreign languages."[8]

Sometimes autobiographies become idealizations. If the author wants to emphasize a family's success, taboo subjects are often not mentioned. For example, most women are reluctant to discuss unwanted pregnancies and abortions with other family members. These are personal tribulations they do not want future generations to remember.

What about the role of women in the emigration? The authors in this anthology were able to cope with horrific circumstances, partly because of the gender-related skills they had learned while growing up. Foreign languages, sewing, cooking, and household management proved very useful to them. In some of the autobiographies, comparisons between the male and female family members are notable. The story of Marthe and Alice Brill contrasts with that of Erich Brill, husband and father.

This book is not a study of feminine aesthetics nor of autobiographical theory. Rather, it is an anthology of women's autobiographies. I have attempted to provide these personal histories with a critical and historical framework, in that I focus on *identity* of German-Jewish women in the Third Reich, on their experiences in the context of World War II and its aftermath, and on the genre in which they chose to tell their stories. The memoirs in this collection are a particularly rich source of cultural history, in that these women write with considerable candor about public humiliation as it affected their private lives.

Jews in Germany faced an uncertain and threatening future after 1933, and their situation continued to deteriorate as the regime took hold. A dramatic example of the oppression of German-Jewish women was the sexual abuse in concentration camps. Although personnel treated Jews inhumanely regardless of gender, women suffered specific brutality. Hertha Spier describes the sexual sadism of Amon Goeth at Plaszow: "The roll calls continued. Commandant Goeth often selected the prettiest girls from the fifth row for the white house. After he abused them, he killed them so no one would find out."[9]

We learn that Hertha Spier is the only person of a family of seven to stay alive. Whether or not victims survived in concentration camps was often quite arbitrary. However, studies indicate that some survival strategies were gender related.[10] For example, memoirs and medical reports suggest that women tolerated hunger and endured starvation better than men. This has been attributed to their ability to share sparse provisions. Hertha Spier mentions how she and her sister Gisi could make their bread last the entire day.

Another sphere in which women reacted differently from men was their bonding with one another. Spier describes how the women standing at the role call (*Appell*) in Auschwitz would remain close to each other to stay warm until the *Sturmführer* arrived. They would also change places so the same woman would not have to stand at the end of the row in freezing weather. Hertha Spier writes about herself as well as the other victims, and we learn what happened to thousands through the testimony of one.

Eva Hirschberg's husband was arrested and sent to Sachsenhausen immediately after the *Kristallnacht*. Extreme situations such as this forced her, and others like her, to act. She survived by doing things she would not have done under normal circumstances. "Before this, I would never have thought that I was capable of negotiating independently with bankers and of visiting revenue offices and police stations."[11] She explains how important her relationships with other women became, how they worked together after their husbands' internment, and how she converted her apartment into an office to aid other Jewish women applying for emigration.

Being a Jew in the thirties grew more and more dangerous because of the propaganda campaign—as in *Der Stürmer*—that spread the most vicious anti-Semitism and depicted Jews as caricatures. The social pressure for women to appear attractive was strong at the time and, for cosmetic reasons, Trudi Landau underwent plastic surgery in Cologne. Her sense of identity was influenced by Nazi propaganda; she wanted to change the shape of her nose. "At any rate, my immediate concern was to have my Jewish nose 'aryanized.' Such a transformation would allow me to overcome all apprehension."[12] Of course, plastic surgery then was not as popular or as sophisticated as it is today. The ideals of female beauty influenced her decision. Nevertheless, surgery to eliminate a feature that was characteristic of an ethnic stereotype probably saved her life.

I have never met another person who had the same experience, that is, who had plastic surgery in Nazi Germany in order to stay alive. I'm sure that I wouldn't have survived the war without having had the operation, because before this everyone could see that I was Jewish. After the

15

operation, not only did I look different, but I also had a different outlook on life.[13]

Ilza Czapska recounts her family's odyssey in Poland during the
chaos of war. Because Ilza had three children at the time, she often

Poland under German occupation. From *The Destruction
of the European Jews* by Raul Hilberg, 3 vols. New York:
Holmes and Meier Publishers, Inc., 1985. © 1985 by
Raul Hilberg. Reprinted by permission of the publisher.

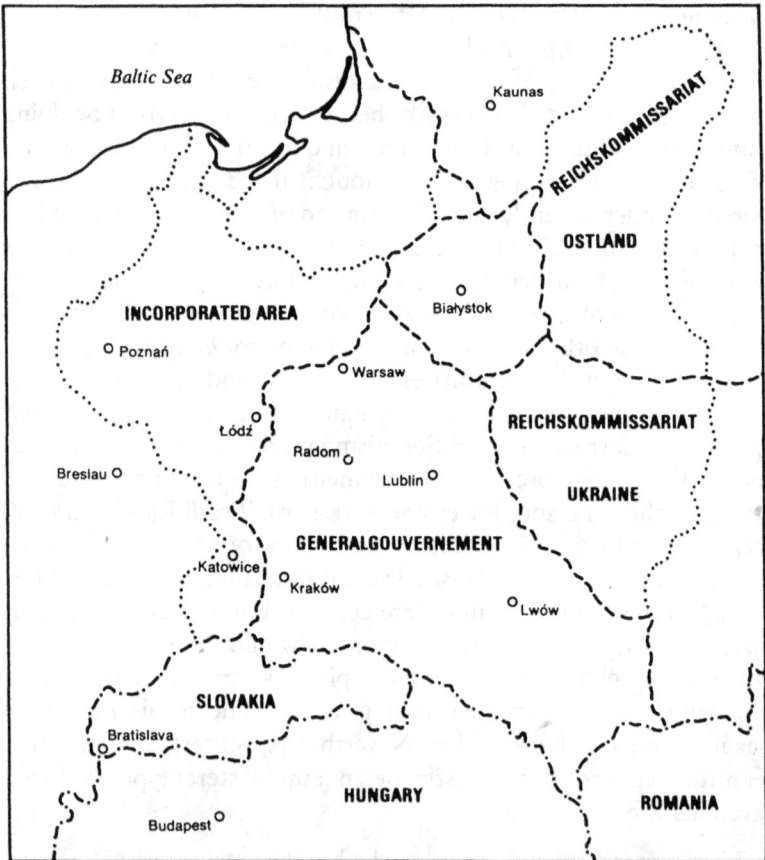

includes their points of view, giving her story a broader context. We see the war through the eyes of a mother, who is intent on saving her family. For example, when the German civil administration confiscates the family property in Poznan and orders them to leave, she confesses: "It was a good thing for me that I had to worry about the children, especially Janek who was then three, so that I had no time to engage in morbid thoughts."[14] Like other authors in this book, Czapska's autobiography was written to keep the history of her family alive, and as a gift to her children and grandchildren.

Käte Kaphan also explores a child's world in the story of the little Jewish girl, and Alice Brill Czapski reveals the intimate thoughts of a young girl when she quotes from her diary of the 1930s. This inclusion of a child's perspective—the recreation of the child's *Weltanschauung*—enriches the memoirs and gives us a deeper insight into the trauma of displacement.

Alice Brill Czapski now lives in São Paulo. Her narrative, "Memories from 1933–1945," reveals the endless hardship that she and her mother endured. Not only do we learn about a child's life in exile but also about the problems and challenges her mother faced as secretary for the newly founded Relief Committee for Jewish Immigrants in São Paulo. Her mother's work involved finding shelter and jobs for those who had left Germany almost penniless. As a refugee, she felt deep sympathy for the plight of these people, and knew that they had to adapt to the new conditions in order to survive.

Renée-Marie Croose Parry vividly describes what life was like for a girl in Nazi Germany, and as a woman in Brazil. The focus of her memoir is the young Renée-Marie, although the understanding of the mature author permeates the narrative.

> Up to my twentieth year, all I could do was to think out how to win through the morrow, to stave off disharmony, to do the right thing under observing, critical, or even hostile eyes; to please, and always make the correct impression. I was, in fact, not living my own life—life was living me."[15]

In Brazil, she is overwhelmed by the exotic Rio de Janeiro of the 1940s. The scents, sights, and sounds are a world apart from those of Nazi Germany. Working in a third-world country introduces her to the inequities of gender and class. Writing today, she often refers to her young self as another person with a different view of the world. By meeting both wealthy and indigent women, she learns the limitations of gender.

Dramatic examples of political and social inequity in her new country are borne in on her as a result of her arrest during the carnival of March 1943. She spends a total of two and a half months in various prisons in and around Rio de Janeiro, and is never told why she is being detained. Her incarcerations in the Police for Foreigners, the *detenção* at the Central Police, the eighteenth-century Casa de Correção, the women's prison of Bangú, and again at the

Brazil, © 1995 by Katherine Morris.

detenção reveal to her the fundamental injustice and arbitrariness of dictatorships. She meets and cohabits with political prisoners, with wives who killed their husbands, with prostitutes and murderers. Although she is thrilled and relieved upon her release, and her life in Rio returns more or less to normal, she realizes that she will not want to stay in Brazil forever.

After almost four and a half years in Brazil, she becomes aware that despite her imprisonment and the painful separation from her parents, exile has provided her with invaluable experiences. Having mastered two additional languages and met innumerable people from different countries and classes, she has grown more self-sufficient. She has also learned that injustice is not limited to Nazi Germany, and that in many countries in the world, including Brazil, there is a disparity between the way things are and the way they should be.

> My departure from Rio caused me no regrets; neither did I feel bitterness. . . . I would certainly not miss the macho double standard; the disdain for working women that classed them unfit for admission to "society"; nor the constant and painful irritation about my own impotence vis-à-vis the obscene disparity between the rich and the poor, and the deplorable role of the Catholic Church, then standing silent, if not colluding in the persecution of those involved with progressive initiatives.[16]

Hilde Wiedemann was also entangled in Brazilian politics before and during World War II. She describes what it was like to be a German citizen in Brazil after the country decided to support the Allied cause. Unlike Renée-Marie Croose Parry, who had immigrated to Brazil as the pro forma wife of a Brazilian in 1942, Wiedemann had immigrated to Brazil with her family as early as 1933. They started a new life on a farm in Paraná, working on the land. Having lived in many different urban and rural settings, Hilde became witness to the tumultuous social changes taking place in Latin America's largest country in the 1940s.

Wiedemann's autobiography begins in Germany with the story of her parents and grandparents. As in other memoirs, we learn about her explicit character as a young woman in the 1930s and 1940s and her implicit character as a mature woman in 1966. She begins with the familiar: "The writing room is small, the desk fits into the corner to the right of the window. . . . I open the filing cabinet and carefully place some family documents on the table."[17]

Käte Kaphan tells a different story. She emigrated from Nazi Germany in 1936, and arrived in the port of Santos with her husband and their three children. After a brief stay in São Paulo, they traveled on a night train to the lush and wild interior. While still in Germany, the Kaphans had purchased land from a large English landholder, the Paraná Plantation Company Limited of London.

The area around Rolândia in northern Paraná became a refuge for German Jews escaping the Nazi regime in the 1930s.[18] Most of the settlers had been professionals, and came from cities such as Berlin, Frankfurt, and Hamburg. The verdant jungle in Brazil contrasted sharply with the art galleries and opera houses they had enjoyed at home. Käte Kaphan conveys her first impressions of the country, and explains why growing coffee was such a gamble. She recorded her remembrances in her essay "Immigration into the Brazilian Jungle" in 1956, twenty years after the events took place.

The restitution (*Wiedergutmachung*) is seldom referred to in personal histories. Trudi Landau describes how she applied for such reparations, how long it took, and how difficult it was for her and her mother to file these claims for their possessions seized by the Nazis. After the state of Israel was formed, reparations from Germany became a divisive issue for many Jews. Many survivors suspected that Germany did not really wish to atone for the past, and that reparations were but part of Germany's political stratagem to be accepted by the international community after World War II. Those who favored indemnification, particularly Israel's Premier David Ben-Gurion, argued that the Allied powers were not going to defend the interests of the Jews or Israel, and that vast sums were needed for reconstruction and rehabilitation.[19] War restitution has been included in this volume because it was an aspect of postwar life that, although rarely mentioned, affected the rehabilitation of victims.

While this anthology tells us much about the profound dilemmas suffered by Jews during the Nazi period, more important is what these memoirs disclose about the women themselves. Although autobiography involves retelling the past, the women are implicitly describing their present condition.[20] Many of the authors are *explicit* about the *act* of writing. Wiedemann begins her memoir by describing the room in which she writes, and later interrupts her narrative to discuss *why* she is telling the story. "This is just a small part of Salvador. I should write about its academic life, its artists, its modern architecture, its industry, . . . and about much more. But then I would never have a chance to discuss our life in Recife, where we lived for more than 20 years."[21] Alice Brill Czapski looks back with the help of papers she had composed as a girl. "My diary of those days was still written in Gothic letters. . . . It is an accurate account of every day life on ship and of all places we visited: Madeira, Tenerife, Tétouan, Ceuta, Casablanca and the Spanish coast from Malaga to Barcelona, from where we crossed by boat to Majorca."[22] Ilza Czapska states in 1978: "I want to write down my memories for all of my children, and not in a broad outline, but in detail, with all of the small and unimportant events that have stayed in my memory that were typical for the children and for the atmosphere that we lived in at the time."[23]

The narratives force the reader to think of such autobiographies in a new way—both formally and conceptually. For the women in this book, as well as countless others trapped in World War II, the personal became the political. The authors paint an objective picture of their culture, but at the same time tell a subjective story of their lives as émigrés.

To live in exile was to be uprooted. Displacement forced women out of their domestic life into a transitional mode of existence. The memoirs reflect a desire to explain the inexplicable, and force us to think of broader issues such as women's marginality and the body politic. Although history is their backdrop, what compelled the authors to express themselves was the need to record their personal stories. These intelligent and sensitive women offer unique insights into the female experience of war, persecution, and exile. Often there is a frank confession of a life not so predictable, and a marriage not so perfect. Finally, these autobiographies help shape the future of women's history, and of Jewish, and German history. Such incorporation into the human record not only redeems the marginality of these women refugees, but confers a special meaning upon their lives.

Editor's Note: The editing of the women's texts was, whenever possible, kept to a minimum, in order not to impinge on the authenticity of the original manuscripts. All translations were made from the German originals.

PART 1

PERSECUTION
AND
EXILE

TRUDI LANDAU

Trudi Landau (née Trude Joseph) was born in Cologne on May 2, 1920. She conveys how her experience shaped her identity, and how the pain of the dichotomy of being German and Jewish intensified as anti-Jewish sentiment grew stronger in the 1930s. Hitler's Germany fomented racial hatred in many ways, and one of the most effective was through the sophisticated use of propaganda. The various representations of the "stereotypical Jew" affected how the author viewed herself and compelled her to seek plastic surgery.

Although Jews were central to the Nazi world view, anti-Semitism was not Hitler's invention—it had its roots in earlier times. Martin Luther, the father of the Protestant Reformation, portrayed Jews as bloodthirsty and evil. He also referred to them as "plague" or "pestilence."[1] This comparison of Jews with vermin continued in the nineteenth century. The Reichstag of 1895 had an anti-Semitic faction that promoted a measure to exclude foreign Jews, whom the speaker, Ahlwardt, referred to as "cholera germs."[2] Ahlwardt also made it clear that the anti-Semites opposed the Jews not because of their religion, but because of their race.[3]

The eighteenth and nineteenth centuries brought some legislation in favor of the Jews—they were emancipated in 1781, and in 1871 the constitution of the German Reich declared their equal status before the law—however, in Imperial Germany anti-Semitism was evident in the army, in the schools, and in the universities.

Why a nation such as Germany tried to destroy its Jewish citizens is a question that will never be answered satisfactorily. Anti-

24

Jewish racism goes as far back as the seventeenth century, when caricatures of Jews appeared in cartoons. However, the "theoretical" basis of racism appeared in the nineteenth century.[4] The phrase, *Die Juden sind unser Unglück* [the Jews are our misfortune], was coined by the Wilhelminian historian Heinrich von Treitschke in Berlin. His historical treatise *German History in the Nineteenth Century* was overflowing with anti-Jewish rhetoric: he described Jews as dangerous to Germany's culture and economy. More importantly, his position as an influential historian made anti-Semitism more respectable.[5]

Treitschke was not the only critic of the era. Others, such as Chamberlain, Stoecker, Duehring, and Marr criticized the spiritual emptiness of German society and blamed the Jews for this state of affairs.[6] After the National Socialists came to power, racial anti-Semitism became part of government policy, and Jews were increasingly persecuted. They were no longer protected under the law—they had become second-class citizens.[7]

In 1927, young Trude moved with her mother and father to Opladen and stayed there until the end of 1938. For many years, her parents did not think of leaving the town where they were esteemed members of the community and where anti-Semitism was not especially prevalent. However, actions against the Jews, such as the Nazi boycotts, affected the family business, and the Josephs were eventually forced to leave.

The Nazi Party initially organized the national boycott against Jewish-owned businesses on March 29, 1933. Julius Streicher chaired the boycott committee that included such members as Heinrich Himmler. On April 1, SA and SS guards stood vigil in front of certain businesses to "inform" customers that the owners were Jewish. One of the reasons for the campaign was to "persuade" doubting members of the bureaucracy of the supposed popular hostility against the Jews, as well as to pressure Jewish merchants to sell their businesses to non-Jews.[8] It did not produce the desired effect instantaneously.

The boycott demonstrated how important Jewish business was to the German economy. Hitler called it off after twenty-four hours.[9] Although the immediate consequences were negligible in economic terms, the boycott increased the pressure on Jewish merchants to sell out. Eventually in the mid-1930s, many Jews sold their businesses because of the control of supplies, the psychological effect of the boycott, and general apprehension about the future. A special market emerged for the selling of these *Objekte,* or objects, as Jewish businesses came to be called.[10] The boycott of 1933, although not successful for the Nazi party at the time, was one of the many manifestations of anti-Semitic government policy, and an ominous sign of things to come.

After the *Kristallnacht* of 1938, Hitler's attacks against the Jews could no longer be seen as random or unplanned. The Nazi dictatorship gradually took away the rights of its Jewish citizens. Two striking examples of persecution were the *J* stamped on Jewish passports and the yellow Star of David Jews were required to wear.

> I know and have lived the life of a Jew in Hitler's Germany. I still have my passport #3917 delivered by the German Embassy in Brussels, Belgium, on December 2, 1939. It had a red *J* for Jew on the first page. My maiden name was lengthened compulsorily with the biblical name "Sara." Every Jewish woman was obliged to use this name as a matter of insult from the Nazi point of view, just as every Jewish man was obliged to use the name "Israel." I was no longer living in Germany when Jews were required to wear the yellow star on their chest for immediate identification. In France, from 1943 on, I had been living under a false name provided by *la Résistance.*[11]

In 1939, Trude fled Germany with her father and escaped to Brussels, where the Belgian Jewish Committee provided them a monthly sum to buy food and live in a rented room. Trude's mother had already fled to Palestine in November 1938 on a tourist visa, and it was decided that her husband would join her there. However, their plans were changed when the Germans invaded Belgium in May of 1940. The young Trude returned home one day to find a message from her father lying on the table, that he had been incarcerated as a civilian prisoner of war. He signed the note: "Bleibe brav. Dein Vater" [Be good. Your father].

Albert Joseph was taken to France with other German civilian prisoners and held in a camp near Elne (St. Cyprien) in the south. Trude visited him there after she was released from Gurs in August 1940. In the same year, he was moved from St. Cyprien to Récébédou, near Toulouse, and subsequently to Drancy/Paris, from whence he was deported and sent to the concentration camp of Majdanek near Lublin in March 1943.[12]

Trude lived in exile in Belgium and France until the end of the war. In November 1945, she and her husband Jean embarked for Brazil and arrived in São Paulo on January 1, 1946. She was reunited with her mother in São Paulo in 1949 at the age of twenty-nine.

Trudi Landau's early experience as a political refugee sensitized her to the plight of others, and in São Paulo at the age of fifty-five she began to write for various Jewish newspapers. Gradually she became involved in the case of Vlado Herzog, a Jewish journalist who was tortured and killed by the Brazilian dictatorship.[13] She now resides in São Paulo with her husband.

CHILDHOOD IN GERMANY

BY TRUDI LANDAU

Today it may sound incredible, but until after the war I had never thought of myself as being a citizen of any nation other than Germany. I knew, of course, that my family and most of my parents' friends were Jewish, but Judaism was simply a religion to me, like Catholicism and Protestantism. At that time I had never met a member of any other religious sect such as a Buddhist, a Moslem or a Taoist, let alone a member of any unusual faith such as animism. In Christian surroundings, everyone who was not baptized was considered a pagan and would go to hell if he died without having been baptized, so we collected money at school for Catholic missions in Africa to save those little kids for Christianity and for paradise.

The three principle religious denominations in Cologne were Catholicism, Protestantism, and Judaism, with their corresponding cemeteries, churches, synagogues, and schools. I finished my first year in grade school there and then, in 1927, moved to Opladen. I was seven when I moved with my family to this small town of 18,000 inhabitants, 18 kilometers from Cologne. My parents opened a men's clothing store (*Herrenkonfektion*) in Opladen. Only a few Jewish families lived there, maybe a dozen, perhaps less. I was sent to the *Marienschule*, a school run by Catholic nuns (because there was no Jewish school), and I stayed in the Catholic school for ten years and completed what was called *das Einjährige*. Had life continued in a normal fashion, I would have finished my *Abitur* in three years and thereafter would have been ready to enter the university, but it was already 1936 and our future was uncertain. Also the business (which had been expanded to sell women's clothing) was not going well because of Nazi boycotts, and my parents couldn't afford my tuition. So I switched over to a one-year course at a commercial school where I learned bookkeeping, shorthand, and typing.

The notion that we Jews were not German was even more ridiculous in my case, because I was the best pupil in my German class. My papers were always read to the class as examples of good prose. My talent for writing was already apparent at that time, but I did not recognize it. I practiced only when I wrote thousands of letters to friends and relatives scattered all over the world.

Later on, in Brazil, I heard the reproach that the German Jews had been "Germans" first and Jews second, and therefore "it served them right when they were told they were not Germans." But who could we have been otherwise? My father had fought for Kaiser and fatherland during World War I. He had been wounded on the front and had been given the Iron Cross for bravery. Unfortunately, he even acquired malaria in the fields, from which he suffered recurrent attacks of fever, headaches, and chills about once a month.

My grandparents and great-grandparents many generations back had been born in a place called Nettesheim. Also, my mother's family, the Stiels of the city of Eschweiler, had lived in the Rhineland for centuries. I learned this on my sixtieth birthday, when the daughter of Willy Stiel, Chava Efrat of Tel-Aviv, told me that the family was of Sephardic origin and had left Spain around 1500 trying to escape the Inquisition. Our ancestors were Jews who had settled in France and Germany. When I was a youngster, of course, I had never heard of Ashkenazic or Sephardic Jews and never thought about our heritage, so how could I have imagined myself a citizen of any other nation but Germany?

Everything I knew was from German books: my outlook on life, my education, my concept of ethics, honesty and honor were all German. I think I am very German even now, although I became a Brazilian citizen in 1951, and I am still Jewish above all.

As a child I used to sing: "Deutschland, Deutschland über alles" with all my heart, but today I no longer feel anything for Germany, even though I have a few German friends in Brazil and in Germany. Like everyone else, I remember numbers and count in the language I learned first, which was German. When I still believed in God, I prayed in German. Even when I saw my dead son lying on his bed, my first thought was in German: "Nun hat er endlich Ruhe." (Now he is finally at peace.) I know that if I should live to an old age like my mother and should lose my short-term memory, I will only remember the German language.

Passport photo of Trudi Landau, 1945.
Courtesy of Trudi Landau.

I was not curious about my heritage and knew nothing of Jewish history, maybe because the religious instruction I had was minimal. I took a streetcar once a week to Wiesdorf, where a Jewish teacher taught the children in the area. We learned Hebrew and studied the Bible, but whenever I could I didn't attend, pretending to have a headache or using bad weather as an excuse. Anyway, the lessons had a strictly religious outlook, not a philosophical one. The Old Testament was something very ancient, and at that time I did not know that it was also the history of the Jewish people.

Other factors encouraged me to avoid accepting my Jewish identity. In front of our house on the Menschendahlerstra*β*e was a small square where a wooden crucifix stood. One day I was playing with one of the children and he told me, either innocently or by parental suggestion, that the Jews nailed "our Savior" to the cross. That was in 1930 when I was ten years old, before the Nazi regime came to power. But I never forgot it and probably assumed part of the shame for such a vile act. I never asked anyone about it, including my parents. Of course, I wasn't familiar with the New Testament because I had never attended a Christian service.

Maybe I was sorry because I wasn't like everyone else and didn't celebrate the same holidays. The other children took part in two or three processions a year on *Maria Himmelfahrt* and

Fronleichnam dressed as little angels with wings and flower tiaras in their hair. I could only observe. I had a Protestant friend by the name of Ilse Tillmann who invited me to her home frequently and especially at Christmas time. I saw the tree decorated with candles and ornaments and ate sweets and nuts.

I felt better on secular holidays when we chanted patriotic songs. I sang the German national anthem (*Deutschland, Deutschland über alles*) with all my heart, because Germany was my beloved fatherland.

One must understand that our position was completely different from that of the Jews in Poland, Russia, Rumania or even of American Jews who had escaped Eastern Europe. These Jews had lived in more or less closed communities, were somewhat more religious, and their culture revolved around the Yiddish language. They also had their own cuisine and their own music. So, of course, they represented a nation within another nation. Yiddish was unknown to us, and I didn't know that it even existed. When I first heard it many years later, I thought it was a badly pronounced German as is sometimes spoken by foreigners.

After the war I also heard the reproach that German Jews considered themselves superior to Polish Jews. That might have been true of the adults at the time (I was only a teenager), but this feeling would be analogous to an educated person feeling superior relative to someone who is uneducated. This is a social judgment. It always disgusts a person who has good table manners to see someone with poor etiquette; such a response is not conscious but instinctive. I first met Polish Jews after the war in Brazil, and I think it is unfair to stigmatize German Jews as "high-nosed" and preponderant. They were proud of being honest, well-bred, and straight forward, and they loved their country.

The fact that Hitler took away their nationality, their possessions, their freedom and their life could not have retroactively taught them a lesson they should have known beforehand. Without the Nazis, the German Jews would have continued to be who they were and what they were, and would have continued to contribute their best to all sections of public and private enterprise. They would never have thought of leaving the country or hating their compatriots. It was one thing to be German by nationality, but it was quite another to be Jewish by religion. Under normal circumstances, there were no restrictions imposed upon them. They could travel and work, and those few who were Zionists at that time could go to Palestine.

After I escaped being killed by the Nazis, unlike my father and twelve other relatives who died in camps like Auschwitz, Sobibor, and Theresienstadt (one cousin survived Auschwitz and lives today in Amsterdam), I have not to this day been able to listen to the German national anthem, even though the first verse is no longer sung. They sing the last one, I think, which goes: "Einigkeit und Recht und Freiheit, für das Deutsche Vaterland." Whenever it is played on television during soccer games, I have to leave the room. It makes me feel like crying when I remember all the harm they did to us. I have no sense of belonging there anymore, nor do I like to be classified as German. They killed every feeling of that kind in me. I do not go to the extreme of not speaking German or boycotting German products, as many of us did in the first years after the war. I remember when the first Volkswagen was manufactured in Brazil, many Jews would not hear of buying one and were even outraged when they heard of someone who had. I have been driving my 1971 Volkswagen for nearly twenty years now. They are no longer manufactured.

The concept of being Jewish by race was perfected by Hitler. Before him, most anti-Semitic hostilities had been based on religion. The Jew who was baptized to become Christian was no longer a Jew. But during the Third Reich, religion as a whole was of no importance any more. Hitler established new values, the Jews being on the lowest end of the scale. When he spoke of the French, he always used the phrase, "the decadent French." When he spoke of the Russians, he used the phrase, "the Russian subhumans." With repetition, this gradually became interpreted as eternal truth. Furthermore, the Jews were to be blamed for all the misery and all the wrongs that had been perpetrated. If one reads the literature about it today, one can only smile bitterly, because the intelligent nation of Germany believed it at the time. All art, music, painting, or drama produced by Jews was *fremd*, or alien. Sigmund Freud's theories were despicable and diabolic. Books by Jewish authors were burnt and their publication prohibited. The phrase, *Die Juden sind unser Unglück* (The Jews are our misfortune), was coined and printed and repeated in newspapers and speeches without really explaining who, when, where, or why. It was just published and accepted.[1]

Trudi and Jean Landau, France, 1942.
Courtesy of Trudi Landau.

After the war we were asked why we did not react to all of this from the beginning, and why we did nothing to defend ourselves. How can one fight against lies and absurdities believed by a whole nation? The only escape was to leave Germany, and many Jews did. They went to every conceivable place, wherever they had a relative or wherever they could acquire a visa. America had then, as it has today, a quota system, and I was on a waiting list for several years to immigrate to the United States, but the war intervened. I had an uncle, mother's brother Jack Stiel, who lived in Los Angeles. I met him and his family in 1954 in Cabazon, California. I also had cousins on my mother's side who would have been able to send me an affidavit, but after the war I had lost their address and did not even remember their names.

For many years my parents did not think of leaving Opladen, where anti-Semitism was not so strong. They were well-loved and esteemed members of the community. Mother participated in the women's bowling league and father participated in carnival festivities. He was a very happy person who told many jokes, and everyone enjoyed his company. The one who suffered most was me, but my parents did not know it. What I went through as a child was published in 1978 in the São Paulo morning paper, *Folha de São Paulo*. After the film *Holocaust* had been aired on television, I was asked to write about my personal experience. The two stories appeared later in my book, *Crônicas do meu tempo*, published in 1981.

THOUGHTS ON JEWISH IDENTITY

My father often called my mother Nas (short for German *Nase*, nose), because one of her most remarkable experiences as a young woman was having plastic surgery on her nose. In 1912 she had her crooked nose remodeled by someone who is today known as the father of plastic surgery. His last name was Joseph, and he was known throughout Germany as *Nasenjoseph*, because of the many nose operations he performed. He was the first one to correct ugly or misshapen noses through a procedure which is still employed today.

My mother was a very emancipated woman by the standards of the day. At the age of twenty-three she went by herself from Eschweiler to Berlin to have plastic surgery performed on her nose, which was unfashionably large. If I remember correctly, it cost her 1000 marks, no small expenditure at the time. Anyway, my mother had a relatively small, common nose after this operation.

Of course, when I was a child, I had never been conscious of what type of nose I had. Only after Hitler had come to power and the Nazis had started the infernal propaganda campaign against the Jews, did I notice that the caricatures pictured Jews with large noses. According to the stereotypes printed in the party newspaper, *Der Stürmer*, my physiognomy was characteristic of a race that was allegedly guilty of all the world's evils.

I started putting my hand over my nose as though I were hiding something shameful, just like people who have no teeth cover their mouths. I only felt at ease at the movies, where it was dark. In 1939 my father and I were living in a rented room in Cologne-Ehrenfeld because we had left our home and most of our possessions in Opladen and were getting ready to leave Germany. There I met a Jewish boy who had had a nose operation and he told me that I could do the same. I will never forget what he said to me: "After you have this operation, you will not only be an intelligent girl but also a pretty one as well." This, of course, meant that he did not consider me pretty. I didn't care about intelligence—beauty was more important. At any rate, my immediate concern was to have my Jewish nose "aryanized." Such a transformation would allow me to overcome all apprehension.

I went to the surgeon whom the boy had mentioned. Dr. Grabowski had a practice in Cologne, and I told him the truth about my problem. He laughed when I described my mother's operation with Dr. Joseph in Berlin, because he had been one of his students. Naturally, I didn't have much money but he made me a special offer. I think he felt sorry for me. I had the operation on August 24, 1939, a day I will never forget. He took before and after photographs of my profile for his archives as well as for comparative purposes.

I didn't tell my father about the operation, because I didn't want to alarm him and didn't want him talking me out of it. So I left him a note, explaining that I was staying with a girlfriend and would call him later in the afternoon. I wasn't afraid of the operation because I thought that getting rid of my large nose would be worth it. I lay down on the operating table, having full confidence in the doctor. I received only local anesthesia and was conscious during the entire procedure.

Dr. Grabowski and his assistants worked on me for quite some time. First, they made an incision on both sides of the inner nostrils. Then they drew the skin up high on the outer nostrils to leave the bone clear. They sawed the piece that had caused my nose to appear crooked, and after that did something on both sides of the bone that made a terrible noise in my head. Then they cut part of the skin to make the nose smaller.

I lay a few hours in bed, and when I was able to get up I called my father and told him what I had done. At first, he didn't understand me. I had cotton in my nose and I sounded as if I had a bad cold. When he finally realized what had happened and where I was, he was speechless. I went home soon after that, but at night I had to use an apparatus that pressed my nose together. Of course, my face was swollen and I had black and blue marks around my eyes, but a week later World War II started and then nobody really cared what I looked like. A few people who saw me noticed that my face looked different but didn't realize why. It only proves that I attached more importance to it than was necessary.

In October my father and I fled to Belgium. After that, people whom I met did not realize that I was a new person. I wasn't conscious of it either, at least until after the war, because for many years I was fleeing from danger. I have never met another person who had the same experience, that is, who had plastic surgery in Nazi Germany in order to stay alive. I'm sure that I wouldn't have survived the war without having had the operation, because before this everyone could see that I was Jewish. After the operation not only did I look different, but I also had a different outlook on life.

It would be science fiction to describe what my life with that nose would have been like in Germany under normal circumstances. I suppose that without Hitler I would have become a writer or a psychologist, or both. These were the things that interested me until the age of nineteen. The young girl with the melancholy face, high forehead, and huge nose was buried on August 24, 1939. I became "frivolous," by the standards of the time—standards that saw the German *Frau* as a woman who did not use lipstick or other artificial things to make her more attractive. She was "clean" and natural, on the outside as well as on the inside. I was a product of the moral principles of the time, the Nazi principles that had accompanied me since 1933. To me there were two kinds of women: wives and whores.

I felt certain that with my new nose and by combing my hair over my forehead, no one would suspect me of being Jewish. I smiled easier because I had rid myself of a heavy burden. My appearance would not put me in immediate danger, because I looked like an average person whom no one would remember after seeing only once.

In a certain way, my new nose changed my behavior and destiny. Maybe I did things the wrong way because I had given up my personality and taken on a fictitious one. Only in 1973, when my only child died and everything seemed to cave in on me, did I start anew. Perhaps I spiritually regained my old nose and returned to myself as nature had made me. I became a conscious Jewish woman and acted as one. Since 1975 I have been fighting anti-Semitism and dictatorship in this country with my typewriter.

ILZA CZAPSKA

Ilza Czapska was born on November 30, 1896 in Schockwitz, Silesia, a region of Poland that was part of Germany in the late nineteenth century. Although Czapska's grandparents were Jewish, both her parents were baptized as Christians when they were children. This particular aspect of her family history became important when the Germans invaded. The Nazis created race laws specifically for Poland that were different from German laws. According to Nazi racial theory, a Jew in Poland was anyone whose father and/or mother had been, or still was, Jewish. Ilza became a Polish citizen through marriage, although never denying her Jewish ancestry. Since her parents were baptized Christians she was not considered Jewish by the Nazis, but a citizen of Poland. However, her mother, Ella Dyrenfurth, was nevertheless classified a Jewess in Germany and killed in Theresienstadt.

Hitler's invasion of Poland in 1939 was traumatic for the Czapski* family. Ilza Czapska combines the personal with the political, weaving intimate family details with problems created by persecution and war. The role of her children was important in that they drew her attention away from the ever present dangers, and forced her to concentrate on the burdens of everyday life.

Czapska describes an odyssey typical of refugees trying to flee Europe for distant lands. She was persecuted as a landowner in the

*The Slavic family, or male surname, here is spelled "Czapski," whereas Ilza's female surname is spelled "Czapska."

region the Nazis had chosen to settle "ethnic Germans." In fact, her testimony provides an individual view of Hitler's plan for Poland. All Polish landowners in her vicinity were imprisoned in Dobrzyca, an internment camp in western Poland between Breslau and Poznan, and their farms were confiscated. One goal of the Nazis was to gain *Lebensraum* (living space) for the "Germanic master race" at the expense of the "Jewish-Bolshevist establishment" and Jews in general in eastern Europe.[1] For the Nazis, Poles were much lower on the social scale than Germans, and still lower were the Polish Jews. It mattered little to the Nazis if Poles were injured or killed as a result of actions against Jews.[2]

Czapska distinguishes between levels of authority in occupied Poland. She contrasts the older German veteran reserves (*Landsturmmänner*) with the younger, more brutal ethnic Germans (*Volksdeutsche*) and compares the so-called general government (*Generalgouvernement*) with the ruthless German civil administration (*Zivilverwaltung*). Such details elucidate the Nazi pillage and the liquidation of Jews in Poland, which were quick and savage.

As early as September 19, 1939, Security Police Chief Heydrich and General Quartermaster Wagner met and agreed upon a "cleanup once and for all" of "Jews, intelligentsia, clergy, nobility."[3] The following day the Commander-in-Chief of the Army stated that "the ghetto idea exists in broad outline; details are not yet clear."[4] The Heydrich plan consisted of two phases: first, approximately 600,000 Jews were to be transported from the incorporated territories to those of the *Generalgouvernement*, a procedure that would increase the number of Jews there to 2,000,000. In a second phase, these 2,000,000 Jews were to be crowded into the ghettos.[5]

Czapska and her family became part of an evacuation program that began in December 1939 in order to clear Jews, Poles, and *Roma* (Gypsies) from the Reich and the incorporated territories, for dispatch to the land designated by the *Generalgouvernement*. The depopulated regions, such as the incorporated area that the Czapskis left, were to be repopulated with the "returning" ethnic Germans of the Baltic states.[6]

The Czapski family left the Poznan (Posen) province, an area of western Poland that was annexed by the Reich in 1939 and included in the Warthegau. The territorial administrative unit of Warthegau existed until liberation in 1945. Between September 14 and October 25, 1939, Arthur Greiser was head of the civil administration, an adjunct to the military commander of Posen (*Zivilverwaltung beim Militärbefehlshaber Posen*). Later Greiser became the local Reich commissioner (*Reichsstatthalter*) of the Warthegau, and, finally, regional Nazi party leader or *Gauleiter*. The Warthegau was planned as an experiment in National Socialism, a place where Greiser assiduously employed racist methods in dealing with the local population. People were divided into *Übermenschen*, or "superior persons," and *Untermenschen*, or "inferior persons." The Germans, of course, were the only members of the first group, while Poles, Jews, and Roma were members of the second.[7]

The German authorities in the Warthegau persecuted the Poles economically and socially. The Nazis ruthlessly enforced such drastic measures as expropriating 95.5 percent of all Polish property, closing schools, restricting the use of the Polish language in public affairs, imposing curfews, and banning travel. The actions were so harsh that the region was known as *Straflager Warthegau*, or Warthegau penal camp. During the occupation many Poles were sent to concentration camps—and over 70,000 were killed.[8]

The fate of Jews in the area was especially tragic. Persecution began in the first four months of the war, and ended in a process of annihilation. Chelmno was the extermination camp in the Warthegau. A total of 380,000 Jews in the region were executed, and only 5,000 Jews remained alive after the war.[9]

Czapska's view of the political situation discloses much more than an individual experience. She accurately illustrates the problems many refugees encountered in Europe between 1939 and 1945: the almost impossible task of obtaining transit and exit visas from various countries, the endless bureaucracy, and the turbulence of war. Death, displacement, and exile were the harsh realities many Jewish and gentile families had to face, and she is aware that her story ends much more happily than most.

OUR JOURNEY FROM OBRA TO BRAZIL, 1939–41

BY ILZA CZAPSKA

It was Janek who asked me to write down all that had happened to us on our way from Obra to Brazil because he was too small at the time to recollect everything from this memorable period.[1] But while I am at it, I want to write down my memories for all of my children, and not in a broad outline, but in detail, with all of the small and unimportant events that have stayed in my memory that were typical for the children and for the atmosphere that we lived in at the time.

It was in 1939 when my husband went on a trip to Brazil. He didn't anticipate an immediate outbreak of war, but the times were precarious. Frederyk begged me not to stay in Obra under any circumstances if the political situation grew worse. He said that we should leave Obra, which was too close to the German border, and flee in the other direction on the other side of the Vistula. It was assumed that the Poles would definitely stop the German invasion.

So at the beginning of August, I packed up the entire family and we went to a summer health resort on the Vistula to await further news. When the situation grew more unfavorable at the end of August, it became clear that I needed to look for accommodations in a strategically unimportant and quiet place. At the last minute, we found a barely furnished house in a summer settlement in Stara Wies[2] that I was able to rent for a few months. Once again I returned to Obra to pack many of our personal belongings in suitcases and to settle a few things with my husband's administrator, our dependable Papa Marwitz.

War anxiety was in the air. This made all traveling difficult, but luckily I managed to get to Obra and aided by our chauffeur, picked up the suitcases at the train station in Warsaw. We fixed up the small house in Stara Wies the best we could and picked up our dinner from the train station assistant, Duray, who later turned out to be an important person for us. Then we waited anxiously without a radio or a newspaper.

The impact of the first bomb, which shook the entire house, made us realize that the war was now no longer a terrifying dream but a reality. Soon began the days when more and more bombs fell in our vicinity, and the otherwise brave Julek became deathly pale with each hit. At this time increasing numbers of trains traveled through Stara Wies filled with refugees; the Germans shot at the poor people inside and on top of the train cars with their machine guns. Our friend Stern, now a refugee from Poznan, arrived one day in his car and told tales of horror, followed by word that the Germans were advancing in lightning fashion from all sides, not only from the west. One day at noon, it must have been the fifth or sixth of September 1939, Erhard Stern voiced the news: "The Germans are in the immediate vicinity, get in the car quickly and flee to the east!"

We had an average sized Willis, hastily packed it full with our most important things, and had more than enough passengers for the small car: Oo, the three children and myself, Roma with the small Evunja, and Dyba.[3] Because the first part of the road was sandy, Julek and Genia walked, and we met them at the railroad crossing. Janek was lying in bed with a high fever, and normally I wouldn't have taken him out of his room. But it was useless to worry about it under these circumstances, so we proceeded into the unknown.

The Polish people were understandably very edgy, and the fear of spies was widespread. It almost became our undoing, because when a soldier spoke to me and I answered in my broken Polish, he immediately thought we were informers. He summoned other soldiers, confiscated the car, demanded that Dyba be watched, and that we all drive to the next commander's office in Garvolin immediately! Our insisting that our two children were not there didn't make the slightest impression on the military men, and I was terrified by the thought that I would probably never see the children again if I had to leave them in the confusion of war. But luckily none of the soldiers could drive, and since Dyba simply refused to proceed without the children, the transport pulled out and Julek and Genia soon caught up with us. Speechless about the situation and the military escort, the two were somehow stuffed into the packed car. Thus began the ride to Garvolin, a ride that none of us would forget.

When we reached the main road to Garvolin, we found ourselves in an indescribable chaos. The night had become pitch-black and the only light was a ghastly glow emanating from the burning villages nearby; the street was packed with pedestrians, riders on horses, and vehicles of every shape and size. The civilian population was fleeing from Warsaw in the direction of Lublin and from Lublin in the direction of Warsaw, so our car made progress at a snail's pace, and we were always in danger of a collision.

That is what things looked like outside of the car. Inside, the feverish Janek was constantly throwing up, but he managed to whimper quietly on my lap while the small Evunja, whose pacifier was lost in the tumult, screamed piercingly. The larger children crouched in a position that was difficult to endure for a long period of time.

But as so often happens in life, the banality of the situation pushed itself into the foreground and the predominant thought was:

"If only Evunja would stop screaming." And so it happened that all of us thought less of the danger of the situation than of finding Evunja's pacifier in the chaos of the car. Unfortunately, the search was in vain.

Suddenly the car was stopped by a Polish officer who asked why a private car had a military escort. Then something totally unexpected happened. When the officer listened to our story and confirmed that it concerned the Frederyk Czapski family of Obra, he said that he knew this family, that is, he knew the father by reputation and that we were definitely not spies. He sent the soldiers away with harsh words and recommended that Dyba drive immediately behind him under his escort.

There I experienced for the first time, as many times later, how Frederyk helped us even when he was far, far away. It gave me a feeling of peace and security that never left me in those difficult months. Shortly before we reached Garvolin, the officer told us to turn onto a country road he had pointed out. In a few minutes we thought we were in another world: feeling a total stillness devoid of human activity on this forest road while witnessing a fiery blaze behind us in the darkness of night. Ahead of us was tranquility and silence! We drove in this manner until the gasoline ran out, which was only a few kilometers. We stopped in a large village off the beaten path that was filled with refugees, and finally ended up in an empty room in a farmhouse with an assigned kitchen. Because no other straw could be found, we made two piles of pea straw on the floor. For the next few weeks we remained there in an unbelievable filth: bitten by fleas and bedbugs and surrounded by an unimaginable number of flies from the kitchen.

It wasn't wonderful in Domaszewnice, but we were lucky that neither the Germans nor the Russians found us and, with the exception of the first few days, that nobody had been injured by bombs or machine gunfire. Janek no longer had a fever, but he had bloody diarrhea that scared him and brought him down. He got well again, thanks to the good teacher who gave us some rice and a piece of soap, a precious commodity at the time. Other than that, Dyba watched out for us like a father. He walked for hours to procure meat and bread so that we didn't starve. But we were cut off from the entire world, and the only source of information was the teacher's radio that didn't work very well. Countless refugees assembled in front of it in the darkness, holding their breath so they wouldn't miss one word of the faint voice on the air. As soon as one of us

heard a foreign language, we looked for someone among the listen-
ers who understood it. What we learned, of course, was depressing
—Poland was totally conquered and destroyed. Julek almost always
accompanied me on nightly visits to the teacher's house in the village, and he, too, will probably never forget the atmosphere of
these evenings.

In addition to this picture of our life in Domaszewnice there is
the painstaking way we camouflaged our car, the pig hole in the
middle of the barnyard that Evunja fell into now and then, Oo's efforts to try to find a place to bathe, and the fight to discover a spot
that could be used as a bathroom. Oo had her seventieth birthday at
this time; we had imagined a wonderful party for her but found ourselves in the most unpleasant of circumstances.

After the report about the armistice was confirmed, came the
big question: what now? I was in need of a man's advice and tried to
make contact with refugees who could assess the situation better
than I. One particular gentleman who was interested in us managed
to find a better place for our family nearby on a small piece of property and advised us to start communicating with the people in Obra
as soon as possible. We had already done that anyway, for we had
given a letter to the first ones returning in order to let our friends in
Obra know that we were still alive and living in Domaszewnice with
no money. We really didn't know whether the letter would arrive
or not. The days went by, and we had almost given up hope. But
one day a bicycle stopped at our front door, and there stood our
secretary from Obra, Robert Falkenberg!

When they received our letter in Obra, Robert went and obtained money for us. He had given up his appointment as Ethnic
German in Kozmin in order to come to Domaszewnice, and our
secretary Miss Dybizbanska had baked a cake for the children. So
Falkenberg had bicycled for fourteen days through half of Poland in
the midst of all the postwar confusion, and now he was standing in
front of us alive and well with the squashed cake in his hands! What
a joy it was! Never in our lives had we eaten such a delicious treat,
not only because it was a good confection made of butter, flour, and
eggs, but also because it was a tangible expression of the grateful
solidarity of Frederyk's coworkers in Obra. They were still attached
to our family even when it caused them great difficulty.

Moreover, Falkenberg brought some good news: nothing in
Obra had been destroyed. The German troops had rushed through
and searched for my husband, whose name was on their death list

42

because of his known animosity toward Hitler. But when they ascertained that he wasn't there, nothing further happened. Papa Marwitz kept working as an administrator in Obra, and the Dyba family was alive and healthy and hadn't fled. How happy Dyba was to hear about his loved ones, after despairing of ever seeing them again. He thought that they had probably died while trying to escape, just like the hundreds of people whose fate we had observed in Stara Wies.

So it seemed that the *return to Obra* was the only thing to do. After all, what could we undertake in eastern Poland without any money? We then prepared for the return trip home, and the car was made ready. Thanks to our knowledge of the German language we were able to obtain gasoline from the occupying troops and our dear Willis was packed full with Oo, Roma, Evunja, the three children, myself, Dyba, and also Falkenberg and his bicycle! We didn't make progress very rapidly and it wasn't comfortable but we were getting closer to our goal. I really can't remember details of this trip, only being in a house the evening German soldiers came in as we were retiring. While making room for them I suddenly heard my name—it was the young teacher from Petersdorf. He had recognized me and now looked after us!

After about three days we arrived in familiar territory and drove through Walkow, our church village, and through the village of Obra. The atmosphere became very festive and we automatically sang a song of thanks. Finally we stood before the house. Papa Marwitz and Stacho came running out: but it wasn't the reception we had been expecting. Instead we were greeted by disturbed and worried faces. They informed us that only a few days earlier the German civil administration had confiscated Obra and that a certain Herr Schreiber, the so-called giver of life and death, was there and we no longer had the right to enter our home!

Of course we despaired, but it wasn't the best time to indulge gloomy thoughts. Because it was late in the evening, my most immediate worry was where we would spend the night. Schreiber was sleeping in my bedroom, but I was able to press for permission to use the other bedroom for one night only. I was subsequently allowed to live in Oo's house and to take my personal belongings there. We managed to obtain the right to be granted food rations in specie, as happened in former days, when our itinerant workers had received a minimum wage of about 10 zloty for meat and other items. The next day I gathered clothes and belongings and we set ourselves up in the villa. I was determined not to take the situation so hard. We had, after all, lost the war, and there were people in far worse predicaments. Compared to the time we had spent in Domaszewnice, the villa seemed like paradise.

I drove to Krotoszyn (seat of the municipality) in a borrowed farmer's wagon. A neighbor of ours had become the district mayor, and the confiscation of goods was under his control. I tried to get him to improve our financial situation, but my pleas fell upon deaf ears. The majority of the population of Obra was very kind to us and brought us butter, bread, eggs, and other provisions secretly at night so that we in no way suffered. In fact it was just the opposite—we felt surrounded by affection and helpfulness. In total secrecy, a good-willed neighbor had butchered a pig for us, and we thought that we would be able to spend the winter there peacefully with such rations.

Then one morning at the end of October, Schreiber appeared at the villa with two policemen and demanded that we pack our suitcases immediately and bring them downstairs. We were allowed to take the bedding along as well. They told us that Oo, and the children and I were to be transported to a camp in half an hour, refusing to give us any more information. Schreiber and the policemen searched through everything for money and jewelry, but found little since we didn't have much of value. So we climbed into our carriage for the last time with Janiec, the driver, and headed for an unknown, hostile destination. Our suitcases were in Stara Wies, and I could only throw a bundle together, but in the haste of departure I forgot to take the bedding. I realized it at once, but Janiec wasn't allowed to turn back. They promised to send it to us, however.

Where were we going? That was the gnawing question and it was a good thing for me that I had to worry about the children, especially Janek who was then three, so that I had no time to engage in morbid thoughts. I was very conscious at the time that the most important thing was to keep the children healthy in body and mind and bring them through this period safely. So that they would not be overcome with fear, it was of the utmost importance that they see their mother as calm and unafraid. I don't know if I succeeded totally, but I always sensed with the deepest thanks that God had protected the children and spared them some truly horrifying experiences that could have left them emotionally disturbed. All three lived through this period mentally unharmed.

So we drove in the direction of the unknown, but it turned out not to be as bad as I had expected. Instead of being transported to a faraway place, the carriage stopped in front of the mansion in Dobrzyca, a wealthy estate in the vicinity of Kozmin.[4] We were told that the house had been cleaned out, and that the only things to be found in the individual rooms were straw sacks. All the landowner's families were brought there and their possessions confiscated. The Germans didn't want them near the workers and assembled them there to avoid unrest. Later other families came because the Germans didn't want to leave them in their former neighborhood, for some reason or other.

For the time being, we were in good company. We were the only family not of Polish blood and therefore held a different position. We were also the only family without a father, and I felt somewhat deserted but, in general, most of the families were nice. The supervision of the camp was in the hands of Herr Schreiber, who was especially ill-disposed toward us. Mr. Chelkowski was in the inner administration and his actions were above reproach. All services including the cooking had to be done by the interned Polish ladies, who took turns working in the kitchen. Because of Janek, I was not obliged to perform any communal duties.

The sanitary conditions there were extremely precarious: the toilet was the park, and washing facilities were—the lake! This was unbearable when it was below freezing. The boarding was extremely simple: there was a minimum amount of money set aside for us, and most of the time we only had potatoes cooked one way or another. However, I don't remember ever starving. We didn't have any dishes, but managed to get a pan that we used when food was distributed and then used spoons. Oo couldn't decide whether to eat out of the pan, and I will never forget how happy she was when she found the bottom of an old vase in the compost heap in the park. When turned upside down it served as a bowl.

Luckily we had a small room for ourselves, and after a while Roma and Evunja were brought to the camp. We stayed warm by stoking a big wood-burning stove with wood that the men had chopped in the park, and we slept better fully clothed on our piles of straw than we thought possible. I'll never forget Sundays, because we then had real streusel cake, which was like a comforting greeting from a better world.

We got our bread from the Polish baker in the small town of Dobrzyca, where it was picked up in baskets. This was our only contact with the outside world. It was also the way that gifts, hidden under the bread, were smuggled into the refugee camp. The women of the camp had devised an arrangement with the friendly baker. Every day he would save a little bit of flour and in one way or another butter and sugar. So on Sunday afternoons we had streusel cake!

The most unpleasant moments there were the body searches of the first days along with the eventual confiscation of all valuables, the room revisions, and other such situations that made us feel like we were at someone else's mercy. At that time it seemed very terrible and humiliating to us, but today we know that it was a harmless sojourn compared to the German concentration camps.

The older German veteran reserves were in charge of the surveillance of the camp. They turned a blind eye to the smuggling of gifts, and we trusted them. Suddenly they were replaced by younger Ethnic Germans. Only later did we learn why: the German civil administration didn't know what to do with the camp refugees and thought the simplest solution would be execution. One night they ordered the guards to line them up against a wall. But the old German veterans refused to shoot civilians, especially women and children, so the command wasn't carried out. However, the military sentinels were removed and the young Ethnic Germans took over night duty and tormented us when they could.

Our personal situation was especially precarious because Schreiber was angry at us, and the inspection of our room by the SS left me with disagreeable memories. What malicious comments they made about our Christmas tree with the Advent ornaments that decorated our bleak room! Rumors spread that with proof of livelihood one could leave the camp in order to travel past the Vistula, so I decided to fill out the necessary papers declaring my bank account in Warsaw. I never received an answer to my travel request, but I later learned that my bank account, which was unknown to the Germans up to that time, was confiscated immediately.

I don't know what kinds of memories my children still have about the camp, however, I am certain they were awed with the exemplary attitude of the Czartoryski family, especially with the eighty-year-old niece of Kaiser Franz Josef of Austria, who spent her days on the layer of straw in quiet dignity without complaint. They were probably impressed, too, by the adroit way the young countesses scrubbed the rooms and stairs. I'm sure they remember

46

the exciting story about the camp visit of the young countess's fiancé better than I.

Julek's days in the camp were filled with helpful activities such as carrying wood, and the grownups remember him as a desirable young helper for all jobs. I don't know how Genia spent her time there, because Janek was always at my side. The long evenings were most often spent in the dark because the fire from the stove gave off little light, and candles were a luxury impossible to come by. I tried to make the time pass more quickly by telling stories and singing songs. One time the vicar gave us a big church candle, and how wonderful it was. The most beautiful moments at this time were receiving the gifts from Obra!

Schreiber forbade any contact from Obra under penalty of death, but we did receive warm clothes and a sum of money collected in the village. Among these practical items was, more importantly, the invaluable spiritual support that made us conscious of the friends near us.

Ilza Czapska with oldest son Juljan, youngest son
Janek, and daughter Genia, ca. 1942.
Courtesy of Alice Brill Czapski.

One day the most unbelievable thing happened. Some prisoners went to fetch rolls in the bakery to be distributed among us. As usual, they were accompanied by a guard. That day, biting into the bread, we found a piece of paper hidden inside with my husband's address at a hotel in Paris! This was a very special event, as we had not the slightest idea of his whereabouts! We would have suffered terrible consequences had Schreiber found out that father was not in neutral Brazil but in the enemy territory of France. According to the laws of that period, having contact with someone in a hostile country meant the death penalty.

Days and weeks of anxiety and insecurity passed slowly, and we concerned ourselves with the small problems of day-to-day existence. Then one day we were told that the next day we would receive a double ration of bread, and that the entire camp would be transported east! We packed up our possessions. Where were we going? It was a burning question, because it was very cold in December and a concentration camp in the east far away from helpful friends would have been very dangerous for the children, especially for Janek and Evunja, because both were still very small and delicate. But anxiety wouldn't help the situation.

We were brought to Kozmin where a passenger train was waiting. Later we were informed that the civil administration had proposed cattle cars but the military administration prevailed and passenger trains were sent. Women and children were packed into the cars as tightly as possible, while men and young people, (Julek among them), were separated from us and traveled in the baggage car, if I remember correctly. The Ethnic Germans traveled along as guards. The doors were shut, and then we were on our way, to the east!

No one told us where we were going. Before leaving Kozmin I was able to write a postcard describing our evacuation to my mother Ella, and put it in the mailbox. Unfortunately this news also reached my husband who was now trying to sustain communication through Switzerland and Sweden. The information, of course, put him on the edge of despair.

We rode toward the east, day and night and night and day! The children remained courageous and didn't complain much about being hungry or thirsty. Janek and Evunja, this time *with* a pacifier, slept on their mother's lap. Genia didn't have it so good, and we didn't know what was happening to Julek. The train stopped in Warsaw and traveled on, always farther east. Where were we going? Suddenly it stopped in the middle of nowhere and all people from a particular place—let's say Kozmin—had to get out into the snow. Then we traveled on. After some time we stopped again at a small station, it wasn't a city, one couldn't see a village and again some of the refugees were obliged to get out. Where were they going?

Eventually the train was almost empty, there were only the camp inmates inside and we could at least stretch ourselves out on the benches. Roma became friendly with an Ethnic German guard, but even he said that he didn't know where we were headed. One talked of tin barracks still farther east, but all the worry didn't help us. We had to wait patiently. Finally the train stopped again and the people from Camp Dobrzyca had to get out! Now came the verdict! We stood there irresolute on the train platform: then something totally unforeseen occurred. A man came up and asked us in Polish if we wanted to get into the car provided for women and small children that would bring us to the schoolhouse, in the next village, where a warm meal was waiting![5]

We weren't in a camp but with friends and in freedom! We couldn't believe it—it wasn't a dream but reality. The German civil administration, in their sadistic way, did not tell us that the Dobrzyca camp would be disbanded and the inmates deported to eastern Poland. What anxiety and distress could have been avoided had we known about this from the beginning! In this part of Poland where the so-called general government ruled, the Germans only exercised a loose supervision for the time being. This meant that the Polish people could live there freely, and that the individual municipalities were supposed to take care of the deportees from western Poland.

Now at least we were in a friendly environment. After eating a delicious hot soup I went to look for a place to stay and managed to find a room for Oo, Janek, and Evunja in the home of the nice wife of the local doctor. The older children and I slept on straw at the home of a farmer who wanted to take care of us. In the morning he gave us such a huge bowl of milk and potato porridge that Genia and I didn't know what to do with all of it. However, Julek saved us with his big appetite and helped us empty the bowl. Oo told me that Janek had fallen asleep immediately. The next morning the doctor's wife offered him a cup of milk, but before gulping it down greedily, he first inquired politely whether his mother had also drunk some.

The immediate danger of the camp had disappeared—we were free, but didn't know what to do for the time being. We could stay in the present community as refugees, but the well-intentioned people of Dobrzyca advised us not to wait until our freedom was once again taken away. They suggested we try to distance ourselves from the crowd of refugees as quickly as possible. Because we weren't that far from Stara Wies, where we had rented the house before the war had broken out, we decided to go there. We hoped that our money would last for the journey and left the next morning, riding to the train station in a rented farmer's wagon. We were able to get seats in the overcrowded train, thanks to Roma's skill in dealing with men and the fact that she could prove she was the wife of a German soldier.

We arrived at the train station of Celestinow, which was about two kilometers from Stara Wies, as it was getting dark. There we rented a sleigh for Oo and the two small children and the rest of us walked on the somewhat familiar forest path to Stara Wies. We entered the Duray's home late in the evening. He had long taken us for dead, and there was great joy and excitement on our return.

Duray informed us that we couldn't go back to the old house because it was being used by "robbers" as a hideout. He told us to stay with him. Those good people, in the joy of seeing us again, didn't know what to do. Mrs. Duray wanted to have Oo sleep with her in her own bed under a warm down blanket, and it wasn't easy to find another arrangement that wouldn't hurt her feelings. Finally we were all put up in the small room that was well insulated against the winter cold but was hermetically sealed. Mr. Duray, of course, shared the room with all of us: six adults and four children. Oo awakened at 6:00 the next morning, happy about her rest on the sofa where she had slept very soundly. I then realized how she had adapted herself to the new conditions.

Duray managed to find shelter for us in the upper story of a summer house that was empty, which had a small but very warm room that served as Oo's bedroom and the living room during the day. It was next to the cold attic where Julek stayed and next to another room that was just as cold, where the rest of us slept, including Evunja in her big suitcase. The living room was chaos. One fell over children crawling or sitting on the ground or even tripped over one's own feet. But it was warm and comfortable considering the frigid weather outside. I asked the local landowners for heating coal and necessary staples as "charitable gifts." We even managed to obtain bacon and sausage from people returning clandestinely from Obra, where the pig had been butchered shortly before our deportation. All in all, everything was agreeable in Stara Wies, far away from need and misery as long as we stayed in our forest seclusion and didn't travel to Warsaw.

But travelling to Warsaw was something I had to do, of course, because we had no money. Stara Wies was about an hour away from the Polish capital, and as soon as I found a place to stay and knew that my family was safe, I went to Warsaw on borrowed funds. The purpose of my trip was to find Mrs. Kruszewska and try to withdraw some money from my account. I'll never forget this first trip: I went to the bank and heard that my assets and safety deposit box had been confiscated and that I didn't own a penny. I was despondent. Then a bank clerk added: "By the way, a man came in today and asked about your account." "Who could that be?" I inquired. Because I pleaded, they looked into the matter and discovered it was a lawyer from Breslau who was trying to transfer my inheritance to Poland. He came to Warsaw as a German official because Uncle Werner, my brother who still lived in Germany, had asked him to look into my account. This was a big help in time of need!

I actually met the lawyer in the hotel. Due to the fact that I was an old client, he helped me with the German authorities. Not only did I receive my jewelry from the safe to dispose of as I wished, but I also got a monthly sum that would ensure a modest income. He returned to Breslau the next day and through him I could give my mother Ella news of my whereabouts and let her know that we hadn't been sent off to a death camp but were alive and well in Stara Wies. She received the news on December 24, and I'm certain that she had never been so thankful as she was at this Christmas.

I looked around and also found our friends, the Kruszewskis: from that day on their home became my refuge in Warsaw. They offered me money, and because I didn't want to sell the jewelry so quickly, I could do a little Christmas shopping. When I arrived back in Stara Wies, I felt like Santa Claus with so many useful and coveted items. Oh, this early time in Stara Wies! It was like a fairy tale, because I've forgotten to describe how the gracious Durays, on the first morning we drank coffee together, suddenly pulled our suitcases out from under the beds. They even apologized because some things were missing! The Durays had gone to our house after the German and Polish troops had marched through, packed up everything, and stored it away just in case. There wasn't much missing.

Just a few days earlier, all we had were the clothes on our backs, but now we owned suitcases filled with everything we needed. Not only that, we had the best pictures of my husband and mother and other things of sentimental value. How wealthy we felt!

Later on I had to make many trips to Warsaw. Standing outside on the platform at a temperature of -30 degrees Celsius, I saw such inhumane suffering in the city that I always returned to Stara Wies half-sick. Once Julek was with me because the tailor was supposed to make him a suit. There was a lot of typhus going around in Warsaw and we hadn't been vaccinated. When Julek came down with a high fever two days later we were very anxious for hours, but it was only the flu, and he recovered quickly. Once we went by sleigh to Otwock to do some shopping at the market. It was bitter cold, and it made a lasting impression on the children. Because of the frigid weather, I almost couldn't make the trip. The children asked me very reasonable questions about buying this or that. I answered as follows: "Buy what you want, do what you want, I don't care, I'm freezing!"

But it was warm in our room. Roma somehow succeeded in making German soldiers toss charcoal briquettes to us as they traveled by in trains. It was a good addition to our wood. Oo also taught the children how to play bridge in order to pass the time. Little Janek, of course, participated in some way, usually saying "five aces" or something similar. We had regular correspondence with my mother and with friends. I'll never forget the time when I read a letter out loud from a girlfriend who sympathized with our plight. Julek asked astounded: "But why? Things are going well for us!" That was the most wonderful thing that anyone could have said to me.

Initially there were no Germans in Stara Wies, but then they confiscated the sawmill. Because the mill was in our immediate vicinity, it was unavoidable that we would come into contact with the occupying troops, and they wanted to know why we were there. When we explained our situation, they couldn't believe that our property, which had been in the family for generations (not just from 1918), was taken away. "But you received money for it," they exclaimed. "No, we didn't get a thing for it," we answered. "That can't be, justice reigns in Germany!" they retorted. And even though we were living proof of the opposite, not one of these Germans lost total faith in Hitler or his righteous actions.

So the weeks and months passed . . . and then came a surprise. One day in Warsaw I was told that I should go to the Hungarian consulate where a visa was waiting for me. Hungary? I didn't know a soul in Hungary. Then a letter arrived with an utterly unfamiliar signature. It read as if it were written by a close friend and said that someone anxiously awaited our arrival, and that everything had been prepared for our welcome. The puzzle was solved a few days later when we received word from my husband indirectly through Switzerland. He had managed, with indescribable difficulties, to get us a permanent visa for France. Naturally, we couldn't acquire an authorization from the Germans to travel to France, an enemy country, and that is why Hungary came into the picture.

Now the efforts for the exit papers began. Many times I had to take the troublesome trip to Krakow where the German passport office was, only to find out that the Hungarian transit visa wasn't enough to leave Poland, and that I had to have a final visa. What a disappointment it was both for Frederyk and for us! He would always let us know indirectly that the Brazilian permanent visa had been granted, but Berlin stated that it wasn't there. Finally, after months of effort from Uncle Werner, a civil servant ascertained that it was at the Brazilian legation and had not been sent to the consulate. I had proof of the permanent visa in my hand, nevertheless, the German authorities made the acquisition of the exit permit difficult, and time was running out. There were always new, complicating stipulations developing that put our immigration into question.

I traveled to Krakow to visit a gentleman who, I was told, worked secretly with the German passport office. I explained our situation to him. "Do you want to have your exit papers by this evening?" he inquired. This question seemed fantastic. "Of course, if possible," I rejoined excitedly. Possible it was, but way too expensive, and therefore out of the question. I begged and protested, but to no avail. Then he thumbed through my passport playfully. "Czapski? I worked together with a Mr. Czapski in the Polish-South American Board of Trade. Are you related to him?" Now the ice was broken. Even if all of my previous pleading hadn't worked, my husband's name did. The man refused a personal payment and took only what a German passport officer needed, a sum I managed to obtain with difficulty. By evening I really had my passport with the exit visa stamp in hand. Although I still needed the permission to take my luggage along, I didn't want to waste any more time and preferred to take the risk of having complications with luggage at the border than delay our trip out of the country. So we departed as soon as possible.

Uncle Krischan Christiansen had just left Turkey and showed up unexpectedly one day in Stara Wies. He helped us with the departure. The final hours before we left were chaotic because we received a telegram from Uncle Werner stating that the Italian border could close at any moment. It changed our travel plans at the very last minute: we couldn't first travel to my mother in Breslau, but we had to travel through Berlin as quickly as possible to pick up the Brazilian visa and then leave Germany. Uncle Werner greeted the children in Frankfurt an der Oder and then took them to their grandmother in Breslau. I traveled to Berlin and afterwards returned to Breslau.

These were emotional days. We said goodbye to poor Oo in Warsaw. She still had a German passport, making an entry permit for France impossible, so she stayed in Stara Wies with Roma and Eva. Difficult, too, was saying farewell to my mother Ella in Breslau, who probably knew this would be our last goodbye. She remained strong and dignified, as was her nature, and I consoled her by saying: "Think of us as traveling to happiness!" But it was a heart-wrenching moment for both of us, one of the most difficult in our lives.

Uncle Werner gave us enough money to last until Budapest and accompanied us to the border. We traveled in the sleeper car of the Orient Express to make things easier with luggage inspection, and it worked out well. Customs officials greeted us in light blue uniforms and silver helmets and looked like messengers from another world. A different universe it was indeed: Budapest in all its opulence, the grand hotel, the city, all far away from the war.

We needed a few days to take care of passport formalities, and then took a train through Yugoslavia and Italy, where we stayed one night on the French border. It was here that we learned that my husband was no longer in Paris but in a Polish officer's camp in Vichy. So we changed our travel plans and one evening our dream came true. We arrived at about 10:00 P.M. in a train station and there stood Frederyk. He took sleepy Janek in his arms and brought us to the hotel!

My husband had gotten permission to live with us in a private hotel, and these weeks were the happiest of his life. By devoting all his strength to it and overcoming almost insurmountable obstacles, he brought us out of German-occupied Poland into France. Now we were healthy and happy and in his arms in Vichy, even though he had at times in the past feared the worst. After great effort he succeeded in getting into the Polish army in France, despite his bad Polish that betrayed German heritage. Instead of remaining an unknown, destitute refugee sitting in a Paris hotel despondent about his family and unable to fight against Hitler, now he was living respectably among other officers and proud of his wife and children!

Julek was with him a lot and probably enjoyed being known and liked among the circle of officers as the eldest son. Genia was usually with Janek but the time in Vichy was certainly pleasant for her. As for myself, I couldn't totally enjoy the situation, even though I was so happy to be with my husband again. The thought never left me that he was an officer, that we were in the midst of a war, and that we could be separated any day. I would have preferred my husband travelling to Brazil with us right away, but it wasn't in his nature to stand aside passively and not commit himself to the general good. He believed, because he wasn't of purely Polish heritage, that he could help the future of Polish children if he returned to Poland as a Polish officer.

It was interesting how Janek got accustomed to the situation. He had been used to speaking German with me, but when we arrived in France I told him that he could visit father only if he spoke Polish with me. The small four-year-old managed to pull through, and surprisingly after a few months he had forgotten so much German that he didn't understand much of it. Later he would speak brokenly and laboriously until I insisted that he start learning it again.

We couldn't enjoy this peaceful togetherness in Vichy for very long. Soon the war news became highly disturbing. I'll never forget a midday meal we had in our small hotel when we heard Pétain's voice over the radio admitting the danger of the situation. All of those listening were deeply moved and rose together to sing the Marseillaise.

Suddenly the first refugees arrived from the north and their numbers increased daily. Day and night, cars and passengers of every kind passed by our hotel in slow motion because all the roads were so crowded that nobody could move quickly. Now and then there were air raids and the nightly sirens made a lasting impression, leaving us with many vivid memories. We now had to decide what we were going to do and we chose another separation because

Frederyk didn't want to risk us being in Vichy when the Germans arrived. He was as an officer bound to orders from above, so we decided to travel to Bordeaux and from there through Spain to Portugal. He would then try to meet us there as soon as possible.

We dispatched a few of our suitcases so that we wouldn't be burdened with too much luggage on our journey. We kept a small piece of luggage that contained the best and most important pieces of clothing. In the event our other bags got lost, we would have enough items for one year. In addition to this suitcase, my purse was the most important piece of luggage . . . attached to this was a night potty. It wasn't an attractive piece to carry but it was indispensable for Janek, and to Genia's dismay, she was the one who always had to carry it! So equipped, my husband drove us one evening to the train station, whereupon he returned immediately to Vichy because of an alert. Then the *second part of our Odyssey began.*

The evening express train that was supposed to bring us to Bordeaux was set off course and we spent the night in a waiting room expecting the next train. When one arrived early in the morning heading in the direction of Bordeaux, we took it to get out of the dangerous Vichy zone. A few Polish gentlemen who had also been waiting advised us to leave quickly. We didn't know that my husband's group had received orders to drive south and that they would arrive a half hour later in a car to try to pick us up. So we sat in a crowded train that progressed leisurely in an unknown direction. After twenty-four hours we determined that we must have gone in a circle and were once again near Vichy. A few Polish officers climbed aboard but unfortunately Frederyk was not one of them.

The following days and nights were total confusion. We could no longer travel to Bordeaux because it had just become part of the German-occupied zone. There were no longer scheduled trains. Every train traveled a few hours and then we were told to get out, whereupon we had to find out when and where another one would be available. At most of the train stations there were straw beds for emergencies as a relief action for "mother and child," and thanks to Janek's presence we could stretch out there.

Julek was always given the job of finding out how we could travel farther and had an exceptional talent for doing this. Not only did he find a steaming engine on outlying tracks, but also train cars that were prepared for departure. He always managed to discover seats for us on the most crowded trains, or at the very least for Janek and me. Janek remembers this period as a time of abrupt

56

awakenings followed by train hunts. All of us would scramble to reach the car at the very last minute, fearing that we might miss the train. It was a recurring event in those turbulent days. This trip was especially rough for the children: they were never rested, there wasn't enough to eat, and they always had to carry baggage in a rush.

After seemingly endless days in Bayonne, we finally arrived near the Spanish border. I wanted to take our suitcase and go to the shelter for "mother and child" that was in town about a half hour away from the train station. There were no porters or carts and Julek went on strike for the first time because he didn't want to carry the suitcase anymore. I really felt sorry for the children because I knew how exhausted they were. I decided that we should first eat something decent in the train station restaurant. When I saw so many suitcases piled up I asked if I could leave my luggage there, because the official baggage storage was closed. After eating an exorbitant and atrocious meal we went to the shelter without our suitcase, and the children slept for a few hours. But I was nervous about our baggage, and when the children woke up refreshed, we decided to go pick up the luggage and keep it with us in the shelter.

How can I describe the horror I felt when we walked into the train station restaurant and didn't see one piece of luggage! The employees refused to take any responsibility and looking for it would have been senseless. So we had to live with the fact that we only had the things we were wearing on our backs . . . including my purse and the night potty! It seemed like a dreadful situation but I later realized that the big suitcase would have been an almost unportable ballast in the coming days. Julek made inquiries in town and heard news that the Polish officers from Vichy were staying there. What excitement it was for us! But unfortunately Frederyk wasn't among them and the Germans were supposed to arrive at any moment. Because Julek was a young man and in particular danger, I couldn't risk staying there any longer in the hope of meeting my husband. So we left the very next morning on the last train to the Handaye border station.

Later I learned that Frederyk arrived there with a transport from Vichy on the day we left. From the small harbor, he then took a ship to England. Had we met him then, what a different course our lives would have followed. But it wasn't meant to be.

The train station at the border was filled with refugees, all desperately trying to get across before the German onslaught. Trains weren't travelling across the frontier anymore, and the crossing on the main road located about a half hour away from the train station was closed. The entire place was so crowded with misplaced persons that it was indescribable. They came to the border in an endless stream of vehicles: the owners wanted to abandon their cars there in order to save themselves on foot. Food was almost impossible to get, and a room was unthinkable. I was happy because I managed to find a place on a bench in a waiting room where I could hold Janek on my lap. From time to time the older children would also find a place to sit, or they would simply lie down on the floor.

Now and then a rumor circulated that the borders were opening. Everyone rushed off and waited there for a few hours, sometimes in pouring rain, but returned deeply disappointed and even more afraid. These days and nights were dreadful, and my strength was running out. I'll never forget what Janek said to me then: "I really like this! I don't have to go to bed and I can always sleep on Mommy's lap." I was profoundly thankful that I had the task of protecting such a young creature, and that I wasn't transferring my anxiety to him.

And yet another person became very important to me during this period who reminded me that there was something else in the world besides fear, terror, and being hunted. Near us on the bench in the waiting room was a mulatto, a French citizen who had all of his papers in order and was on his way to a French colony. He didn't try to get over the border, even when it was suddenly opened. He was waiting for—his bicycle. He had dispatched it on the train and didn't want to leave France without it. How soothing it was to experience this. There was still a world where someone waited patiently for his bicycle. And he didn't wait in vain: four days later it really arrived and he rode away quite happily across the border.

Our situation wasn't as satisfactory. We tried to travel to Spain on the first train that went across the border because we had a Spanish transit visa, but without a visa for Portugal the Spaniards wouldn't let us in. We were sent back and ended up in the same train station. In the meantime, the French had closed the waiting room, so we sat on the street. I wanted to try one last time to acquire the Portuguese visa and befriended a lady who was in the same situation. She had connections with the Portuguese consulate in Bayonne. What a struggle it was to make the trip with a taxi driver who demanded an enormous sum, and what a difficult decision it was to leave three children behind without their mother.

Julek was a godsend. I could give him money and tell him to look for a place to stay that night, something that was no longer impossible, because most of the refugees who had visas had already crossed the border.

Because I couldn't say when I would be back the next day, I told Julek to meet me at the train station. My trip was upsetting and came to nothing. I didn't have paid proof of passage from Portugal to Brazil and realized that we would have to stay in France with our permanent visa for the time being. I returned late that evening and was more than happy to meet Julek in front of the terminal. After he had found lodging for the children, he returned there on the chance that I might come back that night. My son had some disturbing news for me: during my absence the refugees had been put in the mayor's vehicles and sent to Lourdes because the border locality had been included within the German-occupied zone. The troops were anticipated at any moment.

It seemed that we were the only ones who had been left behind and now had to figure out how to travel out of the occupied zone at our own expense. When day broke, I started searching and I succeeded in finding some others in the same situation. So, together with a diplomat, a mulatto, and a German refugee lady, we took a car. After a protracted discussion, the owner agreed to drive us part of the way to the border of the presumed occupied zone without demanding an astronomical price. I quickly woke up the children and we set out. Soon we arrived in a little town that seemed friendly. We went to a small hotel and spent a comfortable night after I had gone shopping for underwear. It was high time we changed it since what we were wearing was all we had.

We really liked the village and decided to stay there. Our female travel companion took the responsibility of going to the town mayor the next morning to get some information about accommodations. She came back quickly; there were plenty of lodgings available, but the town had been included in the occupied zone, and the last bus was leaving there in half an hour! Once again I got the children ready in a rush so that we could catch the bus that was, of course, packed. When we arrived at our destination, we weren't allowed to get out because the place was filled with refugees. The vehicle drove to the nearest larger city, and stopped in front of the closed train station. The women sat on the lawn while Julek and the diplomat went to look for a place to stay. When they came back hours later with nothing, I went looking for a place for Janek so that at least he could have a roof over his head. As for the older children, nothing terrible would happen if they slept outside in the mild June night.

So I took Janek by the hand and felt confident that someone would open a door for the child. But this walk became what was for me one of the most depressing memories of my life: I rang endless doorbells and went to hotels asking only if I could spend the night on one of the many chairs in the hallway. Everywhere I heard a curt "no!" In the meantime, the diplomat had received information that a bus was bound for Pau that evening. The prospects of finding a room in one of the small towns near Pau seemed better. Once again we took to the road and got out of the bus in the town of Gan.

A waiter in one of the cafes, while escorting us to the door, stated flatly that Janek couldn't spend the night there on a bench. Afterwards, the German refugee and I did manage to find a place for him with a friendly butcher's wife. Julek and the diplomat spent the night wandering back and forth in front of the town hall, and the next evening they stayed in a barn somewhere. After that we finally managed to find a room outside of Gan, in a place called the Old Lady of Gan.

What happened there is worth mentioning. We rented two rooms with the German refugee, our traveling companion, for an exorbitant fee. We were allowed to cook in the fireplace in the kitchen. The property was situated beautifully, right next to a water mill, but the solitary old lady who lived there was like a greedy old witch from mythology. Everything on her property was old and starving: chickens, pigs, oxen, etc. We lived a quiet and peaceful life there and went shopping in Gan. Genia took over the "kitchen," and tried cooking a meal over an open fire in the fireplace for the first time. Now and then we let cars take us to and from the beautiful city of Pau. It was here that I had my first lessons in Portuguese from a friendly old priest whose passion was repairing old watches. We took wonderful walks in the picturesque countryside and the children recuperated. But the tranquility was only superficial: we were cut off from the entire world, we had no contact with my husband, and there was not much chance that he would find us. The money that he had given us before we left was almost gone, and the attempts at getting a visa didn't work. In short, our situation wasn't rosy.

So I decided to accept the invitation of our friend Ehrlich, who owned property near Montauban. I had hesitated to get in touch with him because I didn't know if it would put me in a dangerous situation, because they were still being watched by the Germans. But their estate was in the unoccupied zone and they invited us so hospitably to stay with them, that I finally decided to go there. It was a great comfort for me once again to be in a warm and humane atmosphere with helpful people.

The Ehrlichs lived in a large and beautiful home with very little furniture. Although they led a simple and difficult life, we were taken in without hesitation and felt like family. The children helped with the cows and pigs, took turns picking grapes at the neighbors, and Julek and even Janek took a great liking to Ruth Ehrlich. Because Montauban was a direct link to Bordeaux, we tried several times to get back our luggage that we had dispatched on our trip from Vichy to Bordeaux. After we sent a letter to the Germans written in German, something amazing happened. We got back our suitcases! The few things from Poland that we still have today were those things that we had in Stara Wies and then in Vichy. Those were the "unimportant" items that we had lost, and they had found us again. Thus it happened that peculiar things like the table cloth that my parents brought me from India, and this or that item of elegant clothing found their way to Brazil, and other more important things were gone forever.

Suddenly we were rich, and every piece of clothing from the suitcases was a gift. In the meantime, I tried to work on our departure. It just wouldn't work out for us to have the Spanish and Portuguese transit visas and the French exit visa all at the same time. There was always one missing even if we managed to get the other. Finally it seemed like it was going to work out. We packed our bags and set out on our way . . . but returned the same day. In the meantime, the French exit visa was no longer valid for the border we had to cross. But no one had told us that the day before! What luck that we were living with the Ehrlichs and could continue to stay there—it would have been a horrible situation otherwise.

Since our arrival, the Ehrlichs had sold their property for cash and rented a small house. We moved in even though it was crowded for them. They also loaned us money so that we could work on our emigration. Then came the winter of 1940–41 that was frigid and snowy. We were cold and glad to have the thick Polish sheepskins that had found their way back to us in our suitcases. Finally we learned of a ship that would travel directly from Marseille to Rio de

Janeiro, which did away with the necessity of transit visas, so I decided to take this trip and booked places for us on the *Alsina*.

In order for the ship to be able to travel safely, it had to get permission from all warring powers, so it took weeks then months before the company could tell us the departure date. We climbed aboard the ship at the beginning of January 1941, assuming that we would arrive in Rio within three weeks. We didn't know that we wouldn't leave the *Alsina* for five months. The ship was, of course, completely occupied with people from many countries and classes, from poor Spanish emigrants to the former president of Spain, Zamorra and his family. Most of the travelers were German emigrants, although a group of Polish engineers and some French were also on board. Many of the higher-class passengers stayed in the third-class sleeping rooms.

We were fortunate because we had a small third-class cabin with four beds all to ourselves. The room was so tiny and the ceiling so low that we couldn't sit up in bed, so when Janek was sick, as was often the case, I had to lie down next to him. The quarters were made still smaller by a huge ventilating system that took fresh air from our cabin to the rest of the ship. We had good air, a great benefit in a cabin with no windows, however, less advantageous were the water pipes that went through our room and the water bursts that occurred from time to time covering our beds and suitcases. But this happened later during the voyage.

At first we traveled to Dakar, Senegal via Oran, Algeria. The sea was rough, and with the exception of Julek who remained strong, our cabin was a collection of seasick passengers. We were all happy to arrive in Dakar and to once again walk on land. Genia was frightened of the many dark people, and Janek was surprised that even the babies were already black. For me, the first impression of the colorful splendor and abundance of the native marketplace was an unforgettable sight. We thought that we would be leaving the next day and were astounded when our departure was postponed daily. Then they told us that the continuing voyage was cancelled until further notice, that our travel tickets only included room and board for three weeks, and that we had to pay for the additional "hotel."

This created great agitation. Only a few passengers had money at their disposal, and the wildest rumors were going around about what would happen to those who couldn't pay. After endless telegrams and difficulties, the additional demand for payment was dropped and all of us stayed on ship.

It would be going too far to discuss the details of our months on the *Alsina* in the port of Dakar, but the anxiety of the passengers increased daily. After all, we were at war and none of us knew what the next hour would bring. Each day brought new gossip about our fate and novel attempts to continue the voyage: suggestions of other routes, renting of an Argentine ship to be financed by the passengers, attempts to reach the nearest English colony with sailboats, procurement of visas for the republic of Liberia. The passengers tried everything.

At the same time, the food was getting worse and worse. Even the sick received neither rice nor potatoes. The main source of nutrition was poorly prepared fish and the half-cooked *poichis*, a kind of pea. Each traveler received a small ration of sugar every day, along with a limited supply of bread. In short, our stay was unpleasant. We were allowed to go ashore only once a week, and even then we weren't allowed to buy anything. When we returned to the harbor, we had to go through customs, and a routine was started among the passengers to smuggle eggs and jam. There was such comradery among those on ship that the management didn't succeed in keeping second- and third-class passengers separated. As time went on, work and study groups formed: a type of tailor's workshop was introduced, naturally without machines. The Polish director Ziembinski staged a pleasant show, and everyone tried his best to stay busy.

Janek had many friends, especially Mr. Schur who was particularly taken with him. All of the older children were also popular. In spite of the "social" life on the *Alsina*, the uneasiness of the voyagers was not abated. I didn't want to expose myself to this anxiety, and tried to stay away from the others as much as possible by playing with Janek. It must have been because of this that I got through the months better than most of the others. I was, of course, terribly anxious about Frederyk but was almost always confident that we would all stay healthy and see each other again. At this time we once again had communication with my husband, who was granted a leave of absence from the army because of his age. On the way to Brazil, his ship was bombed and he had to return to England. From there he flew to Lisbon where he discovered that his Brazilian permanent visa had expired because he hadn't emigrated within the time limit, and the visa wouldn't be renewed.

It was a terrible situation for Frederyk, but a good one for us to have him near us, if only by correspondence. He pressed the *Alsina* authorities to have us treated just as well as the French on board. They received preferential treatment over the other foreigners, a situation that had great significance for us later.

Months passed without any noticeable change in our lives. The *Alsina* would move in the harbor from one docking place to another, that was all. It got hotter, and the people on ship got sicker. Four babies were born from mothers who had anticipated being in Brazil long before. An anecdote concerning Janek is a good illustration of what life was like at this time. I sketched a picture, or was it Genia? It was a dining room with a bedroom and a closet. "Mommy," he asked, "what is a dining hall?" "A room where one eats," I replied. "But why, doesn't one eat in the kitchen?" he inquired. When he looked at the closet he asked the same question. When I explained to him that one hangs one's clothes in a closet, he found it terribly odd. "But Mommy, we hang clothes on a line!" Then I suddenly realized that since our departure from Obra, with the exception of the time spent in Vichy, we had always hung our clothes on a line!

The weather became hotter and hotter and one dared not go on land without headgear. To spare the expense, the passengers lent each other their hats. One felt part of a big family, and some of our friendships lasted longer than the time we spent aboard the *Alsina*, such as our close relationship with Mrs. Rozenowicz.

At the beginning of June there appeared an announcement on the bulletin board with the upsetting news that the *Alsina* and its passengers had to travel back to Casablanca! What was behind it? Slowly they began to unload the ship. It was no longer a secret to the passengers that the *Alsina* had contraband on board. That was the reason why our trip kept on being postponed. What could we expect in Casablanca? The atmosphere on ship was that of anxiety and optimism. Finally the torturous journey came to an end and we had beautiful weather with tranquil seas.

But then came the great disappointment in Casablanca. All passengers had to disembark and were "housed" in a camp of the Foreign Legion, until they could find another way to continue their journey. These were terrifying hours, obstinacy did not help and even the old and sick had to leave. Only the French were allowed to stay in Casablanca, as well as a few who received preferential treatment. Thanks to my husband's intervention we now belonged to the lucky group and were treated like the French. The farewell from our fellow passengers who faced an uncertain future was difficult, and I was impressed that most of our acquaintances did not oppose this special treatment but instead wished us luck.

We were allowed to roam freely for one week in Casablanca, and after this week if we had not yet left Morocco we would have to go back to the camp. Would we be able to get out in one week? Ships didn't stop in Morocco; one could only leave from Spain, and the few ships leaving from Spain were almost always full.

Julek's efficiency stood the test in this situation. He succeeded in taking care of all formalities quickly so when the initial ships came, he was always one of the first to disembark and therefore one of the first to get to the Travel Agency. Thanks to Julek we got the last reservations on the middle deck of the *Cabo Buena Esperança*, which was supposed to leave in the next few days. But we had no money, and the reservations had to be paid in dollars within forty-eight hours! How lucky we were that Frederyk was within reach! I was almost certain that he would be able to come up with the money, even though I knew that he was destitute. You can just imagine what a state of alarm he was in when he received our telegram that told him that everything depended on getting the money. We faced either an ocean voyage and freedom, or a refugee camp for an unknown period of time.

My husband came through, and our journey was secured. We experienced a few interesting days in the city of Casablanca, with its picturesque alleys and quaint leather stores. This is where we bought a briefcase for Julek. Janek was so used to being on the ship that he didn't say "we're going into town," but rather "we're going ashore." He called the top stories of the hotel the "upper deck."

When the day of departure arrived, we went via Tangier to Cadiz to board the ship with a few other passengers from the *Alsina* who were in the same situation. Tangier, being neutral, seemed mythical. However, we encountered another obstacle here. Something happened that Frederyk had always feared: our permanent visa had expired because we had been unable to enter Brazil within the three months after it had been issued. The *Alsina* commander's certification that we had been impeded by "higher powers" made no difference. Did we once again have to endure disappointment when we were so close to our goal? It was an exceedingly tense situation.

Finally, all the complaining and pleading of the *Alsina* passengers caused the consul to change his mind. He didn't give us another visa, but also didn't prevent us from boarding the ship. In other words, he signed his name to the passenger list that served as a rudimentary register for the shipping company that would be sent to the authorities in Rio. They would then decide whether we would be able to disembark or not.

Luckily at that time, we had no idea of how precarious our situation was, and were happy to finally be on a ship sailing for Rio. The vessel was more than overcrowded. Some beds had been sold twice, and a few of the passengers had to sleep on the deck. Finally we were given beds in the immediate vicinity of the toilets, and it was really awful. Janek has bad memories of this trip. But we had bread and even butter for breakfast; any meal at all was better than nothing. Nevertheless, for the *Alsina* passengers it seemed like a luxury. Besides, what difference did it make *how* we were traveling? The main point was that we were traveling!

The weather was agreeable, and during the voyage we received a telegram stating that father was on a ship to Rio that had left a week later than ours. The telegram did not have a signature, and I did not realize what it meant, thinking it might be from some fellow passengers from the *Alsina*. When I finally understood it was my husband's, I experienced a deep feeling of gratitude. Without further incident, we arrived in the harbor of Rio de Janeiro on July 10, 1941. After a few delays, we were allowed to disembark and were received by Mr. Vogel, whom we had telegrammed about our arrival. He was utterly astonished by our message, because he had heard "reliable" news about the sinking of our ship and the death of the passengers. Thanks to him, the police didn't find us and bring us to a camp because of our expired visas. We remained "untraceable" for a few days until the danger had passed. After much running around, our situation was put in order and our permanent visa declared valid.

The other passengers of the *Alsina* who arrived later were not so lucky, and most of them were not allowed to disembark. But we were there, and Frederyk actually arrived one week later! I can still see him standing in front of me. He stood on the deck and waived his handkerchief like a flag above his head to greet us from afar. That evening we sent a telegram to my mother Ella in Breslau reading: "united!" This word described all the pain and sorrow that occurred in the past and was replaced by the blessing of a reunion.

Thus began our life in Brazil: a life of great struggle and unappeased homesickness most of all for Frederyk during the first few years. It was also a life of strength and joy that emanated from my children, who made Brazil their new home. And it seems to have been a success: the most important values of the old world were combined with the atmosphere and challenges of the new.

Translated by Katherine Morris

KÄTE KAPHAN

Käte Kaphan describes the trauma of persecution through the eyes of her daughter, a schoolgirl under the National Socialist regime. The identity of the mother is closely bound to that of the young girl, and the lives of both are drastically reshaped by the Nazi policy toward Jews. The author defines herself through a mother/daughter relationship, and in this way gives voice to her child. It is the true story of Kaphan's daughter Annemarie, and the humiliation she suffered shortly before their emigration.

Children's points of view are often absent in the memoirs of men. As Rahel Straus stated in her memoir of Imperial Germany: "For a man, his career is the main content of his life, everything else is secondary." And she continues: "I have often found that in the biography of a man, even in an autobiography, his children are hardly mentioned."[1] A child's world view is what enriches so many of the texts in this anthology, but what is unusual about Kaphan's story is that she does not focus on her own childhood, but on that of her daughter.

After the Nazis came to power, they passed laws to change the school system in order to benefit "Aryan" students by decreeing the segregation of Germans and Jews. On April 25, 1933, one of the most important racial ordinances came into effect. The Law against Overcrowding of German Schools reduced the number of "non-Aryans" in each college or school to the proportion of "non-Aryans" in the German population as a whole.[2] Primary schools were not affected, but in the high schools (*Gymnasien*), universities, and technical institutes, an acceptance quota for Jews (*numerus clausus*) was fixed at 1.5 percent of the total enrollment in order to reduce progressively the size of the total Jewish student body.[3] Exceptions to the 1.5 percent rule were made in cities where the percentage of Jews in the community exceeded 5 percent of the total population.

Because of the new law, Jews were forced to set up their own schools. By 1936, more than 50 percent of Jewish students from ages six to fourteen attended schools run by the Jewish community. Although some Jewish children were still allowed to attend German schools, the position of the Jew in the Nazi school system was not enviable. The anti-Semitic curriculum included racial theory that emphasized the inferiority of Jews. For example, some students learned that all Jews were communists, and that Jews were responsible for World War I, inflation, and the unjust armistice of 1918.[4] By November 1938, the remaining Jewish students were expelled from the German school system. Thereafter, Jews were only permitted to attend Jewish schools.[5] The story of Annemarie Kaphan shows how Jewish children suffered isolation and racism in school during the National Socialist regime.

Käte Kaphan (née Manasse) was born in Dramburg, Pomerania in 1906. Although her brother Ernst attended the Gymnasium, Käte attended middle school because there was no college preparatory school for girls in the town. At fifteen, she became engaged to Heinrich Kaphan, a young man thirteen years her senior who had been a soldier in World War I. He was one of the few Jewish farmers in the area, and owned land near Dramburg. At her parent's insistence, she waited three years and married him at the age of eighteen. The couple lived on a farm, Emilienhof, near Dramburg until their emigration in 1936. Between 1924–36, Käte Kaphan had three children and lived as a farmer's wife in Pomerania.

Her father, who had managed a business selling farm products in Dramburg, died in 1935. A few months after his burial, *der Stürmer* printed a notice about him, including the names of the non-Jews who had attended his funeral. This page of the Nazi paper was posted in the marketplace of Dramburg. After that incident, few townspeople dared to greet the Manasses on the street or to visit their home.

The Kaphans and Käte's brother started making preparations to leave Germany. While they evaded a cruel fate, very few of their relatives escaped the Holocaust. Käte's mother later joined the

Kaphans in Brazil.[6] Ernst Manasse immigrated to America and now resides in Durham, North Carolina.

THE LITTLE JEWISH GIRL

BY KÄTE KAPHAN

Her name was Annemarie, and she played happily with the other children in the school yard. She had blues eyes and blond hair just like most of her schoolmates. In class she sat next to the other children. She wore glasses on her lightly freckled nose and sat close to the chalkboard so that she could see it well.

Annemarie was not always happy, since she was terribly homesick. Her parents lived in the country and she had to live with her grandparents in order to attend school. It was only on Saturday, after school, that she was allowed to take the train home, only to return once again early Monday morning. But that meant something wonderful: in the morning, while it was still quite dark, she sat between her parents, warmly wrapped and indescribably secure as they drove to the station. How she loved that half hour.

Each time she sat in the poorly lit train car, so small and alone, she fought back the tears as they welled up inside her, and she reminded herself that another week had begun and soon it would be Sunday again.

Annemarie liked school. Learning was fun for her. If the homework was a bit difficult, her grandfather would help her. But he was a little too strict, she thought, and as soon as he really pushed her, she would have tears in her eyes. She cried so easily! Almost as easily as her little brother. They all teased him about it, and she always felt somewhat ashamed for him.

But Annemarie's tears would dry as fast they flowed. There was always something to look forward to. There was the play that was supposed to be performed in front of the whole class, a wonderful play with a chorus and angels and a moon and stars. The children barely had time to get their homework done each afternoon before they had to go back to school. Not even the best toboggan-run or the frozen river, which was perfect for ice skating, could keep them away. The Christmas play came first, and it was such fun that it outshone everything else. She even refused to be saddened when one of the kids would shout "Jew girl" at her, which was happening more

70

often now. "If God made me this way, it must be for the best," she once said to a schoolmate who had heard the shout.

A week before Christmas vacation near the end of rehearsal for the performance, the teacher, his voice sounding as if nothing were wrong, said: "Of course the three Jewish girls don't need to make any clothes since they won't be allowed to participate."

Among the jumble of the other kids, the three girls stood struck with horror. This was absolutely impossible. Why did they suddenly not belong? Until today they had been allowed to participate just like the other children. "You three can go," said the teacher. "I think," Annemarie said as she and the other two children left the school, "that my heart stopped beating when he said that." "Mine too," said little Inge.

Käte Manasse (age fourteen?) and brother
Ernst Manasse (age twelve?), ca. 1920,
Dramburg, Pomerania. Courtesy of Ernst Manasse.

By the time Annemarie ran all the way home, her cheeks red from the cold of the winter day and the upsetting news, her mother was already there. "Were you practicing again for your performance? You've hardly got time for your homework anymore," she kidded. "They won't let us be in it, Inge, Hilde and me," said Annemarie and then she cried inconsolably in her mother's arms, devastated by the feeling that she had been so horribly embarrassed in front of the other children. "I never want to go back to school, never, ever." "It's mandatory," her mother said, her heart breaking, "you've got to go." Her daughter had reached a lonely point. Her little girl had to accept her fate. Not even her mother could help her now. What a tragic realization for the mother and the daughter, a realization so deep that it reached the very roots of the connection between mother and child.

The next day Annemarie went to school by herself, and even when they were together, the three Jewish children were alone now, each of them carrying the heavy burden of being outcasts, spurned and despised by the others in the class.

After Christmas vacation the three girls were no longer allowed to sit next to the others. They sat in the last row. "I can't read the board from here," said Annemarie, but the teacher only shrugged his shoulders. Annemarie didn't cry anymore. She fought against it with all her might; she did not want anyone to see how badly she had been hurt.

But one day she did cry even though she really did not want to because her teacher, who used to be so friendly to her, was standing right there. It happened when she asked him to return her "poetry album," which she had loaned him a long time ago so that he could write a few words in it. "I don't remember what I did with it," he said, "it's probably gone." Her beloved poetry album. Her teacher and her schoolmates had written such lovely poems in it, and she had always kept it so carefully, afraid that the leather jacket would get dirty. Now it was gone. The teacher didn't even seem to know if he'd ever had it.

Little Annemarie cried then, aware of his coldhearted and inhuman indifference in the way he said "I don't even know if I have it any more . . ." You could tell that each day, each hour in school was torture for the children. They were no longer cheerful and carefree. Their childhood had been stolen. Security and trust in the fairness of adults, the basis of a child's happiness, had been replaced by the fear that had been planted in their young hearts.

72

At the end of the year the class was supposed to write an essay. The three little Jewish girls, outcasts who sat despised in the last row, were supposed to write an essay titled "In celebration of January 30."[1] What an absurd thing to ask for, what cruel cynicism. Unless you remember that the parents of these Jewish children lived in constant danger, it would be hard to believe that they decided to make the children write the essay. "It won't help. Unless we want to risk everything, the children have to write it," the parents said, disgusted by the betrayal of their own decision, but scared of the unavoidable consequences if they did otherwise.

Annemarie's parents did not let her write the essay. Annemarie's mother said: "It would be better for you to be thrown out of school than to write that essay," and, when Annemarie said she was scared, she added "write some other paper. Write about something else, whatever you've been doing in class, just tell them that your mother would not let you write that essay."

It was as if the teacher was looking right through her when, almost dying of fear, she whispered to him what her mother had said. From then on the teacher treated her as if she were not even there. He would not look at her homework. While the other children were trying to outdo each other to show how much they learned, their hands flailing wildly in the air, she raised her hand modestly when she knew the answer, one finger extended; but he would not call on her. It made no sense to keep trying.

At first Annemarie had not realized that it was being done on purpose. But eventually it became clear to her. And one day, after school, she put her knapsack on and never went to back to school. Annemarie was able to emigrate to a far-away country. Both of her Jewish schoolmates died along with their parents in concentration camps.

Translated by Matthew Kaplan

RENÉE-MARIE CROOSE PARRY

For many, exile and war were experienced at a young age. Renée-Marie Croose Parry (née Hausenstein) describes what life was like in Bavaria as the daughter of a Jewish mother, and how she later escaped from Germany to Brazil. Croose Parry starts with her youth in the 1920s and 1930s and continues up to her arrival in the United States in 1946 at the age of twenty-four.

The fact that she was unusual by virtue of her maternal Jewish inheritance became clear to her when she was about fourteen. One day, as a student at the Lyceum of the Missionary Benedictines in Tutzing, she found her classmates and teachers discussing who would enlist in and attend the functions of the *Bund Deutscher Mädchen* (League of German Girls). Of course, Renée-Marie would not, and could not, join.

The League of German Girls was a constituent organization of the *Hitlerjugend* (Hitler Youth). There had been forerunners of the League in the 1920s, such as girls' organizations with National Socialist tendencies; however, in 1930, the *Völkischer Beobachter* announced that the organization had been renamed as part of the Hitler Youth.[1]

The major aim of the League of German Girls was to instruct young women in the ideals of National Socialism: obedience, discipline, fulfillment of duty, and self-sacrifice to the party. After 1936, the emphasis was on becoming healthy, suitable housewives. Until 1939, the primary goal of the League was to educate and train women to become mothers of "racially pure" children, and to raise them as good National Socialists. The Hitler Youth motto for girls was: "Be faithful, Be pure, Be German!"[2] One-third of the educational program was devoted to ideological training—schooling that emphasized the difference between "Aryans" and "non-Aryans."

In such an environment, not only did the young Renée-Marie feel like an outcast because of her mother's Jewish ancestry, but also because of her father's occupation as an uncompromising writer and art historian. The most dramatic and shocking realization of her plight occurred when her father was reviled by the Nazi authorities at the infamous Exhibition of Degenerate Art in Munich in 1937.

Since Hitler's rise to power in January of 1933, the suppression of modern art in Germany became part of the Nazi's political program. In 1933, Göring condemned the Bauhaus movement as a "breeding ground for cultural Bolshevism."[3] Hitler's first speech against "degenerate art" was given in Nuremberg in 1934. Degeneration (*Entartung*) was originally a medical term in the National Socialist vocabulary, a term used to describe human deterioration caused by "racial mixing and the decline of physical and mental capacity based on heredity and race."[4] The term "degenerate" became a Nazi catchword and later an official designation for non-naturalistic modern art, particularly art that was innovative or socially critical, such as Dadaism or Expressionism.

Gradually, the works of the "degenerate" artists such as Max Beckmann, Otto Dix, and Paul Klee were systematically removed from public collections and galleries. In the summer of 1937, Adolf Ziegler, the president of the Reich Chamber of Fine Arts, assembled paintings, graphics, and sculptures under the title of "Degenerate Art" for display in the Hofgarten in Munich. Twenty-five of the leading German museums were required to give up materials for this exhibition. Beginning in 1937, German and foreign works of modern art were expropriated under the label of "degenerate art." Some were sold abroad by dealers to line the pockets of Nazi politicians, some were sold by auction in Lucerne, and the rest were burned in Berlin in 1939.[5]

The Nazi attacks against innovative art were not solely directed against the works of art themselves, but also against the artists and those who supported them. These artists were dismissed from their jobs in museums and teaching institutions, and deprived of their degrees and honors. The Nazi dictatorship marked the end of an era in Germany, the end of an epoch that had allowed free discussion of politics and poetry, the end of respect for the individual and the intellectual, and the end of a period that cultivated a savoir faire in the world of culture and art, a world in which Germany was preeminent. It was also the end of normal family life for Renée-Marie Hausenstein.

OSTRACISM AND EXILE

BY RENÉE-MARIE CROOSE PARRY*

A Perilous Start

The port of Lisbon, where we had embarked in the early days of March, 1942, was already far behind us as, all too gently, we glided away from the war that was tearing the fabric of European civilization asunder. It had taken a strong dose of fatalism to entrust our lives to the *Siqueira Campos*, an old German ship which Brazil had kept, among other reparations, after the first World War. It had been rumored that half of the passengers were too frightened to risk the voyage, and hoped to be able to stay on in the safety of neutral Portugal. As would soon become apparent, their fears were justified. Following Brazil's termination of diplomatic relations with Germany some weeks earlier, Hitler's government had announced that any vessel which could not readily be identified by its flag would be torpedoed without warning, a fate that befell the ship that sailed from Lisbon immediately before us. In this threatening situation, the Captain had decided to camouflage the *Siqueira Campos*, thus causing our delayed departure while the ship was painted battle gray and her portholes blackened. When we were finally summoned to leave, the first sight of the old ship came as a shock. She looked more like a battleship ready to sail for war, than a liner about to carry us safely across the ocean. I was assigned a cabin near the center of the main deck, and was pleased to have it to myself. Whatever fears and trepidations we had felt soon evaporated, thanks mostly to the friendliness of the Brazilian crew. Over dinner we talked about our debt to providence for having brought us this far. We drank to our future, holding on to our youthful and insouciant faith that we would be alright if we could survive the first most dangerous days and reach the open seas.

---

*I wish to thank my husband, Kenneth, for the many hours spent in going through these pages with me, and for all the editorial and linguistic improvements he suggested.

Back in my cabin, I unpacked and arranged my belongings for a good start to the three week voyage to Rio de Janeiro. Relieved after the long wait, I quickly fell into a deep sleep. But it was not to last. A thunderous and bellowing noise, coming from the entrails of the ship right underneath my cabin, made me leap from my bed. My first thought was that we had been hit by a torpedo, and that the ship would sink. In a sleepy stupor, I raced onto the deck, and back again to pick up the bag that contained my most precious and irreplaceable papers and possessions. Once more, I heard the same rumblings, followed by a pounding clatter as if rocks were striking metal. Back on deck I saw no fire, no smoke, and not a single member of the crew. The night was cold and clear, and the chill distracted my mind, helping to allay my panic. The noise stopped. I realized I would now have to wait for morning to find out what had happened. I reassured myself that if something had seriously gone wrong, someone would have come to warn and instruct the passengers. I managed to subdue my worries, and fell asleep again. I don't know how long I slept before I was jolted out of bed once more by the same shattering din. It followed the previous pattern, and abated after several minutes. I looked outside, but no one could be seen. I tried to pacify my thoughts and sleep till morning.

It must have been about eight when I rang the bell. The steward knocked almost immediately. I opened the door to a slender man in a smart, dark blue uniform with golden braiding and buttons, who addressed me in French. When I asked what had caused the horrendous noise in the middle of the night, his simple explanation quickly dispelled my fears. What, in fact, had ruined my sleep was the sound of large clinkers from the furnaces that drove the turbines, which, on this ancient ship, were discharged at intervals straight into the sea! Alas, the chute carrying this debris passed close underneath my cabin. When I asked why I had not been alerted the evening before, to be spared such a harrowing experience, I was told a long and intricate tale depicting the many disadvantages of all the other cabins. Having weighed the pros and cons of moving, I decided to stay on the main deck. I was occupying the only cabin with immediate access to the open air and skies, which also allowed me to avoid the narrow passage ways and cumbersome thresholds under the heavy safety doors on the lower levels. Besides, I could always stuff my ears with cotton wool!

I was barely twenty when I crossed the Atlantic aboard this ship, travelling with a group of Brazilian students of German origin, which included an aeronautical engineer whom I had met at Munich University, and with whom I had entered into a pro forma marriage to make possible my escape from Germany. I had left behind a father and mother, who, more than anything, wanted their daughter to survive. My escape would allow them to confront together whatever peril might befall them, without endangering their only child. And here I was, carried forward by circumstance, having torn myself away, somehow, from parents and friends, from familiar environments and customs—and, not least, from grievous remembrances and fears . . .

Growing up in Bavaria

My early childhood might have appeared normal outwardly, but inwardly it was a time of turmoil. My often withdrawn, but always caring, father—a leading art historian and author of many books—was already fifty when I was only ten. My mother, a native of Brussels, who ruled her household with precision, acumen, and style, was in her early forties. In 1932 my parents rented a house on a hill at the edge of the forest high above Tutzing, with views of Starnberger See and the Bavarian Alps. As was explained to me a few years later, it had been hoped that with the Nazi movement growing we would be less conspicuous and our lives more tenable, if we moved from Munich to the countryside. I delighted in my escape from the city. During long walks on the wooded lake-side with my young and loving nanny, Gusti, we picked mussel shells from among the withering leaves that had fallen ankle-deep from the gigantic oaks and beeches along the lake shore. I relished the nutty, musty odor, when our shoes stirred the brown, decaying mass of leaves. These mussels, known in German as "Gemeine Teichmuscheln"—*Anodonta Cygnea*, which today is a protected species—concealed scintillating mother-of-pearl interiors, and became objects of deep fascination, one of my first binding links with nature. The country-fresh simplicity and genuine devotion, that Gusti brought to our relationship, created a bond that was to give more emotional security and stability to my life. Alas, the idyllic years in this beautiful corner of Bavaria: the excursions on Benediktenwand, the broad and gently contoured mountain range some twenty miles Southwest beyond the lake—upon whose outline I would often watch the light of the setting sun from my balcony; the skiing in the foothills of the Alps; the swimming and sailing; the convivial and delicious meals in local inns of Starnberger See *Renken,* lightly breaded, pan-fried fish caught only in our lake; the carefree innocence of these enjoyments was to suffer an abrupt end.

It had been a perfect sunny morning for our recreation-break in the courtyard of the convent school. We were eating slices of thick brown bread spread with home-made raspberry jam, prepared for us by the sisters to bridge the time between early breakfast and the end of our school day at one. Then, suddenly, like a bolt from the blue, my whole life would be changed. I was about to receive sentence of separation from my peers. One of my class-mates, a girl from the town of Weilheim, turned towards me and shouted with a pitched voice: "Du Judenweib!"—"You Jewish wench!"—spitting on the ground before me. It must have happened in my fifth year of enrollment at the Lyceum of the Missionary Benedictines, when I was about fourteen. For a few seconds, which felt like many long minutes, I stood immobilized. Stunned and confused, I could not understand what was happening to me. A thousand thoughts raced through my mind. I knew that my mother looked foreign. She was one of the few women in the village who wore make-up, which used to worry me. My father once told me that some of the villagers spoke ill of her, saying that she was false; but he hastened to state categorically that nothing could be farther from the truth. In order to escape the staring eyes and jeers of the girls surrounding me, I turned and ran for home, up Station Street, along the railway track, through the tunnel, and up the steep lane leading to our house, poised on a small plateau above the village. I opened the front door and called my parents with a breathless, tearful voice. Why did others seem to know things that I did not know? If indeed I were Jewish, why had I not been told? I was angry and crushed. I thought my life was coming to an end.

It took me several years, and the endurance of many whispered innuendos and secretive exchanges, so prevalent at the time, really to understand *why,* and *how,* my mother's ancestry should suddenly have changed my whole existence. Waking up to the dangers of our situation, which my parents had kept hidden from me for the sole purpose of safeguarding a happy and unencumbered childhood, seemed harder now than had my eyes been opened from the beginning in 1933, when—upon Hitler's rise to power—my parents' much delayed return from a study tour in Greece might have been explained to me in terms of the new reality.[1] But I was then alone with Gusti and my paternal grandmother, Clara—and only eleven years of age. Though my father was a Protestant, and my mother Jewish, by race if not by faith, my parents had believed it would be wise to bring up their child in harmony with the predominant religion of the region, which, at the time, was Roman Catholic.

That day, my parents talked to me for hours, trying to calm my troubled mind. We sat in my father's study at the long table, on which he was preparing the layouts for the next issues of the weekly Literary and Woman's Supplements he edited for the old *Frankfurter Zeitung*. He explained to me some of the details of my mother's background: her upbringing with her brother by her early widowed mother in Brussels, where he had met my mother in 1916, herself a young widow of World War I, whose first husband, Richard Lipper, had fought the Germans and succumbed to fatal wounds in Flanders; and, further back into the past century, when my mother's maternal grandfather, Rabbi Isaak Rülf, organized extensive aid, and health and educational facilities for the multitude of Russian Jews, then fleeing from the pogroms in pre-revolutionary Russia.[2] Among the books Isaak Rülf had written, the most important were five volumes on metaphysics.[3] My father then described his own precarious situation as a writer, and told me how his refusal of a request by the Ministry of Propaganda to delete Jewish artists from future editions of his comprehensive and widely read Art History,[4] had caused the withdrawal and destruction of all his books, and his expulsion from the National Society of Writers,[5] which made it impossible for him to publish any further books in Germany. I heard his words and saw my mother nodding supportively, but it took years and many more questions until I was able to interiorize and fully comprehend the meaning of what had been imparted to me. This process was gravely undermined by a further occurrence when a regular summer visitor to the village, whom I would often meet on the way to the public bathing place on the lake shore, stopped me one day to enquire whether I was the daughter of Wilhelm Hausenstein, and then asked whether I was the child of his first or present wife. Thrown completely off balance, I mumbled, "His present wife . . ." running off as fast as I could. An insidious doubt had been planted in my tender and vulnerable psyche, which it would take me a long time to resolve.

Later that afternoon, my parents went to see the Mother Superior at the Lyceum to inform her of the morning's incident. Besides genuine apologies, they received every assurance that such behavior on the part of my class mates would not be allowed to occur again.

But a spell had been cast. When I went back to school, the question of enlistment and attendance at the functions of the *Bund Deutscher Mädchen*—the Hitler youth organization for girls, was being discussed, again setting me apart as the only non-member. Happily my parents decided that I should spend my final year, from 1937 to 1938, in the convent school of St. Irmengard in Garmisch-Partenkirchen, where, we had been told, Princess Roslie zu Öttingen and Ines von Stauffenberg, neither of whom belonged to the BDM, would be among my class mates. The new experience of communal life as a boarding pupil helped me to feel accepted, and I blossomed in the absence of the constricting pressures deriving from the generation gap and anxious atmosphere at home.

At the school in Tutzing we had already begun to read parts of the daily newspapers in class as the regime required, and, although the news had previously held little interest for me, I now paid more attention, trying to find out what in our readings might be of consequence to our lives. My parents, who had always avoided discussing politics in my presence, and in that of the cook and maid, for fear of repercussions should an unguarded word slip over their lips at the wrong moment, now tried to draw me into conversations to help objectify my understanding of our situation and of my father's work for the newspaper in Frankfurt.

I had lived in such blissful ignorance! I knew, of course, of Hitler's role as chancellor of Germany, and probably had seen a few pictures in the papers, but little else. There was no television then, and I would have found it difficult in those early years to describe Hitler's appearance, had it not been for a visit to *Zirkus Krone* in Munich. This great circus had been part of the cultural history of the city since the beginning of the century, and my parents its regular patrons since 1921. Frieda and Carl Krone warmly received us at the entrance door, and, having taken us aside, warned us that Hitler would be attending the performance incognito. They apologized for having to give him the box normally reserved for us. That evening, Frieda Krone led us personally to the seats immediately in front of our usual box. Hitler was to arrive after the lights were dimmed. My father entreated me not to turn my head. But at barely twelve years of age, this was an invitation. My eyes were glued upon the entrance to the arena. Hitler appeared within minutes, after the band had finished playing the grand overture. He wore a dull moss green, belted raincoat, and, together with his aides, was escorted to the box behind us by an official of the circus. Having waited

Renée-Marie Hausenstein (age fourteen)
on the Ilkahöhe above Tutzing.
Courtesy of Renée-Marie Croose Parry.

Wilhelm Hausenstein and daughter Renée-Marie
in the *Buchenhaus* garden, summer, 1934.
Courtesy of Renée-Marie Croose Parry.

impatiently, and trusting that by now all eyes would be firmly focussed on the performance in the ring, I turned my head very
slowly to catch a glimpse of Hitler's face. He was sitting two yards
away, with only a low wooden banister separating his seat from
ours. He noticed my furtive glance almost immediately, and looked
straight into my eyes with a bemused and kindly smile. I felt a mis-
chievous satisfaction as I turned again toward the ring. After the
circus I remarked to my parents, not without a faint smirk of pride,
how friendly Hitler seemed, and how he had smiled at me. But I received no reply . . .

From the moment that I was living in the full knowledge of my
Jewish ancestry, remembrances from the past began to push into
the foreground of my mind, as if to seek integration into their
rightful place. One such memory concerned my father's closest
friend, the Jewish philosopher and physician, Max Picard, who had
been living in the Italian part of Switzerland, the Ticino, since the
early twenties. When Hitler came to power, Max was forced to give
up his visits to his close friend and companion, Dora König, whose
house in Starnberg lay but a twenty minute train ride from our village. Henceforth, Dora would travel across the Alps to be with him.
A year or two passed, with almost daily exchanges of letters and
postcards between Max and my father. Then, one day without
warning, having overcome his fears and brushed aside all reason,
Max appeared at our door in Tutzing, driven by the overwhelming
need for live communication with his friends. I remember hearing
the doorbell—and, shortly afterwards, the most heartrending sobs,
that seemed to emanate from my father's study. Fearful of what
might have happened, I flew down the two flights of stairs, stopped
to collect myself, and quietly peered through the study door, holding my breath as I stood on the threshold. There, in the distant corner of the room, sat the familiar figure of Max Picard—in whose
honor my parents had given me my second name, Maximiliane. He
sat crouched in wordless grief, with his hands folded tightly over his
knees, and tears streaming down his face. My parents, who were
kneeling on the floor in front of him, begged him to explain his un-
controllable despair. The more they asked, the more he wept. After
a while, having become aware of my presence, my mother turned
her distraught face towards me, and with a gesture of the hand indicated that I had better leave the room.

Only a year or two later, after the cruel incident in school had
set in train the discovery of my Jewish heritage, did my father

enlarge on his earlier veiled explanations, confiding what Max had said after regaining his composure. His mind, father told me, had been overwhelmed by visions of an unspeakable future, of a catastrophe of immeasurable proportions. Max had not elaborated. He had simply repeated over and over again: "Es ist schrecklich! Was ich kommen sehe ist schrecklich!"—"It is terrible! What I see coming is terrible!" Neither my parents' nor my own imagination could, *at that moment in time*, have fathomed the depth or the dimensions of the horrors that were to come. Looking back upon this visit, we had no doubt that as Max sat in my father's reading chair, trembling with the pain of his vision, his living body had indeed presaged the ordeals, and the gruesome, cruel death, that had begun to descend upon the Jewish race. I never sit down in my father's armchair, which is still kept in his study nearly sixty years later, without reflecting on the flow of tears Max Picard shed in it—in prophecy of the great mourning . . .

Another memory from those years, which is still stronger than that of the whistling whine of the first bombs I heard fall upon Munich, is a visit with my parents to the "Exhibition of Degenerate Art" in Munich, in 1937. I remember stepping up a narrow staircase facing a horribly contorted Christ, the sight of whom struck me with fear. I walked between my father and mother, looking at paintings by Nolde, Schmidt-Rottluff, Kandinsky, Kirchner and others, whose work I had not yet learned to understand. My father suddenly stood still and pressed my hand. We had reached a wall without paintings, tautly lined with sack-cloth. Rows of names I did not recognize were displayed in big black shiny letters, line after line, until the name of my father sprang to my eyes: WILHELM HAUSENSTEIN . . . My heart began to pound. I do not think my father had anticipated finding the names of writers and critics included there. But the organizers had obviously chosen to make a point by indicting those who had praised in their books and articles—as my father had done with Paul Klee and many others—the "degenerate" artists being reviled in the exhibition. After this demoralizing experience, my parents took the train to Munich as rarely as possible. My father's work was demanding: in addition to editing the weekly supplements for the *Frankfurter Zeitung* from his home, he would take the train to Frankfurt to work with Martha Bertina, his able, witty, and congenial assistant, for a few days each month. She was eventually to sign as editor in his stead, so as to limit the exposure of his name. More and more frequently he wrote his articles under various pseudonyms. However, my father's mental battles of nine years to exclude even a hint of compromise with the regime ended in early 1943, when he, my godfather Benno Reifenberg, himself half Jewish, and Dolf Sternberger, who, like my father, was married to a Jewess, were all summarily dismissed upon the order of Joseph Goebbels, Hitler's Minister of Propaganda. After Hitler's defeat two dissertations were to be written on the subject, analyzing the phenomenon of the supplements' integrity in the face of all the pressures which had been brought to bear upon the editor and correspondents during the Nazi period. One thesis is entirely devoted to the woman's page, *Die Frau*;[6] while the other describes *The Spiritual Resistance in the Cultural Coverage of the Frankfurter Zeitung Against the Dictatorship of the Totalitarian State, 1933–1943.*[7]

My late teens were lived in a state of hurtful and damaging dichotomy. By temperament I was willful, passionate, and happiest when active with others in the wide expanse of nature: skiing, sailing, climbing; escaping what I perceived as the limiting, dampening atmosphere at home, where my parents carried on their lives under the ever present threat of new Nazi policies and their consequences, especially as rumors about affected friends and colleagues pressed in on them.

A very frightening event added further strain to these unfathomable dangers. My parents, my paternal grandmother, and I were having dinner in the downstairs dining-room, when we noticed a crackling noise coming from upstairs. We had occasionally been plagued by *Siebenschläfer*, rodents suggesting a cross between a rat and a squirrel, which sometimes kept us from falling asleep by rolling acorns around the attic floor to store them for winter. Since none of us had had the heart to put up traps, we had tried to find more humane, albeit ineffective, ways of containment. When the cook opened the door to bring in the main dish of our meal, the noise sounded quite ominous. Racing upstairs, my father called down at the top of his voice: "Bring up every available vessel with water! The attic is on fire!" We rushed to fill all the pots and pitchers we could find in the kitchen, the scullery, and the cellar. Unfortunately, it was a weekend, when the local firemen gathered around their *Stammtisch* for a few, or more, rounds of beer. It took them more than half an hour to arrive at our house, their helmets dangling from their forearms. And then, no one knew where to connect the hoses for water. One of the men said in broad Bavarian dialect: "Yeah, if we had water we could extinguish the fire!" Another remembered that a plumber, Herr Ferdinand Bustin—"the Jew" as he was known—was familiar with the property and might be consulted. In the meantime reinforcements were called from the district town of Starnberg, while huge flames leapt from the attic into the night sky, and thick black smoke began to permeate the top floor.

Suddenly, my mother was nowhere to be seen. My frantic father found her overcome by fumes on the top stairs with a full bucket beside her. She was conscious enough to walk down with his help. Twenty minutes later "the Jew" arrived, and the hoses filled with water. As the firemen fought the blaze, my former schoolmate and first childhood sweetheart Günther, son of Dr. Georg Brendel, the leading physician in our village, arrived to convey his father's proposal that we move to his sanatorium on Main Street—an act of considerable civic courage at the time. Indeed, we were to be his paying guests for almost six months. It was never established to our satisfaction whether the fire had been caused by a flying spark from the old chimney, or whether we were the victims of arson.

We had hardly moved back into the now restored and modernized old house, before another event wrenched our hearts. We sat at table eating lunch, when a thunderous roar, followed by a thump that shook the house and everything in it, made us race out into the garden. A few yards from the kitchen window, a giant beech tree with its richly foliated, early summer crown, and its light gray, silken trunk, several meters in circumference—after which the home had taken its name of *Buchenhaus*—had crashed down upon the meadow! Thick, foul smelling fumes poured out from the rotten center of its base, turning from black to reddish brown as they rose against the midday sun. In an instant, what had been only seconds earlier a majestic, formidable, healthy beech in its prime, shading the house, and a focus of admiration for our visitors, lay on its side, severed from life. Who could have blamed us for seeing a somber symbolism and feeling a foreboding of fates to come, as we stood before the wreckage of our venerable tree.

My father was to immortalize this tragic and prescient incision in our lives in an essay on the fallen tree, *Ein Baum ist gefallen*,[8] though he could not have foreseen that the owner of the house, Lieutenant Colonel Cäsar von Hofacker, would be put to death a few years later for having taken part in the careful planning and preparations of his cousin's plot to kill Hitler. Claus Graf von Stauffenberg and his heroic friends and colleagues, who, on July 20,

1944 led the unsuccessful attempt on Hitler's life, were tortured and brutally murdered before the year's end. Cäsar von Hofacker's death sentence was pronounced on August 30, and he was killed on December 20 in Berlin-Plötzensee—hung up on a butcher's hook, as were his courageous comrades in the dark cellars of the Nazi apparatus, in order to procure visual evidence for Hitler of his revenge.[9]

It will probably never be known whether my parents' tenancy of Cäsar von Hofacker's country house had drawn the attention of some investigating Nazi bureaucrat to them, and whether this had anything to do with the arrival in January 1945 of two letters addressed to my mother, a prompt reply to the first of which would almost certainly have led to my parents' death. They were written upon the order of the *Geheime Staatspolizei* (the Gestapo), as stated in the second letter, which was signed, *Der Vertrauensmann: Theodor Israel Koronczyk*, under the letterhead, *"Vertrauensmann der Reichsvereinigung der Juden in Deutschland,"* (The Trusted Person of the State Association of Jews in Germany). Hiding the first letter of January 4 from my father, who at the time was in bed due to an aggravation of his heart condition, my mother had the presence of mind to burn it, together with an enclosed questionnaire. She justified this action to herself aware that mail was being lost in bombing raids every day, and hoping against hope that her name might be forgotten in the growing turmoil of the last months of the war. But the second letter of January 22, which my parents received together on the twenty-sixth, implied such grave consequences for my mother if the form were not filled out and returned immediately, that my father felt compelled to hurry to Munich with the completed document. Upon arrival at Hiltenspergerstrasse 53, the address from which the letters had been sent, he discovered that the building had been severely damaged in an Allied bombing raid, and was still smoldering. According to a note my father attached to the second letter in his file, Koronczyk was nowhere to be found, and he therefore gave the envelope to a small pale woman, in her half-destroyed apartment across the corridor from Koronczyk's quarters. She promised my father to give the letter to him or his wife at the earliest possible moment. Such was my father's anguished fear for my mother's life, that he recapitulated the action he had taken in a registered letter to Koronczyk the same day. Miraculously, my parents never heard from "The Trusted Person" again, saved most probably through the time gained by my mother's decision to throw the first letter into the stove, given the rapidly deteriorating conditions all around them.[10]

In her 103d year, my mother reminded me that before taking the life-or-death letter to Koronczyk, my father knelt on the floor before her, and, holding her hands, said that if she were to be taken away he would remain by her side to the end. In a veiled entry in his diary—my parents lived in the constant expectation of a house search and had to destroy many treasured letters, including some from Rainer Maria Rilke—my father wrote that January 26 "was one of the most terrible days of my life." Again, a month later, on February 25, he added: "The weeks that lie behind me belong to the most dreadful I remember from my entire life. [. . .] I am still so blocked by this experience, that I am unable to record here how much we have suffered. I must postpone it to a later, more quiet moment, assuming that I shall live to experience such a respite and the distance from these events it would bring me."[11]

Shortly after my sixteenth birthday, I returned home from Garmisch, having passed my final exams. While my father cleared the way with three professors at the University of Munich, to enable me to attend lectures informally as a guest-student—German literature and theater under Kutscher; the history of Greek art under Buschor; and Spanish art with Kehrer—I was relegated to the kitchen to learn the art of cooking. I never regretted those six months at the side of Libosa, our buxom, red-cheeked, Bavarian cook. She taught me to differentiate between the gentle, enduring heat of *Briketten*, made of compressed dried peat from the neighboring moorlands, and the fast sharp heat generated by wood. She also introduced me to the subtleties of removing one or more of the iron rings to lower the pan or pot into the fire for even faster frying. But, unfortunately, the skills of dealing with an enormous country stove would be wasted on me as a future city dweller, although this introduction to the culinary arts became the basis upon which I would later improvise my own recipes around the world.

The two years at Munich University, though immensely broadening, and a real cultural immersion, did not provide me with the rigors of academic training, since as a guest student I could not participate in seminars, nor be subject to the grading process—disciplines I needed. To avoid awkward questions from on high, and any embarrassment to my professors, my attendance having been noticed and frowned upon, my parents encouraged me to enroll at the *Sabel* commercial school, where I could acquire secretarial skills.

Simultaneously, I joined a private English course, and attended the Munich fashion school to learn the rudiments of dressmaking.[12]

It was hard to question these arrangements. My parents wanted me to receive the best and broadest education possible, without calling undue attention to my existence. I remember their frequent exhortations to conduct myself as self-effacingly and modestly as possible—which was contrary to my "taking charge" and "hands on" nature. I wonder how I managed to do so well, always yearning to be elsewhere, beyond, out there in the world. Sailing on the Starnberger See was such an escape, and luckily my young friends in Tutzing frequently invited me to join them. But one brilliant summer day in 1940, this too was to be taken from me. The president of the Yacht Club, with whom I had often sailed, advised me with an air of benign sheepishness that, under the circumstances, I should save myself and members of the club "any embarrassment" by not accepting further invitations.

As door after door to the outside world and to open conviviality closed before me, and as my innate *joie de vivre* was more and more reined in at home because of parental concerns and fears of exposure, a brief New Year's holiday in the Arlberg mountains was to open a new page in my life. I was invited to ski with friends: with Jochen and with two half-Jewish sisters, though on their father's side—a fearfully significant difference under Hitler. However, Helga and her younger sister were so blond and blue-eyed that they had once been chosen from their class to present the visiting Führer with a bunch of flowers, which, as they delighted in telling, earned them an approving smile and tap on the cheek, Hitler having admired these little model Aryans! Arriving at the valley station of Langen in the late afternoon, we took a mule-drawn sled, with brass bells tinkling on the bridles. We glided over slushy snow up a winding road through intermittent tunnels, the openings to the valley overhung with layers of fresh snow and giant icicles glistening in the rays of the dark orange, setting sun. As the chill of night descended, the runners of our carriage began to crunch the snow. It took well over an hour to climb to the height of 1,750 meters, where the small village of Zürs lay embedded in snow between steep and rolling slopes, now assuming hues of cold metallic blue. The concierge at the Hotel Lorünser led us to the annex, a cozy, picture book chalet with tiny double windows and dark green, carved wooden shutters, which would be closed each night to keep in the warmth. My bed was crowned by a mountainous, white damask covered eiderdown. On the marble top of an old chest of drawers stood a floral porcelain jug and basin. The rustic wardrobe, painted by peasant hands, showed the names and marriage date of the original owners, more than a century ago. A fragrant warmth, rising from an old, tiled stove in the groundfloor living-room of the wooden house, enveloped me as I unpacked. Suddenly, the silence was broken by rumbustious laughs and a joyful exchange of greetings in the adjacent room. Jochen's friend had arrived to join our party. I stopped to listen, captivated by the rich, vibrant voice of the stranger. It touched me at the depth of my being. Never before, nor ever after, would the unknown feel so tangible, so immediate, and so inescapable. I realized, even before the door opened, that my life would be thrust into a new and immeasurable future.

Jochen knocked to introduce his friend. As Lupo bent his head to cross the threshold, his Jovian presence exploded the confines of my small, narrow room. His hair reflected the light like polished ebony. The fair olive tint of his skin set off the color of his hazel-gray eyes, as if his ancestry had had its roots in Italy. In conversation these eyes would scintillate with a love of life. And yet they

Hans (Lupo) Count von Hertling between 1939–40.
Courtesy of Renée-Marie Croose Parry.

would frequently assume a sad, distant look—the mark of soldiers who have lain wounded on the battlefield in close encounters with death. In fact, Lupo was recuperating from a severe bullet wound received on the western front, that had grazed and penetrated his back from the left side of the waist up to his right shoulder, miraculously without damage to his spine.

After two weeks of bliss and togetherness, and the convivial companionship of like-minded friends, we descended into the valley—and to the raw reality of Hitler's wars. It was painfully clear to us that there could be no thought of marriage as long as Nazi laws prevailed. In the meantime, Lupo confronted an infinitely worse predicament. His grandfather had been chancellor of Germany, albeit for the short period of one year.[13] Lupo told me that he had come to believe that the progeny of former German leaders were being systematically exposed to the perils of the front, so that, hardly recovered, he would shortly be sent from his base near Vienna to lead his motorized shock troops in the German attack upon the Balkans. Anticipating his departure and prolonged absence at the front, we spent one day in Tutzing for Lupo to meet my parents. Toward evening I took the train with him back to Munich so we might be together until he left for Vienna. As we crossed the square to the main station, we fell upon my friend, Ellen Bühler, and the man she had always hoped to marry. The star of David, imprinted upon yellow cloth, which all Jews were forced to wear, was stitched onto her dark gray overcoat in a way that enabled her to cover it casually by throwing open her lapel. As she realized that I was accompanied by someone she did not know, I caught a glimpse of her humiliated, pained expression, when she quickly moved to hide the star. We embraced, and I introduced Lupo. Having gained confidence in the course of our conversation, she told us in whispers that the days to her deportation were numbered, and that she feared to be taken on one of the next transports to Poland. I put my arms around her as we agonized together, searching for words—helpless words. "By God," I said, "there must be something we can do to prevent this from happening!" Her companion lowered his eyes in silent despair. To my distress, we had to leave them hurriedly to catch the train for Vienna. Ellen never returned. After the war, I heard that she had been sent to serve the appetites of German soldiers behind the front-lines, before dying in a concentration camp. She was so young, freckle-faced and pretty when I last saw her, with soft, blue-gray eyes, a delicate, retroussé nose, and dark blond locks tumbling over her forehead. She was gentility and kindness personified.

Lupo and I walked on in silence under a dismal sky. There was no snow on the ground to alleviate the melancholy grayness surrounding us, and there seemed nothing left to say. We clutched each other's hands until they hurt—enduring a double heartbreak; for them, and for us. Lupo too was destined to die. He was killed on April 14, 1941, not far from Mount Olympus, a few minutes after exchanging his seat in the motorcycle sidecar with his driver, to allow him to rest. The driver survived, but Lupo was struck on the temple by British shrapnel. He was buried in Ptolemaïs. Few of his comrades survived. One of them traveled a long way to give me the dreaded news—with a photograph of a bare wooden cross covered by Lupo's helmet at the head of his freshly covered grave. The German army would march into Athens on April 27.

Ellen Bühler in Germany 1939–40.
Courtesy of Renée-Marie Croose Parry.

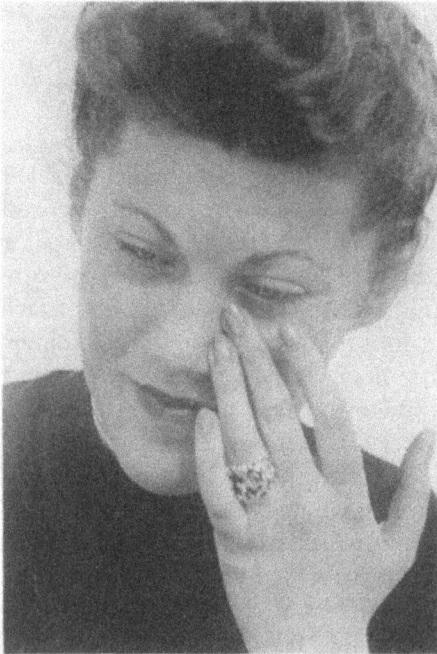

For many months I was reduced to the mere physical existence of eating, drinking, and sleeping—unable to concentrate, to read, or to prepare myself for work in an ever more uncertain future. Deeply troubled by my grief, my father invited me to join him on a short visit to Vienna and Salzburg, hoping that the beauty and resplendent art of these cities, about which he was to write, would help to pull me out of the chasm into which I had fallen.

For several years my parents had admired my clear soprano voice, and the facility with which I learned to sing and memorize some of the most difficult Mozart arias. We agreed that I should visit Erna Morena, well known for her masterful performances during the Munich opera festivals, and particularly for her rendering of Wagner, to seek her opinion on the potential of my voice. She had now retired, and was teaching in her apartment not too far from Pension Olive on Ohmstrasse, where I had often stayed while studying in Munich. She found that I had talent, and emphatically encouraged us; even though my father had stated quite unequivocally that I should only enter upon a singing career if my voice promised to carry me beyond average achievement. As a former critic, he was only too aware of the curse of mediocrity. She reassured him that given time, strict training and relentless practice, I had every chance to succeed. The idea grew on us and might have been pursued, although not without difficulty in our severely reduced circumstances. But it was to be otherwise.

For over ten years my parents had been linked in friendship with Franz Xavier and Frieda Hirschbold, who lived above the hamlet of Leutstetten near Starnberg. Franz Xavier was a civil engineer, a hefty, ebullient native of Bavaria, with a gift for water-divining and astrology, besides being mayor of Leutstetten, the country seat of Rupprecht, Crown Prince of Bavaria. As mayor he would receive early notification of new laws, decrees, and regulations. An anti-Nazi to the core of his being, he kept in touch with many endangered persons, and stood by my parents with advice and courageous help. He warned us in 1941, that he anticipated an escalation of Nazi persecution. The mayor of Tutzing, Walter Herre, the principal greengrocer in the village, was also supportive. It was thanks to such discrete assistance, and the help of several faithful villagers, in whose shops my parents had bought their provisions since 1932, that they were able to survive those terrible years: the Zistl family provided more milk, butter, eggs, and cheese than the ration card allowed; the greengrocer and butcher also gave additional supplies when possible; Franz Lidl, who went out each morning to retrieve *Renken* from his nets, would keep a fish for them; and the Bodemanns were always generous with supplies from their general store. The Catholic parish priest in Landsberg, well known to my parents from his days as chaplain in Tutzing, provided a haven whenever Franz Xavier thought my mother should go into hiding. But such support notwithstanding, my parents were never free of the feeling that our survival hung on the thinnest of threads. A few malicious words from a citizen turned informer, or the whim of an ambitious Nazi functionary in Munich or Berlin, would have spelt disaster. Thus my parents became more and more preoccupied with their desire to ensure at least my survival.

The Escape

My Brazilian and Greek student friends would come from time to time to share a family meal at our table, bringing news of developments in Munich. In late summer of 1941, the Brazilians decided to leave for home as soon as possible, fearing that they might be drafted to fight the war because of their German parentage. Helmut, one of the Brazilians, suggested that I could be taken to safety by joining them on their return to Brazil. As far back as 1936, my father had already considered a proposal by Erwin Rosenthal[14] to take me, together with his wife Margherita and their five children, to another European country, and, eventually, to the United States. Bernardolino, the youngest of the family, had been one of my childhood playmates. But my parents were unable to contemplate such an early separation: I was then barely fourteen.

Helmut suggested that I could accompany him as his fiancée, hoping that an exit permit might be obtained on these grounds. He made no secret of the fact that his parents in São Paulo were proud of the new Germany. His father, who had built up three department stores in major cities of Brazil, had sent a telegram in response to his request for a return ticket, exhorting him to recognize the historic moment he was privileged to witness. German immigrants had not, in general, assimilated into the Brazilian culture, and had not intermarried like so many Portuguese and Italians. They were therefore also inclined to feel that a Brazilian education did not provide the required standards for their children.

After some very cautious investigations by Helmut, and by my father, we came to the conclusion that it was too dangerous to apply

94

for a permit on the basis of an engagement, which would draw attention to my name while I remained under Nazi jurisdiction. Helmut had been in touch with Berlin, where an influential Brazilian of half-German parentage ran an office for trade and liaison between the two countries—and probably much else, in collusion with the Gestapo. At the time, the Brazilian president, Getúlio Vargas, and his administration, were still allied to the Axis cause. Anti-Semitism and anti-communism had emerged in Brazil in the thirties, and had fused to become widespread, supported with considerable enthusiasm by many in the German and Italian colonies.

The advice of Helmut's contact in Berlin was that we should apply in person for my Brazilian visa, once we were married. This was not a step I wanted to take, but Helmut insisted that it was the only possible way out. An agonizing decision had to be made rather quickly, and a date set at Munich City Hall for the autumn. As the marriage ceremony proceeded—a troubling, impersonal, bureaucratic ritual—I stood in awe thinking of my impending escape and my friend's generous determination. I immediately acquired a French, Portuguese grammar, French being my *mother*-tongue, and closer to the language I now wanted to learn in the shortest possible time. In November we took the train to Berlin to have the appropriate entries made in Helmut's passport, and to obtain my Brazilian visa. Senhor Gelser-Netto, as I remember the sound of his name, was sitting at an imposing desk behind which I was shocked to see the Brazilian and Nazi flags—their poles amicably crossed. This explicit arrangement put in relief for me the cruel angularity of the black swastika, set off in white on a red banner, as against the expressive and colorful Brazilian flag with its thoughtful array of symbols. The pairing of the Nazi and Brazilian flags made me shiver, and filled me with foreboding. I hardly opened my mouth as we sat across the large divide separating us from this self-important, stern official, with whom Helmut talked in Portuguese. We left Berlin the following day without having seen the city. All I could think of was to get away, fearful that my good luck might be running out.

Winter came early, and with a vengeance; the coldest I could remember. Heavy snow lay meters deep, aeroplanes were being delayed or cancelled, and we began to fear that we might not reach Lisbon in time to sail on February 22. News from the fronts in Russia was grim. Hitler had counted on the conquest of Moscow well before Christmas 1941. Most soldiers were not clad to fight in temperatures of 30 to 40 degrees centigrade below zero. Among the gruesome tales reaching our ears was one of men, who, trying to take off their footwear, had lost their toes, frozen onto the inner soles of their boots. Being unable to conquer the capital and its reserves of warm clothing before the onslaught of the great Russian winter, an irate Hitler tightened the screws at home. My family's, and especially my mother's, survival grew less certain as the Führer's top echelon met on January 20, 1942 at the Wannsee Villa in Berlin to agree on the "final solution"—the last, insane step to seal the murder of six million of Europe's eleven million Jews.

From the beginning of Hitler's ascent to power, my father, with my mother's active encouragement, had reasoned that if all Germans of integrity and vision were to leave the country, there would be no one left to try and stay the course, and to help rebuild Germany's moral and intellectual base after the Third Reich's inevitable defeat. As the regime's atrocities mounted, he bore more and more heavily the grave responsibility for his wife and daughter. His pain in contemplating the departure of his only child was alleviated only by the knowledge that he would now be free to remain at my mother's side, without having to worry further what might happen to me. It had indeed become very doubtful whether an Aryan husband—and especially one already subject to political persecution—could continue to provide a measure of security for his Jewish spouse. It was quite clear that my planned escape to Brazil had been a wise decision.

Keeping in touch with the airport, our group of six was now instructed to fly from Berlin, where weather conditions had been less fierce. We boarded a train, and after a long and wearying journey were told in Berlin that our flight had been cancelled, with no other prospects during the next few days. We returned to Munich, where all the hotels were filled to capacity, and finally got a little rest in the armchairs of the lobby at Hotel Bayerischer Hof. Trying to stay together and obtain seats for everyone in our small group became very difficult. I found myself fighting the temptation to call my parents in Tutzing to hear their voices once more, and to report the Berlin fiasco. But the last of our goodbyes had been so woefully distressing that I thought it would be better for the three of us not to repeat the wrenching agony—the more acute as we had little hope of ever seeing each other again.

Tired out we arrived at Munich airport in the early morning hours of February 22, 1942, the day our ship was due to sail. When

96

we stood in line at the passport controls, the inspector ordered all passengers with Brazilian documents to step aside. My heart pounded as we looked at one another in dismay. We sat down and went through all the possible reasons for this impasse. After what seemed an eternity, an official came to tell us in a non-committal tone, that we should present ourselves without delay at Police Headquarters in the city. Our complaint that we would miss our boat in Lisbon, and lose the value of our transatlantic passages drew no response. The official repeated the address of the Gestapo, and turned on his heel. We agreed that I should wait in a hotel, rather than draw attention to myself. I suggested that if asked, Helmut could reply that I was inordinately tired, and barely twenty, and that, as my husband, he should be able to speak for me.

Back at the hotel, with no room in sight, I searched for empty armchairs and settees, and strategically distributed the smaller pieces of our luggage to secure resting places for the night. I tried not to imagine my friends' interview, and kept my eyes on the revolving entrance door. After what seemed an interminable wait, they reappeared. Their faces looked calm enough. Watching over our strewn out belongings, I listened breathlessly as they explained: because Brazil had broken off diplomatic relations with Germany, orders had gone out to all immigration controls at airports and borders to hold back anyone with Brazilian passports or visas. Helmut had immediately given the interviewing Gestapo official the name and telephone number of the Brazilian representative in Berlin, who, he hoped, would help ease our passage. After a long wait they were released. Nobody had asked for me. The questions that now remained seemed trivial: was the snow we saw falling in thick flakes, through the tall lobby windows, going to stop in time to allow planes to take off? Was there going to be a plane for us at all? The news from the airport was favorable. We might get to Lyons, and from there to Barcelona and Madrid. The rest would be easy.

Another restless night was followed by an early taxi ride to the airport, and hours of anxious waiting. The air tickets had been altered, but we would probably miss the boat, and lose the passages which had been paid for by the parents in Brazil. Once more I quelled my desire to hear my parents' voices. We got through passport control without a hitch. I began to breathe more easily, when I was suddenly accosted by a man in his mid-forties, of medium build, wearing a well-cut coat of light camel hair and a stylish hat that matched his slick, eel-like approach. He had taken advantage of the fact that I was separated from my friends by a throng of pushing passengers. He spoke quickly with a quiet smooth voice: "I see you're going to Brazil. It would be most helpful to hear from you— say once a month. All information is pertinent! Don't let me down! You are intelligent. You know what I mean . . . " or words to this effect. He slipped a card into my hand with a German name and cryptic address, and vanished into the crowd as fast as he had appeared. Horrendous thoughts flashed through my brain: my parents! I was leaving them behind as pawns. In a single moment I had been blackmailed, and an unpayable mortgage was now weighing down upon my future life. My friends tried to make light of it. I could not. I would be unable to cast off the spell, which turned into a subtle form of psychic torture, relieved only for short periods when letters would arrive from my parents, reassuring me that they were still alive.

Our various flights, my first adventure in the air, passed without mishap. To our great surprise and joy, we found the *Siqueira Campos* still in port, its camouflage far from complete. Our enforced stay in Lisbon had the fortuitous effect of allowing us to see the city and its treasures, and to marvel at the spectacular displays of foods and other goods, which had long been absent from shop windows in Germany. I grew fond of Lisbon with its gentle winter: my gateway to a new, and perhaps easier, life. Our hotel, around the corner from a busy town square, was sumptuous with its fin de siècle atmosphere, and left nothing to be desired. I loved the rich, pure olive oil used so lavishly in Portuguese cooking, and revelled in the great variety of food, especially the colorful, exotic fruits that we had not seen in Germany for several years—if ever. I could have done without the "palm court" music, the lamenting, concertante violins, that catered to the tastes of an affluent middle-aged clientele during lunch and dinner. We had been forewarned by worldly, well-meaning friends that Lisbon, in neutral Portugal, was one of the spy capitals of Europe. Although this may have been the case, I was spared any further intimidating incidents of the type suffered at Munich airport. The mere possession of the card was traumatic, as I continued to agonize whether I dared to tear it up.

I wrote a first, twelve page letter to my parents about all I had seen, enclosing picture postcards of paintings I had enjoyed in the museum. My father was to use one of them by Domingos Antonio de Segueira—a loving portrayal of his daughter, Mariana Benedicta Victoria, at the piano—as the subject of a most sensitive essay, exteriorizing the pain in his own heart.[15] Our wait in Lisbon stretched out over ten days. It was already early March, and we had been instructed to keep in daily contact with the shipping line, as the *Siqueira Campos* was now expected to sail at any time.

Between Two Worlds

It must have been around the sixth of March when we finally embarked. With half the normal number of passengers on board, we had much space to roam, and the service was excellent. I befriended a French family and their seventeen year old daughter, who, like I, had a passion for dancing. The young officers aboard were delighted to teach us the *samba*, and the resident pianist gladly recited his songs in Portuguese and Spanish. Although this was not to lead to an intellectual enrichment of our vocabulary, it at least helped our ear and syntax! If there were spies aboard, German or other, as I heard in later years, I did not have the savvy or psychic prowess to detect them.

The onset of gloomy, rainy weather depressed me, and led to a disturbing introspection, during which I would brood about and question the meaning of my life, the helplessness of the individual at the hands of fate, and the increasing triumph of evil. As had happened so often before on my balcony high above the lake, intense crying spells overcame me. Subconsciously, I longed to understand the world, and myself as a part of it, especially in terms of what had come, and gone, before me. Unable to explain this yearning to myself, I hungered for an englobing knowledge of history that would help me to transcend my feelings of impotence, which, for years, had threatened to overwhelm me. I did not comprehend it then, but came to see it clearly later: the growth and application of my intelligence had been arrested by the constant diversion of psychic energy required to hang on, and to hold my own from one day to another. Up to my twentieth year, all I could do was to think out how to win through the morrow, to stave off disharmony, to do the right thing under observing, critical, or even hostile eyes; to please, and always make the correct impression. I was, in fact, not living my own life— life was living me. A deeply felt desire for acceptance, and the fears for my survival and for that of my family, had narrowed my horizons and forced my attention onto the practicable, the immediate, the now.

Crossing the equator under blue, tropical skies brought a change of mood and the occasion for a special party at the Captain's table. The crew shed their dark wintery uniforms, and appeared in fresh white linen. Everyone's morale seemed to have been given a boost. Thoughts of those burdened teenage years slipped from my consciousness for longer and longer periods of time, as the new climate, the brilliant sunshine with its enveloping warmth, activated my vision of the future. With a tinge of bad conscience, I felt a sense of rebellion rise within me against all the suffering and pain. My Germanic, Brazilian born companions lacked the antennae with which to understand the deeper layers of my state of mind, and there was little conversation amongst us in which I really wanted to share. Although we were sailing together into the future, they too had become part of my travailing past, from which I now longed to escape.

My knowledge of Portuguese improved rapidly as I began to understand others, and to use it in speaking with members of the crew. Unforgettable is the exchange with one of the stewards whom I had summoned one morning to rescue me from what I feared might be a scorpion, or worse, in my cabin. Reaching for my toothbrush—there it sat on the handle, over two inches long, rusty dark brown, with long tentacles gesticulating incessantly, and paralyzing my every limb. As the door opened, a ray of sunlight fell on it, making it look more formidable still, when suddenly it flew into the air and disappeared. The steward laughed: "Não e nada, minha Senhora. E uma barata!" I was not reassured and made him promise to eliminate the creature from my cabin immediately. I walked on deck with my pocket dictionary, but could not find the term *barata*. One of the French-speaking stewards stopped and was greatly amused to introduce me with latino flourish to one of the tropics' omnipresent pests—the common cockroach. He savored telling me that I had better keep them out of my wardrobe, for if there should be a trace of food on any of my dresses, that spot would be devoured, material, yarn, and all. Little did I know then the gigantic sizes Brazilian roaches could attain, and under what circumstances I would be forced to face a teeming swarm of them.

That night at dinner we were briefed about the final days of our voyage. We were to dock in Recife, the most easterly port in northern Brazil, and in Bahía to the south, before sailing on to Rio. The carefree interlude of life aboard ship was coming to an end. I began to visualize the reception I might be given by Helmut's parents, and how they would react to the disclosure that we planned to go our separate ways, with me earning my livelihood in Rio. I slept restlessly. My bunk felt hard and uncomforting as I tossed and turned.

The early dawn was breaking. I stepped out onto the main deck in my white dressing gown, staying near my cabin and leaning against the railing of our small vessel, which had been my home for all of three weeks. The dark blue ocean was smooth, with hardly a ripple. On the horizon, I discerned shadows which, in a few hours time, would turn into the outline of the sub-continent we were approaching. Below me, alongside the ship, and only a few yards away, swam a playful school of dolphins. I knew them from pictures, but was hardly prepared for my solitary witness on this glorious morning. I stood spell-bound as my eyes followed the precise rhythmic movements of these gracious mammals, emerging and leaping in unison to form split second arches over the water, their silken skins glistening in the rising sun as they glided smoothly back into their element, time and time again. I was entranced: it was magical, as if I had escaped into a living fairy tale at the antipodes of hate, of bombs, and smoldering ruins—my senses overcome by the powerful, enthralling scent now emanating from the earth as we drew nearer. I did not know that the earth could smell so strongly— and perhaps it did so only in the tropics. Of course, my nostrils had been sensitized by weeks of exposure to salt-laden breezes and Atlantic storms. I *drank* the air. I imagined that these odors bore the scent of steaming vegetation, of the sweat of herds of cattle and of other animals yet unknown to me, and of throngs of people already working in the heat of the breaking day. The memory of this extraordinary dawn lives with me still—a seminal *mid-way* experience, linking memories of the past with the present, and pointing to a future I could not anticipate. My life was being recast. The severance from everything that had been *home* to me, the traumatizing separation from my parents whom I so feared never to see again, and the acute pain during our last embrace were all beginning to fray the invisible cords binding me to them. Already, the rawness of these emotions was being subdued by new and overpowering experiences, my anguish slipping away imperceptibly, a little more each day, as I was thrust into a totally different and exotic world. Still unaware, I had taken the first steps toward a distant future in which I would consider myself less a citizen than a planetarian—always forced to struggle, but growing to feel more and more at home in the larger world that was now beginning to unfold before me.

PART 2

THE
CONCENTRATION
CAMPS

HERTHA SPIER

Holocaust testimony is an attempt to describe the indescribable. Why do these victims and survivors record their experiences? Many want to assure themselves, and others, of their existence after the Holocaust. The writers prove that they have survived, even though the "final solution" had condemned them to die. In a sense they are saying: "I write, therefore I am."[1]

The personal motives for describing the Holocaust are diverse. Hertha Spier (née Grüber) spent six years in the Krakow ghetto, and in the concentration camps of Plaszow, Auschwitz, and Bergen-Belsen. Like many Holocaust survivors, she writes for her children, yet spares them, and herself, from detailing the experiences.

Hertha Spier's style is simple. She writes of the events that shaped the worst years of her life. At the beginning and at the end of the narrative, Spier describes her current situation: that of an author dealing with what happened, while at the same time trying not to remember too closely. Sometimes she refers to past events and relates how they still affect her present life. Hertha Grüber was young and innocent, and the atrocities she witnessed were unforgettable.

The author lived in the Krakow ghetto until its liquidation on March 13 and 14, 1943. Most of the Jews were deported to Belzec, about two thousand were killed in the streets of Krakow, and the remaining eight thousand were sent to Plaszow. This forced-labor camp was eventually turned into a concentration camp under the supervision of SS *Hauptsturmführer* (Captain) Amon Goeth, who was in charge from February 1943 to September 1944. Goeth was responsible for the most heinous of crimes committed at the camp, such as *Selektionen*, mass murder, and personal participation in the murders.[2] In the summer of 1944 as the Red Army approached, preparations were made to disband the camp. The prisoners were transferred to internment or extermination camps.

In such brutal conditions, women relied on different survival strategies, perhaps the most important being a woman's ability to bond with other women; to share food and extend the meager provisions, as they had learned to do during their prewar experiences at home.[3] Women would also try to protect their identity and self-esteem by maintaining their appearance as best they could.[4] Interest in personal hygiene under the extreme conditions of the camps is difficult to imagine, but this concern becomes evident in Spier's testimony.

The Nazis' goal was to obliterate the individual identity of the camp inmates by shaving their hair, giving them numbers for identification, and forcing them to wear the clothes of dead victims. Shaving was especially humiliating because the women no longer looked like women—they looked like men. "Many memoirists have commented on this trauma as it symbolizes the loss in a concrete way of a woman's socially defined identity."[5]

In some camps the circumstances for women were worse than those for men. Camp Commandant Höss of the women's camp at Auschwitz-Birkenau commented: "general living conditions in the women's camp were incomparably worse [than in the men's camp]. They were far more tightly packed-in and the sanitary and hygienic conditions were notably inferior."[6] In August 1944, a new camp for women was added to Bergen-Belsen. In September and October of 1944, 3,000 Jewish women arrived from Auschwitz and were housed in barracks with no water, no beds, and no facilities. Anne Frank and her sister Margot were among these prisoners; both perished in the typhus epidemic of March 1945.[7]

Hertha Spier's relationship with her sister helped her endure years of persecution. Perhaps one of the most frightening episodes of their internment was the threat of their possible separation when they faced Dr. Mengele at Auschwitz. This concentration camp had more extensive labor requirements than other camps such as Treblinka, and for this reason more people were "saved" for work. The victims were paraded in front of the notorious physician who would make an immediate decision about who would live and who would die.[8]

Some survivors of terrible tragedies, such as the Holocaust, share certain characteristics. Survival is a type of existence, and the desire to bear witness to the ordeal is one of its manifestations. Many record their memories in spite of themselves: they don't think about it, they just do it. The survivors not only speak *for* someone—the loved ones, families, and other victims—but *to* someone—those in the world who will listen.

Hertha Spier's narrative has much in common with the growing corpus of Holocaust testimony. One similarity between her memoir and others is that she often views her experience collectively rather than individually. For example, when she describes her own situation, she frequently relates what is happening to the other Jews. Another similarity is her focus on the present. This enabled her, and many like her, to endure years of hardship.

To some extent, survival in the concentration camps was arbitrary. However, certain studies identify a survivor's instinct or skill—an ability to act "spontaneously and correctly during times of protracted stress and danger."[9] This kind of talent is not limited to race, class, gender, or education. As one survivor of Treblinka maintains:

> It wasn't ruthlessness that enabled an individual to survive—it was an intangible quality, not particular to educated or sophisticated individuals. Anyone might have it. It is perhaps best described as an overriding thirst—perhaps, too, a *talent* for life, and a faith in life.[10]

The author's terse memoir exposes the different ways in which Nazis treated the Jews in the death camps as objects, leading to the most obscene consequences. Hertha Spier now resides in Porto Alegre, Brazil.

HOLOCAUST TESTIMONY:
KRAKOW, PLASZOW, AUSCHWITZ,
AND BERGEN-BELSEN

BY HERTHA SPIER

My dear sons, you have always wanted me to give you an account of my experiences from 1939–1945. I've avoided it in the past, but recently

106

*decided to write this short outline. I hope that you will now understand me
and not always ask why your mother is such a bundle of nerves.*

I lived with my parents, three sisters, and brother in Bielitz. We
fled one week before the outbreak of the war and went to stay with
relatives in Krakow. On September 1, 1939, the German troops
marched into the city. From this moment on, life was hell for us.
One could see the first flag with the iron cross insignia fluttering on
the hillside next to the Wawel castle. We heard a song sung loudly:
"The Jews are going where? They're marching through the Red
Sea and the waves knock them down. The world is at peace."[1]

Our faces turned pale—our only wish was to stay together. We
wore white arm bands with the blue Star of David on our left arms.
Those who weren't wearing them were arrested immediately. On
Yom Kippur, all the men were taken out of their homes to dig
trenches, but luckily we were able to hide our Papa and our brother.
We knew that when the men were finished digging trenches, they
were lined up against the wall and shot.

My sister Eugenie (Jenny) was killed in Ravensbrück, and my
sister Henriette (Jetti) fled to be with her fiancé on the Rumanian
border. But when the Germans marched into Rumania, all the Jews
there were shot. In 1940 my parents, my sister Gisella (Gisi), and
my brother Max and I arrived in the Krakow ghetto and lived in a
section surrounded by a high wall. We worked in groups growing
food, cleaning the streets, and performing other forced labor. One
day, the SS coerced all the old people to leave their apartments and
subsequently deported them. Unfortunately my parents were in this
group, and I will never forget the horrible spectacle of our last
farewell.

Hoping they could possibly save themselves at the border, we
sewed jewelry into Mama's underwear and into Papa's waistband.
Unfortunately, we later heard that they had been shot in the forest.
After this transport came the children's transport, which was dreadful. We witnessed children, big and small, being torn from their
mothers' arms and thrown into big trucks. It was a gruesome sight
to see. The parents screamed and wailed to no avail, and were subsequently driven away with clubs. When this terror ended, the only
people remaining in the ghetto were young healthy people who
were needed to work.

Another concentration camp was hastily built near the ghetto
on the site of a Jewish cemetery. The camp Plaszow was finished

after a short time, and we were transported there, where we worked in the different communities and workshops.

We stood daily at roll call to be counted. I shuddered when Commandant Goeth arrived with his wolfhounds and his troops because he always declared new measures that often took a frightful course.[2]

One morning two thirteen-year-old youths who allegedly whistled on the way to the barracks were executed. The storm leader walking behind them thought they had political motives. These youths were put in the bunker and on the next day were hanged at the drill ground, while their parents and thousands of others watched. We were forced to witness the spectacle or be punished. The dead youths were dragged past my row—an appalling sight to behold.

The next evening we had to run quickly into the barracks because there was a huge fire. Jews in Krakow who weren't wearing their arm bands were rounded up together with other prisoners and driven to the concentration camp in trucks. Gasoline was poured into a large pit and then ignited, and when the many trucks packed with people arrived, each person was shot and fell into the fire. This went on the entire night. We looked outside the windows and all we saw was fire and jumping silhouettes; by counting the shots, we knew how many people had been burned alive.

The next day the pit was still glowing as we walked by it on the way to work. It stank so horribly of human flesh that I can still smell it, and always avoid anything that is glowing or burning. This event was hideous, and I will never forget it.

The roll calls continued. Commandant Goeth often selected the prettiest girls from the fifth row for the white house. After he abused them, he killed them so no one would find out. Often I saw a table standing in the middle of the drill ground where women and men had been whipped (twenty-five on the bare ass as it was called), and I saw a woman lying in the infirmary whose swollen buttocks were purple and blue.

The next day we remained in the barracks for jewelry removal, which meant that we had to give up anything we still owned. I worked in the decorating group. Because I was a handicraft artist before the war and had made things such as leather gloves, belt wallets, and stuffed animals, I was ordered by the authorities to finish different Christmas gifts that were to be sent to Germany.

I made *Kaete-Kruse* dolls in national costume that were about eighty centimeters high. Storm leader John received a stuffed horse I had made as a gift, which was a caricature of him sitting in the saddle.[3] Thereafter I had to make miniature caricatures of different SS men and trembled with fear every day, because I was afraid that this jocular kind of activity would ultimately lead to a death sentence.

I lived in barracks situated on a high rock, and once when I wanted to go down I was thrown over by an SS man who screamed: "You Jew pig, now you'll get a kick in the ass." He hit me with such force that I bounced off the lowest barrack and was thrown many meters. People who saw it picked me up and carried me to the infirmary where I lay for many days in great pain. After that incident, it was torture to stand at roll call or to sit and work for long periods of time.

One day we were assembled at roll call and suddenly ordered to march away. We came to the railroad tracks and were squeezed into each cattle car, 135 per wagon. My sister Gisi was standing in another group but pushed her way into mine, because she had promised Papa that she would look after me. We didn't know where we were going.

It was torture. We were packed like sardines without air, water, or food, and after a long stretch the iron doors were opened; we pulled ourselves out and went to a container of water. Some of the people in the wagon were thrown out dead. Those who had to go to the bathroom were led to the bushes under guard, and others who tried to run away were shot. When the train stopped at its final destination, we climbed out. We knew we had arrived in Auschwitz.

It was the camp with the crematorium and we knew what awaited us. We arrived around evening and were led to a big space where we had to dispose of everything we had. What hurt the most was having to give up our photo album containing pictures of our dear family. Quickly we cut out the heads of our loved ones, wrapped them up in a small piece of cloth, and tied it up with a piece of string. Gisi hid this tiny package in a place where it would be difficult to find. In a similar fashion I wrapped up a few other little pictures and hid them in the soles of my shoes.

After we finished marching we lined up in five rows, trembling one next to the other, and walked until we arrived at the barracks where we had to disrobe. Each female was shaved on the head as well as certain other places with a dull razor. When I saw Gisi without her beautiful curls I began to cry horribly because she looked like a ghost. Now it was my turn. Although my hair fell on the floor and I cried, I didn't protest.

Each woman was given a dress made of rags that belonged to those who had been gassed, and our shoes were exchanged for wooden clogs. Quickly I took the photos from the soles of my shoes and stowed them away. After this entire procedure we went rank and file along a path and saw a powerful fire before us. I told my sister they would definitely burn us now. But being older, she said that it wouldn't happen and consoled me. It was only a sadistic ploy on their part to scare us. We went around the fire and finally arrived at our barracks, where we counted off and afterwards fell dead tired on our plank-beds.

At five in the morning we were awakened with a whistle signal, and like lightning got up and stood rank and file at role call where we were counted and given different instructions. After standing for hours, we were allowed to go back to the barracks. We had nothing to be happy about. They told us we would be shot if we tried to escape, tried to talk to people behind the barbed wire, or didn't follow orders.

The next day a Hungarian girl was the last one from the barracks to get to roll call. When the storm leader who counted us saw that she was late, he called her to the middle of the drill ground and made her kneel and raise her arms. A brick was placed in each hand, then a second, and then a third. She couldn't keep her arms up and they fell a little. The SS man beat her horribly, gave her more bricks, and her arms fell again. He beat her till she lay in a pool of blood, then she was taken away. We stood there, stunned.

A few days later the storm leader came to the barracks. We were too loud for him and he made us go through roll call as punishment. We had to kneel on pebbles while many of the SS men gathered to look at the spectacle. They had a wonderful time. We, on the other hand, couldn't endure the pain but naturally weren't allowed to let it show. All of us returned to the barracks exhausted, with wounded knees.

The following day, three from our plank-bed, myself included, were awakened at three o'clock in the morning to fetch coffee. It was a long way to the kitchen, and when we arrived we saw huge kettles filled with black coffee. I couldn't imagine how we could carry anything so heavy. Wooden beams were placed on our shoulders, the kettle put in the middle, so we could transport this to the huts. When we finished drinking we went to roll call, where we stood until the storm leader finally arrived and counted us. Our rations consisted of the heel of a loaf of black bread and a pat of margarine. At noon we had watery soup, which at least warmed us up.

My sister Gisi and I cut our bread very thin so our food would last the whole day. Our comrades, on the other hand, ate the entire daily portion at once because they wanted to feel full. It was often so cold at roll call that we warmed ourselves with our own body heat. We stood close to one another until, of course, the storm leader came. The last person on the row was the most annoyed because the wind blew on her, but to solve this problem we constantly rotated.

Once when we were at roll call, a woman ran into the electric barbed wire. She immediately turned purple and then very black—it was a gruesome sight.

Often in the afternoons we left through the camp gate under close surveillance to do other jobs in a nearby camp such as carry rocks or gather twigs. One day we were driven out of the barracks and divided into rows. We were afraid we would be gassed and trembled all over. Marching along the main path, we stopped at a barrack where we were tattooed one by one under the left arm. My number was 21646 and Gisi's was 21647: we were no longer human beings, only numbers.

On the drill ground our numbers were called, and we had to report there. The next day was selection, where old and young alike had to strip and stand before Dr. Mengele and his entire staff. He looked at every girl and woman and said only: right, left, right, left. Which meant: right to work, left to death.

We had known for a long time that the ones who went to the left were gassed. Gisi and I were trembling so much that we couldn't speak. We wanted so desperately to stay together. The line stretched for kilometers and we saw the tragedy played out in front of our eyes. The children screamed when the mothers went to the left and the mothers screamed when the daughters went to the left. The sisters who were separated were inconsolable, but the occupying troops found the whole affair very amusing; they imposed their order with clubs upon naked females begging to be allowed to go to the right. Gisi and I went to the right. We were saved. We were lucky, but cried as we saw our suffering comrades standing there being sentenced to death.

They again transferred us to animal cars with 130 persons to each wagon, but we were happy to get away from the camp with the crematorium. For a long time we didn't know where we were going, and this trip was terrifying because we suffered from hunger and thirst. The SS maintained order with clubs. We were powerless. When the train stopped and we were allowed to get out, we rushed like wild animals toward water, not caring whether it was clean or dirty.

I, too, drank water from a stagnant puddle that was on the street. In a few minutes we were standing there in five rows. Afterwards, we marched for hours through a thick forest. The only thing we heard was gunfire and because we weren't allowed to turn around, we thought that the ones in the last rows had already been killed and that our turn was coming. Gisi and I could only think of our dear parents who had also been shot in the forest. Our hearts were pounding. Finally we saw a light and as we approached it saw tents. Our faces beamed with joy because we had once again escaped death.

This concentration camp was called Bergen-Belsen. There were five hundred women per tent, and we were pressed together like sardines. The shelter was erected on the Lüneberger heath amidst flowers of a variety known as *Erika* (heather.)

The time was spent standing at roll call, carrying rocks, and finding wood, among other things. One day there was a strong storm that tore down the tent. Wooden barracks were quickly built, and we lived in these until the end of the war.

Days, weeks, and months passed—there was no end to it. My last duties were in the peeling room, where I peeled potatoes and beets. One week I worked the day shift and the next week the night shift. My hands became purple and swollen from the cold. Sometimes it was possible for me to get a few potatoes and hide them in bread, but in spite of this Gisi and I really suffered from hunger. We were increasingly undernourished, lice ridden, and came down with Ruhr typhoid. Thereafter I was no longer able to work.

One morning while sleeping on the floor next to my sister I stood up and looked down at my dress and my eyes filled with tears. I saw the only dress that I owned covered with shit. Gisi undressed me, went to the latrine and rinsed it out. She held it in the sun and waved it around so that it would dry. But because we were ordered to the drill ground, I put it on wet. That night my sister had such a terrible earache that she screamed with pain. I didn't know what to

112

do, so I sneaked out of the barracks to go to the infirmary for a sleeping pill.

Suddenly a light from the watch tower flashed on me and then I heard a shot. My whole body trembled. I couldn't run, otherwise the SS man would think that I was trying to escape. Arriving at the infirmary, I knocked at the door and I waited a considerable time before the door opened. I begged to high heaven for a sleeping pill, which I received. When I returned to the barracks I fell down on the floor trembling with fear. Two hours later we had to be at roll call again. This went on for a while until we finally were sent to the barracks for the quarantined. We could neither stand nor walk, and three of us were placed on a small plank-bed. The typhus racked our bodies and we wasted away into skeletons.

One hundred dead women were taken away in blankets daily. There were large hills of skeletons in front of the barracks, which is where my sister Gisi ended up two weeks before the liberation on March 29.[4] She died in my arms of hunger and exhaustion. I didn't want to live any more. I became melancholy and fantasized. Gisi was my support through all the years, I loved my sister.

The days went by and I got more and more lice, which built nests on my scalp and on my buttocks. I scratched them and then I had sores, and because of the filth the sores started to fester. I still have scars from it.

Because I didn't receive any more food and the diarrhea tortured me, there was nothing else I could do but lie on the plank-bed and await the end. One day before the war ended, my sleeping companion saved me from starvation and death by giving me potato peels to eat. The German troops had enough to do because the camp was being bombed, so the food rations were left sitting.

I had a small empty sack where I kept my bread and I scratched out the bread crumbs from the inner corners. I was so racked with hunger I saw death before my eyes.

When the English troops moved in and saw the tragedy, they tore the lice-ridden rags from our bodies and transported us in ambulances to the formerly occupied SS camp.[5] The dwellings were changed into hospitals and we were housed eight women per room. They weighed us first—I was 28 kilos. We could neither stand nor walk and were taken immediately to bed.

Every day we were examined and x-ray photos taken. The victims already had pulmonary disease because of malnutrition, exhaustion, and the hours we spent at roll call in the rain, wind, and snow. I had a large spot on my left lung. The doctors were very kind and assured us that with good care and nutritious food we would become healthy immediately.

Every day I received buttered bread sprinkled with sugar, so my heart would get stronger. I was inconsolable and melancholy and didn't care much about anything—I only dreamed of my dear family. Many of them died shortly after the war.

In a few weeks when I could walk again I was led into the bathroom. After I observed myself in the mirror I felt so bad that I went back into my room, holding on to the wall for support. I cried pitifully, because I had seen myself naked in the mirror after so many years. I was starved to a skeleton, so much so that I was afraid of myself. The food I received wasn't enough and I was always hungry, so while sitting in bed I made smocks for the nurses to receive extra rations.

It was announced that all patients with lung disease would be treated by the Swedish Red Cross (*Aktion Bernadott*). On July 15, my birthday, we arrived in Lübeck, and from there we traveled to Malmö where we were quarantined. The Swedish were exceptionally helpful people, and they examined us and took many x-rays. Shortly thereafter we went to a hospital in Karlstadt where we were treated. It was at a convalescent camp in Ahlefors where I got the news that my brother Max had died in Mauthausen. My only hope was dashed. Now I knew that I was the only member of my family of seven who had survived. I went on strike—I didn't want to eat or walk.

My girlfriends watched out for me to make sure I didn't do anything to myself. One day someone told us that there was an arts and crafts exhibition in Stockholm and we were asked to donate various handicrafts. I worked with small pieces of left-over leather and made flowers and bouquets. I had been a handicraft artist before the war and it was such fun for me to work with my hands again. After a short time I received thank you notes from people who liked my work.

A Mrs. Margaret Feychting from Stockholm asked me to make leather flowers for her. We needed to rest a lot, so I worked in bed and sent her small packages every three days. She always sold the leather flowers and I received some money for them, which seemed like a small fortune to me at the time.

This work was a type of sedative because it gave me back some of my self-esteem. With my money I bought oranges and bananas and other things for those in my hospital room. On October 8, 1946, I took a ship that embarked from Göteborg and arrived in Rio de Janeiro on November 8.

These lines represent only a fraction of my experience, because it is impossible for me to immerse myself any deeper into this horrible period of my life. Most unfortunately, I spent six years of my youth in this hell.

Translated by Katherine Morris

EVA HIRSCHBERG

Eva Hirschberg (née Striemer) was born in Breslau, Germany in 1912. Her family moved to Zoppot, the Free City of Danzig, in 1919, where her father started a business. She enrolled as a student at the School for Interpreters in Mannheim, and then continued studying French in Heidelberg. On May 8, 1936, in Berlin, Eva Striemer married Dr. Alfred Hirschberg, the editor-in-chief of a Jewish newspaper *CV-Zeitung*, the official publication of the *Centralverein deutscher Staatsbürger jüdischen Glaubens* or Central Union of German Citzens of Jewish Faith.

This organization was founded in the late nineteenth century to defend Jewish civil rights against the rise of the anti-Semitic movement in Germany. In 1924 it boasted 72,500 members, and at its height the Central Union was the largest and most important association of German Jews.[1] The *Centralverein* represented the liberal Jewish middle class, advocated an integration of German and Jewish identity, and was anti-Zionist until 1933. It was active from 1893 to 1938, until it ceased to exist as an independent group after the *Kristallnacht*. In 1936, the *Centralverein* changed its name to the *Jüdischer Centralverein*.[2] Alfred Hirschberg was its syndic until it closed in 1938.

Alfred Hirschberg was arrested and sent to the concentration camp at Sachsenhausen, where he was held from November 11 to December 5, 1938. Eva's mother, who was living in Zürich at the time, helped them to emigrate in January of 1939: first to Paris, then to London, and finally to Rio de Janeiro.

From their permanent residence in São Paulo, Alfred Hirschberg worked as the syndic of the Congregação Israelita Paulista and editor of the *Crônica Israelita*, with Eva as his private secretary. To help with matters at home, Eva's mother took care of the house and the children, Irene and Gabriela. Alfred Hirschberg died in 1971. Eva Hirschberg continues to live in São Paulo.

"When the Men Were in the Camp" was originally intended to be a chapter in her husband's book about his experience in Sachsenhausen, a book he never finished. Eva Hirschberg recaptures a single dramatic event at a pivotal time in her life, describing her husband's detention in Berlin and his subsequent deportation to Oranienburg in November 1938.

The author begins her narrative with the arrest. What they had feared for years was the increasingly violent assaults against Jews. In 1933, Jews were ordered to surrender their passports and papers so that a large *J* could be printed on them. In April of the same year, Hitler declared a "legal" boycott of all Jewish-owned businesses. In 1935, the Nuremberg Laws prohibited marriages between "Aryans" and "non-Aryans" and took away Jews' rights as citizens. On November 9, 1938, during the *Kristallnacht*—or night of broken glass—a national pogrom was launched and synagogues were burned.

Eva's husband was one of thousands arrested without a warrant. What follows is a picture of how she fought against the injustice on a personal level, and of how the women worked together to free their loved ones. She portrays the sense of panic and fear that consumed the Jews of Berlin after the *Kristallnacht*.

The mixed messages of Nazi leaders heightened the general anxiety—government policies appeared inconsistent, and Hitler's attacks were unpredictable. The entire picture is evident in retrospect, but it was not so clear to Jews in Germany at the time. An example of this confusion was the situation that existed after the proclamation of the Nuremberg Laws and before the 1936 Olympic Games. During this period the Nazi regime deliberately softened its anti-Jewish stance, not as a show of good faith toward Jews, but to pacify foreign governments.[3] Hitler did not want to lose the Olympic Games to another country; the pomp, circumstance, and international acclaim the games would bring to Germany was something that appealed to his penchant for pageantry. Although his private long-term anti-Semitic goals remained unaltered, his public vacillation confused the victims.

Alfred Hirschberg's arrest exemplifies the ominous situation of Jewish men as victims of a fascist government in the late 1930s. Some historians assert that prior to the deportations that began in 1941, the SA, the Gestapo, the police, and city mobs attacked only men.[4]

Even though Jewish males were the prime targets, Nazi violence against female political opponents began as soon as Hitler came to power. For example, Minna Cammens, an SPD Reichstag deputy from Breslau, was arrested for distributing anti-Nazi leaflets in 1933, and was later murdered by the Gestapo.[5] Intimidation tactics were also used against nonpolitical women who were held hostage or arrested because of the actions of male relatives. Gerhard Seger's wife and daughter were incarcerated for one and a half years after he escaped from the Oranienburg concentration camp in 1934.[6] It has been suggested that the Nazis used women hostages to influence the political behavior of men as early as 1933.[7]

Although Eva Hirschberg was not arrested, seeking the release of her husband and applying for emigration was a difficult and dangerous undertaking—especially in Berlin in 1938. Her situation is comparable to that of Ilza Czapska's in that she is constantly concerned about others, and has no time to think about the danger she is in.

Alfred Hirschberg's final release is delayed four weeks, a tactic that was typical of the Nazi bureaucracy in its treatment of Jews. Eva does not let this affect her, and throws herself into her work, concentrating exclusively on securing her husband's freedom and their eventual emigration. Her efforts ultimately prove successful. Hirschberg recaptures one of the most fearful moments in her life, and describes how she copes with the anguish. The author illuminates a political crisis from a personal viewpoint, and illustrates how those with little power negotiated—and sometimes won.

WHEN THE MEN WERE IN THE CAMP

BY EVA HIRSCHBERG

What we had feared for months and years had become reality. We held our breath whenever we heard car brakes or answered the doorbell. I can see my husband now, being taken to the police station between the two good-natured detectives who are hungry, annoyed, and unsuspecting. It didn't matter that we had known for

118

quite some time that this would happen or that he was probably only one of thousands who were rounded up on that day without arrest warrants—his name and address were scribbled in pencil on a scrap of paper. We were dazed, and thought it better not to think because we already knew too much from earlier arrests.

Could I have done anything to help or at least obtain information about the condition of the men arrested? The list of attorneys' addresses that my husband gave me in case this happened was useless. Anyone who had not been picked up was wandering aimlessly through the streets, trying to avoid incarceration.

The helplessness of the first days was the most difficult thing to bear. Where were our husbands? What would they do to them? Would our husbands be set free, and, if so, when and under what conditions? I remember that Alfred specifically forbade me to apply for emigration in the first few weeks. They might only be waiting for the burial of Herr vom Rath,[1] after which they would unconditionally release . . .

Rumors of the most contradictory nature were running through the city: the men were all at the Alexanderplatz.[2] Women had been seen entering the police station with suitcases and coming out a few minutes later without them. It seemed permissible to deliver warm clothes. Of course, we did not want to let the opportunity pass. Four of us took a taxi to deliver the hastily packed suitcases. On the way we were angry with ourselves: one of us forgot slippers, another wool socks, etc. Naturally, once we were in the police station, we had to turn around as soon as we reached the bars where the Jewish section was located. We didn't take the taxi on the way home because cash was in short supply, and our bank accounts were frozen.

And then we heard that they were near Oranienburg, all together in one room. Some of them are supposedly being employed for "light gardening." They still had their hair . . .

In response to the rumor that we could bring our husbands money at the camp gate, I set out immediately but was stopped by some others who had already tried and were unsuccessful. Later on we were allowed to send 20 marks by mail, money that was delivered weeks later.

Another time we ran to the congregation, in vain, where they were supposedly collecting the names of those arrested so that they could start a campaign for the release of all those involved.

Of course the confusion of the first few days was exploited by those trying to make some money. From time to time, we were tempted to try our luck with middlemen. They claimed to have the best connections and promised, for many thousands of marks, to have our spouses set free within three days. Many women clung to these promises in helplessness and despair, and huge sums of money were wasted senselessly.

Later on, relatives with good connections to party members became a source of constant agitation. Time and again they ran to us, hysterical with fear. They had just gotten a phone call from a "friend," who warned them that it would start all over that night. This time the raids would not only be confined to hauling the men away but also to vandalizing our apartments. It took quite a while until we were able to recognize these terrifying reports for what they were, false alarms intended to heighten the mood of panic in the Jewish community.

Was there some method to the internment? Why had many of our acquaintances escaped, and what chance did they have of staying free? Certainly police officers had been sent into houses with long lists, but as people found out about the raids, it became commonplace not to find the man of the house at home. He had been warned by telephone, in many cases by the official himself who had announced his intended visit in order to give the man a chance to disappear. This was done to protest against the incomprehensible orders the official had received to hand over a certain Mr. X to the SS.

When it became clear to the authorities that they were not having much success, they began to try other methods. Each official had to hand over a fixed number of Jews, no matter where or how he found them. No one was safe from being arrested anymore. "The man of the house isn't in? What a pity. But I hear men's voices. We'll take your guests in place of your husband." Anyone who was unfortunate enough to look particularly Jewish was grabbed on the street or in a café. A wild manhunt went on until the desired number was reached.

The fate of those men who remained free was not in the least enviable—they lived like fugitives. There were those who had their appendix removed unnecessarily or faked an illness. Favorite hideouts included households with no men and those the police had already visited. Jews admired and were astonished by "Aryan" friends, distant acquaintances and in many cases, even doormen in their buildings who had the courage to hide them, partly out of pity, and partly in opposition to the senseless raids. Anyone who could not find a somewhat safe place to stay left his house before dawn and walked or drove for hours in the Grunewald forest.

Some friends from next door were living with me, but they didn't feel safe. They slept fully dressed on the couch with the house key in their pockets so they could disappear without a trace in an emergency. This went on for a few days, and then new problems surfaced: such as how does one find a clean shirt without going back to one's apartment? You couldn't go around unshaven since that might give you away on the street! We helped each other and were thankful for the comic relief provided along with the horrible tragedies.

If only someone had recorded our telephone conversations at the time! Since we were almost certain that all private phones were tapped, we did not dare say clearly what we were thinking. The result was something like this: "Good morning, how are you?—Oh, fine, thanks, I'm sure you know how it is. . . . (pause)—So, how is everything else?—Everything else? The same, thanks.—Is Kurt there? No, Kurt is out of town—(does she mean he is in a concentration camp or out on a walk?) Oh well then, goodbye."

If we wanted to go and see someone, we called first. Sometimes we called without saying our names, other times we just mentioned our first name. We had to have a good memory in order to avoid mix-ups.

These weeks were characterized by crowded long-distance telephone booths. You could not walk past a phone that was not being used. The following is the experience of a friend who waited patiently until the person ahead of him finished his call. Out of the booth stepped a man in an overcoat, unshaven, with his portfolio under his arm. One look convinced him that the man waiting to use the phone was in the same situation. He greeted the man with "shalom" and asked whether he could recommend a place to stay for the night.

I was fortunate not to have had a minute alone. There were so many people to take care of—the dinner table was always set—we discussed the situation and offered each other advice and help. I had no time to sit and brood. These were the days that proved friendships, making them deeper and bringing people closer together than had been possible under more normal circumstances. In the evening we sat in front of the radio and wondered if we would be saved by an outside power. We waited to hear how other countries reacted and hoped, if not for immediate aid here at home, for at least a better opportunity to emigrate. Anyone with friends abroad wrote and asked for help.

Through the experience of a woman who worked with my husband and whose husband had also been picked up, we learned that even the constant flow of visitors was dangerous. Many of her co-workers and friends met in her home. The neighbors were watching them and eventually alerted the authorities. What followed was a summons to appear at the Alexanderplatz and an unpleasant interrogation. The officials wrote a report that included the names of the most frequent visitors and then issued a warning. In addition, two acquaintances, both older men, were summoned a few days later and given the responsibility of insuring that Mrs. X would no longer have so many male guests.

Even today I cannot shake the uncanny feeling that comes over me every time I think of my experience with the "black-market mail." It all started when I was approached by a distant acquaintance who asked me to write a few lines for her to deliver to my husband. She said that she had come in contact with the "underground" and had an SS officer at her disposal. I never really figured out what this was all about, however, a short time later I became personally involved.

One evening I received a phone call from a man with a rather sharp sounding voice. He said he had something to tell me about my husband and that I might want to come immediately to the train station to meet him. He was wearing an SS uniform, Heil Hitler! (All this on my telephone that I guarded so fearfully.) I was really in despair, but decided to give it a chance. I took a dark blue coat and a beret, left my money at home, and set out with a pounding heart. A girlfriend came along to watch us from a distance.

A young man in a black coat was actually waiting for me. At first, he seemed intent on trying to intimidate me: he threatened, described scenes from the camp where he was a guard, and emphasized all the things he could do to my husband while playing with his revolver. He was really annoyed, and I later found out why. The party with whom he had made contact initially had not yet paid him the agreed upon sum of money (because he had falsified the amount by adding a zero to it!). I must admit that I felt a bit better when I noticed that the guy wanted money. In return he promised to carry letters back and forth between me and my husband, and as proof he showed me a few lines that my husband had written (I could tell that my husband had agreed to the payments when I saw that his signature contained our pre-arranged sign).

It was only a matter of settling on the amount of the payment. Here I was saved by the freeze on our bank accounts. It was quite impossible for me to raise the sum he demanded, which was in the thousands. If I could pay in installments, 100 marks per letter, then I would agree. We left it at that. Nevertheless, I had to struggle to keep the next appointment with the guy. My friends advised against it, pointing to the great danger involved: once the payments started, the whole affair would spiral out of control. On the other hand, I was concerned about my husband's fate and knew that I was acting with his approval.

What followed were four or five rendezvous with the man. We walked through the busiest streets of Berlin, around the Memorial Church (*Gedächtniskirche*), through the Tiergarten park, and so on. He did not even consider giving me the letter straightaway. First we had to engage in conversation, and I had to listen to him describe hideous scenes from the camps, because he wanted us to get better acquainted. What he really wanted most of all was to come to my apartment. Luckily, my friends were there and they were my best excuse for getting away from him as quickly as possible since they knew nothing about all of this. Nonetheless, news about my husband was of the utmost importance to me. It was, perhaps, even more important that I had some way of letting my husband know about the preparations for his release and our emigration.

After the first weeks of helplessness and sitting around, it finally became clear what I would have to do to obtain Alfred's freedom. Since my husband was neither a veteran nor seriously ill (luckily enough), the only other grounds for his release was the proof that he would soon be emigrating. For that, I needed visas and tickets. If I presented everything at once and went through an interrogation with the Gestapo, then the case would be left to the camp commandant.

The race for the necessary documents was now on. My mother bought visas from Paris. (They were forged, as I read in the German press to my horror on the day before my husband was set free. Luckily the news had not yet made its way to the Gestapo.) I received information about tickets at a very early date. The documents were copied x-number of times, translated, notarized, and the application was submitted. I cannot even begin to say how many pointless applications had already been submitted by despairing wives, all of which tripled the work at the agency and delayed expedition even more.

After the envelope filled with papers was handed in at the Alexanderplatz, another waiting period began. (Because of the high number of applications, some files were misplaced, and it took several weeks of desperate worrying before the mistake was discovered!) I now had my hands full trying to get everything settled since it took several weeks to meet the formal requirements necessary for emigration: getting passports and clearance certificates, paying emigration taxes, and fulfilling the requirements for permission to pack.

In the meantime, the first eyewitness reports from those released were going around. The actor W. was the very first one, and he owed his release to the intervention of Mrs. Göring. It was no small shock the first time I saw a man with a clean-shaven head in front of me and heard his very subdued accounts of what he had been through. One day, the first postcard from the camp arrived, and it contained a few lines with directions for our upcoming emigration. The stamp was posted with the message: "Visit Oranienburg, the summer resort on Lake Stanitz." (This is no joke.)

Despite all the hurrying, despite the fact that I did not waste an hour meeting the requirements that were supposed to lead to the release of my husband, a week, and then another, and then a third and the better part of a fourth went by before it actually happened. During this time, I threw myself into my work, arranging the practical aspects of emigration. Before this, I would never have thought that I was capable of negotiating independently with bankers and of visiting revenue offices and police stations. But when one's husband's fate hangs in the balance, it is probably the same for everyone: nothing scares you away—you are even glad when the once dreaded summons to the Gestapo finally arrives. Things that had been important to you earlier now seem inconsequential. I would never have believed that I would be indifferent when my beloved car was confiscated. I had to sell the car at the last minute because of a decree that forbade Jews from driving.[3] As a result I was cheated out of quite a bit of money on the deal, and this didn't even bother me.

It was more important to save some of our belongings for the future. There was a porter who would transport oversized baggage on foreign-bound trains even if I didn't have a ticket; I had to seize the opportunity quickly. The trunk, which was filled with valuable coats, photos, a typewriter, clothing, etc., was packed overnight and was on its way by morning. I had some anxious moments until I received confirmation from Paris that the trunk had arrived.

With my own application completed, I now had some experience and knew what steps were necessary to complete the process. We decided to turn the apartment into a type of office to give advice to other wives we knew. Women from small towns throughout the country also came seeking help. For the most part, these poor women had to go through much more than we did in the city. In places with only a few Jewish families, people descended on the houses in hordes, destroying or stealing anything of value.

I still don't want to reveal how I finally discovered when I could get my husband back. We lost two days because Saturday was a national holiday and Jews were not allowed to leave their homes. The same was true for Sunday. On Monday, however, I set out for Oranienburg. After losing my way several times, I finally arrived at the camp from the wrong side. Since I had to walk halfway around the camp, I got a good idea of what life was like there. I went past fortified guard towers and saw signs every few feet that read "Do not come any closer on penalty of death." I was carefully scrutinized by the sentry as I saw groups of Jews working and heard sharp commands being given.

It was morning. Not until late afternoon did I see a sad procession walking through the main gate. The men were dressed in wrinkled-up suits, their heads were shaven, and some of them hobbled out supported by their comrades. Guards on both sides made sure that no one looked to the right or left. What I observed from this distance was the daily quota of prisoners to be set free. I had trouble finding my husband among them—the first thing I recognized were his glasses and his portfolio! The guards released them some distance from the camp. I had my husband back again.

Translated by Matthew Kaplan

OLGA BENARIO

Olga Benario is one of the more renowned German-Jewish women to have set foot on Brazilian soil. A dedicated Communist, she became a member of the Communist Youth Movement at the age of fourteen in Munich, her city of birth. Five years later she led a defiant raid on the Moabit Prison in Berlin to free her lover Otto Braun, a Communist intellectual. Benario then traveled to the Soviet Union and became an important Communist activist in Moscow. She was chosen at the age of twenty-six to be the bodyguard for Luís Carlos Prestes, the Communist guerilla leader who was living in the Soviet capital at the time.

What followed was the long trek to Brazil. Together Benario and Prestes journeyed through Europe and North and South America under assumed names. Once in Brazil, Prestes mobilized a Communist revolt against the fascist regime in November 1935, which met with defeat. After months of hiding, they were both seized and arrested in Rio de Janeiro in March 1936. Six months later and seven months pregnant, Olga Benario was deported to Nazi Germany because of her Jewish background and her activities within the German Communist Party. Filinto Müller sent her to Adolf Hitler as a "gift." The rest of her short life was spent behind bars, and her daughter was born in prison. Benario was executed in the gas chambers of Bernburg.

Until recently, the information on Olga Benario has been sketchy. Luís Carlos Prestes is discussed voluminously in many Brazilian history books, but Olga's fate in the hands of two dictatorships was virtually ignored. Only in the former German Democratic Republic was she well known. Numerous schools and factories were named after this Communist heroine. Olga Benario lived the last years of her life in Ravensbrück, and died in 1942 at the age of thirty-three.

The following is the last letter she wrote to her lover and the father of her daughter, Luís Carlos Prestes, and to her daughter, Anita Leocádia Prestes, on the last night in Ravensbrück, before she was put on the bus to Bernburg in February 1942. Moving and eloquent, the message mirrors a courageous and articulate woman facing death. Hopeful facing hopelessness, Benario fought for what she believed in and died pursuing it. Heartwrenching and emotional, the letter is a personal farewell to the two most important people in her life.[1]

LETTER FROM RAVENSBRÜCK

BY OLGA BENARIO

Dear Ones,

Tomorrow I will need all my strength and all my courage. For this reason, I will not be able to think about the things that torment my heart, things dearer to me than my own life. And for this reason, I'm saying good-bye to you now. It's utterly impossible for me to imagine, my dear daughter, that I will never see you again, never squeeze you in my eager arms. I wanted so to be able to comb your hair, to braid your braids—ah, no you have had them cut. But I think you look better with your hair loose anyway, a little bit messy. Above all else, I'm going to make you strong. You should wear sandals or go barefoot, running outdoors with me. Your grandmother won't like this at first, but before long she'll understand. You must respect her and love her all your life, as your father and I do. Every morning we'll do our exercises . . . You see? I've already gone back to dreaming as I do every night, forgetting that this is to say good-bye. And now, when I'm reminded of this, the idea that I will never again be able to hold your warm little body is like death to me.

Carlos, dear Carlos, my love: Will I have to relinquish forever everything good you have given me? Even though I will never have you near me again, it would be a comfort just to have your eyes see me once more. And I want so to see your smile. I want both of you, so much, so much. But what I'd like most is to be able to live one

127

happy day, the three of us together, as I have imagined thousands of times. Can it be possible that I'll never see how proud and happy our daughter makes you feel?

Dear Anita, dear husband. I'm crying under the blankets so that no one will hear me, because it seems that today I don't have the strength to endure something so terrible. Which is precisely why I'm struggling to say good-bye to you now, so I don't have to do it during the last and most difficult hours. After tonight, I want simply to live for whatever brief future I have left. You are the one who taught me, dearest one, what strength of will means, especially when it springs from sources like ours. I have struggled for the just and the good, for the betterment of the world. I promise you now, as I say farewell, that until the last instant I will give you no reason to be ashamed of me. Please understand: preparing for death doesn't mean giving up but rather knowing how to confront it when it arrives. So many things could still happen in the meantime. . . . I will remain firm and determined to live until the last moment. Now I must go to sleep, so tomorrow I can be strong. I kiss you both for the last time.

Olga

PART 3

TRANSFER
TO
BRAZIL

HILDE WIEDEMANN

"The Way Is the Goal" is Hilde Wiedemann's autobiography, and a measure of its content. The author paints a picture of her life in Brazil during the 1930s and 1940s from the perspective of a German-Jewish woman. Perceptive and optimistic, Wiedemann describes an austere existence in the Brazilian wilderness as well as urban life in Rio de Janeiro, São Paulo, Curitiba, and Recife. Although her focus is Brazil, she embroiders her story with the situation in Germany before, during, and after the war and explains how German politics affected the political and social conditions of a faraway land in the southern hemisphere.

Wiedemann and her family arrived in the port of Santos in July 1933. After a few nights in São Paulo, they traveled by train to Castro, in the state of Paraná. In this primitive setting, they embarked on a new life as German colonists and spent nearly seven years earning their living as farmers. She remembers the early days, with all of their expected and unexpected challenges, with a mixture of anxiety and excitement. The difficult pioneer life on a farm in Terra Nova ended with a move to Curitiba in 1939. As World War II approached, and her husband's work was threatened, they settled to in Recife, in the state of Pernambuco, where he started his own business.

When the Wiedemanns arrived in Brazil, the political situation was becoming more and more unstable. In 1930, Brazil was shaken by a coup, and the top military commanders elected Getúlio Vargas as president of the provisional government. He held this post for four years, and during this period, he sought to strengthen his support among collaborators and political allies. The Constituent Assembly of 1933–34 elected Vargas as the first president with a four-year term under the newly drafted second constitution, which was not very different from the first of 1891.[1]

By the mid-1930s, tension had grown between the two opposing parties. The Integralists were a rightist movement with fascist tendencies, and the National Liberation Alliance (Aliança Libertadora Nacional or ALN) was a leftist movement made up of communists, socialists, and miscellaneous radicals. By 1935, street brawls and terrorism were on the increase as the two major parties clashed. In July 1935, the government blocked the ALN by arresting its leaders, raiding offices, and confiscating documents. The communists reacted by staging an insurrection. This became a pretext for Vargas to demand a "state of siege," and revoke normal constitutional rights and privileges.[2]

The new government, endowed with emergency powers, cracked down on the Left with arrests, torture, and trials.[3] Two years later on November 10, 1937, Vargas dissolved the congress and stationed soldiers on its premises. Getúlio Vargas became leader of the Estado Nôvo, a dictatorship that was to last from 1937 to 1945 and resembled in many ways the fascist governments in Europe at the time.

The situation of the German Jews in Brazil grew more precarious because of the anti-Semitic policies of Getúlio Vargas. Wiedemann points out the strange combination of German Jews and Nazi empathizers in Brazil in the 1930s and 1940s. The economic and ideological relations between Brazil and Germany before World War II encouraged anti-Semitism within the Vargas regime. His highly nationalist Estado Nôvo created increasingly restrictive policies toward immigrants, which affected large numbers of Jews who had come to Brazil in the 1930s, mostly from Germany.[4] Brazil was a frontier that offered asylum to numerous opponents of the Third Reich, and Hilde Wiedemann was one of the many German Jews who immigrated there. Brazil attracted 15,000 German Jews in the 1930s, and by 1941 there were 20,000 German-Jewish émigrés in the country.[5]

In late 1937, Vargas introduced new policies to support his regime of national unity and to repress dissent. He burned the state flags, an act symbolic of his antiregionalist policies. He limited cultural activities, decreased the number of foreign language schools, and reduced annual immigration. His National Council of Immigration and Colonization imposed new quotas that were "approximately 50 percent of post-1930 and 10 percent of 1917–30 levels."[6]

At the outbreak of World War II, relations between Brazil and Germany began to shift, and the future of Hilde Wiedemann and her family became uncertain. In the northern port city of Recife, the fascists were just as prevalent as in Rio de Janeiro. The war had created a tense situation, especially for refugees from Germany and Italy. Brazil was now an Allied power, and as such the authorities imprisoned all German men in the city—regardless of their political affiliation. Wiedemann's husband was held for six weeks.

The author explores how the war affected her personally. For years, she and her family had been isolated as foreigners in Brazil, while simultaneously being ostracized by their fellow Germans as anti-Nazi. Highly adaptable, she coped with the situation by forming relationships with her husband's business friends, and with a few American and German-Jewish families. However, she confides that the years in Recife were a strain on her marriage.

Wiedemann's life was an adventure. She escaped European civilization as it stood at the brink of collapse, to embark upon an odyssey in Brazil. Her memoir bears witness to her optimism and dignity, and gives poignant details of her family life. Observant and intelligent, Hilde Wiedemann recaptures facets of daily existence. Aware of ethnic nuances and sensitive to the cultural diversity of Brazil, the author portrays a picture of daily life in a time of global war. Hilde Wiedemann died in 1981. Her three daughters continue to live in Brazil.

The Way Is the Goal

BY HILDE WIEDEMANN

Recife is the capital of Pernambuco and the most important city in the northeast of Brazil. We had come a long way from our little farm. At that time there was no regular air-mail service. By sea, the mail took an average of ten days to reach Rio, and three weeks would generally go by before a letter reached the farm. But it was not just the physical distance that separated us from our farm. We were once again city dwellers in a tropical environment that demanded a new type of adaptation to the dominant lifestyle.

We rented a pretty house in one of the villa suburbs. The kitchen and the rooms necessary for the upkeep of the house were housed in an extension, as was the custom in Recife. The family lived with open windows and doors in the airy coolness of the main house. The branches of an acacia tree, with their large red blooms, created a living roof over the upstairs terrace. Aside from the melon and other fruit trees there was also a mango tree in the garden, which provided shade and a place where the children could practice their climbing skills. A houseboy took care of the heavier housework and sprayed the garden, and a girl helped me in the kitchen.

In those days, I often woke up thinking about the colonial women of the past who began their days at dawn by milking and feeding the cows, while I could just enjoy the pleasant coolness of the morning breeze and listen to the hiss of the water jets spraying the hibiscus hedges with an early morning bath.

It was a good thing that I had developed my knowledge of Portuguese in Curitiba, and that Dorothea had become familiar with the language while in school there, since none of the workers in the stores spoke German any more. The German colony in the city comprised only about 300 families. After diplomatic relations between Germany and Brazil were severed, the German school was closed, and only the club remained until the outbreak of hostilities.

Just as in Rio, we noticed straightaway that the National Socialists set the tone in the colony. The ruling consul was an older man. As moderate as he was, his son was just as avid in his support of the new regime. Since the younger generation studied in the old country for the most part, it was not difficult for the party to find enthusiastic support among young people. You would think that distance would permit Germans living abroad to form clearheaded opinions about events back home. But just the opposite was true. Being separated from home by both time and space caused everything that happened there to be romanticized. Clearheaded thinking was further impeded by the grotesque war games arranged by the most solid family men, and gave free reign to their enthusiasm for running around in uniform. They did this as guests in a country that nourished them.

You can imagine how careful my husband was to keep his family far from this mood of turbulence. Our contacts were limited mostly to my husband's Brazilian business acquaintances and to a few American and German-Jewish families. We found the atmosphere quite stimulating despite the limitations. Of particular interest was the family life of the *Nortistas*, which, in contrast to the South, was still quite traditional. In 1940 there were still very few high-rise apartment buildings.

Most of the families that were financially comfortable had their own houses with large, shady gardens. Almost all of them had several children, and each child who was not yet of school age had his own black nurse. These *amas* were themselves not much more than children, and so their influence was highly questionable. I once watched a neighbor's young son playing with his *ama*. He took the toy that the girl had handed him and kept throwing it onto the cement floor until it broke into pieces. Then came the next toy, which met the same fate. Finally I decided that there were better things to do than play "smash the toy" with such nice things. The *ama* looked astonished: "but his father is a rich man," she answered laughing proudly as she calmly continued her supervision of the destruction.

The bigger children, or at least the boys, were often raised in Catholic boarding schools. After school, the girls stayed at home under their mothers' supervision. They spent their free time sewing and embroidering or preparing the most beautiful sweets and baked goods. One has to have seen a table set for a children's party to understand just what kind of lavishly decorated creations the women in a true Brazilian family could serve. They spent days preparing for these elaborate feasts. It was not just the children who were invited, but whole families took part in the festivities.

I discovered this, much to my chagrin, when we celebrated our youngest girl's birthday after she had started school. Wilhelm and I had put together a Punch and Judy show and had written a play for the occasion which included not only Punch and Judy but also the king's son, a princess, the devil, and a peasant. The king's son even got to sing a beautiful song with guitar accompaniment under the princess's balcony. We grownups had a great time each evening at the rehearsals.

I had invited twenty children and, as the big day approached, I made sure I had cakes and drinks, which were only secondary in my mind. How can I describe the shock I felt when a never-ending stream of cars began to park in front of the house, and whole carloads of kids and other family members started getting out. By the time all twenty of the children I had invited showed up, we had seventy-two guests!

My maid and houseboy outdid themselves on that memorable day. While my husband and I entertained our guests with the

Punch and Judy show, they magically whipped up something quite unusual, and by evening we had a cold buffet that was a hit with both old and young alike. Weeks later children were still coming up to me on the street, their eyes filled with anticipation, and asking "When are you having the next *mamolengo* (Punch and Judy show)?"

When Wilhelm and I were invited to visit other homes, it was at first difficult for me to be good and associate exclusively with other women. At this time, strict segregation of the sexes was still the norm. The men stood around or found a cool place to sit in the garden, where they discussed business or politics. We women sat on the sofas and in the easy chairs and talked about illnesses, domestic help, and children. Sometimes the lady of the house would show off the often beautiful, delicate embroidery that she or her daughter had done. Even in these situations I had to learn how to behave correctly. The first time this happened I expressed my amazement quite freely. I was all the more enthusiastic since I myself had never learned how to make such works of art. Later, as we said goodbye, I found that a packet was being pressed into my hand. I opened it when we got home and discovered all the embroidery that I had so loudly praised.

The graciousness in giving and the hospitality of the northern Brazilians is unimaginable. Of course we Europeans, and especially we Germans, try to excuse ourselves by saying that the Brazilians have never experienced the difficulties of war, that almost all of them grew up on huge estates with numerous servants and without any material worries. In many cases this is true. But there are also countless others who developed exactly the same grace and hospitality in the most modest surroundings.

Thanks to huge, air-conditioned apartment buildings and a shortage of servants, households in the tropics are much the same today as those in cooler areas. But in the Recife of the 1940s things were still done the old-fashioned way. The climate forced people to live in a type of commune, since our lives and the lives of our neighbors were played out in front of open windows and doors. The whole neighborhood heard every noise on the street, every barking dog, every conversation among the help, every concert on the radio. The sound was muffled only by the gardens that surrounded the houses.

Communal life began early each morning in our neighborhood. Our neighbor across the way would yell out his bathroom window to his servants' quarters in a stentorian voice "Fecha a torneira!" [close the faucet]. There was never enough water pressure upstairs for his morning shower, a problem common to all of us who lived in the rapidly growing suburb.[1]

The parrot provided the next act in our morning's entertainment, when Wilhelm soaped his beard before shaving. This amusing enterprise would cause the bird to take off from its perch on the kitchen door and fly up to the bathroom window with the shrillest peels of laughter. Then he would glide a bit and announce to the world "Louro quer café" [Louro wants his coffee], until he was served breakfast.

A short time later, after the various Joãos, Pedros, and Zés had helped their masters get their cars out of the driveways by yelling "abre o portão" [open the gate], and after the children had started on their way to school, the streets would come alive with vendors.

Hilde Wiedemann and her husband in Recife,
state of Pernambuco, Brazil, 1948.
Courtesy of Dorothea Wiedemann.

There was the coal man, whose small, gaunt horse was almost invisible under the sacks of coal piled on his back. Then there was the poultry salesman, whose horse carried a big basket of cackling feathered animals. Fish and fruit salesmen carried their wares themselves on a yoke with a large fully loaded basket on either side.

The woman who called out *"mel de engenho"* [sugar syrup] became a special friend. She was a white-haired negro from the city who was born before 1838, before slavery was abolished, and she still wore slave's clothes: a long calico skirt covered with flounces, a long-sleeved blouse, and a kerchief tied with an African knot. She carried her syrup bucket on her head. Her enviably erect posture ensured that the bucket would be perfectly safe.

At that time it was still quite common for people to carry things on their heads. Whenever I made my weekly trip to the market, which took place in the morning on a shady square not far from our house, our houseboy would accompany me with a large wheel-shaped bamboo basket. He followed me step by step through the aisles of the market with the basket on his head, while I loaded it with our rations for the week—fifty bananas, fifty oranges, coconuts, pineapples, melons, yams, taro root, and vegetables of all types. By the time I was finished, the wheel on his head had been turned into a pyramid that he proudly carried home.

In the afternoon the quiet of the siesta spread across the whole area, and in the evening, too, the streets of the suburb were usually serene. On hot summer evenings many families brought their rocking chairs out onto the sidewalk where the men, comfortable in their slippers and pyjamas, smoked the last cigarette of the day.

The piles of laundry that built up in the house each week could have been a problem for someone new to the tropics. I was lucky. One day two washwomen came to the door and asked if their services were needed. They had no recommendations and they could only give me an approximate description of where they lived, since the streets on the outskirts of the city had no names and the houses had no numbers. I decided to take a chance and gave them a mountain of laundry tied up in a bed sheet. They returned one week later, and it was all snow-white and carefully ironed. Over the course of many years they walked through half the city with large bundles of laundry, including my husband's linen suits. And even in the heat of the summer they would walk with bare feet on the pavement. Not a single piece of laundry was ever lost. How these women managed in the rainy season to bring everything back dry still remains a mystery to me.

A new school year began shortly after our arrival in Recife. We enrolled our children in two schools founded by North American missionaries: the two youngest in a private school not far from home, the oldest in a state-accredited school that was a bit farther away. The instruction in both institutions was good, and the faculty consisted mostly of North Americans. The private school was run by two women who turned out to be true friends after the war broke out. In the first days of the war, all German men were put in prison, and no one knew what was going to happen to their families. The inventories of most German businesses had been destroyed.

In our neighborhood, wandering patriots were throwing rocks through the windows of houses where Germans lived and they even forced their way into some homes. If possible, I wanted to spare my children the terror of such an attack and turned to the school director for advice. I didn't know if we would be in the position to pay for a boarding school. I didn't even know if my husband and I would be brought to a camp or if we would remain in Recife. The director eased my mind. She assured me that she would bear the costs of keeping Elisabeth and Ursula at the boarding school for the duration of the war, if necessary. I did not need to worry, I could just leave them there in her care. I found the same helpful attitude in Dorothea's school. The boarding school took her in without any guarantee that I could pay for her. Over the years we have remained friends with the director and his wife.

The first weeks of the war were equally difficult for all Germans in Recife, whether they were National Socialists or Democrats. Since there was no place else to put them, all Germans were housed in the city jail, eight to ten to a cell. There was hardly enough room for everyone to sleep stretched out on the floor. It was an embarrassing situation for the guards because they didn't know how to handle prisoners who weren't criminals. We women sent blankets, pillows, clothes, and daily meals. Once a week we were allowed to see our husbands for ten minutes with a guard present. We would try to find out how the interrogations had gone, but had to do so in Portuguese.

With the help of some Brazilian friends, my husband was able to get himself released after six weeks. He represented a cooperative building society whose customers were almost exclusively Brazilian, and they urgently demanded that he be allowed to reopen his office. For the first few months, though, the authorities did assign an armed detective to stand next to Wilhelm's desk. After a while he must have been convinced that my husband was not a political threat and he stopped showing up. Through the years he would appear at Christmastime to find out how business was going and to convince himself of the gratitude with which my husband remembered those months they had spent together.

Within the first few years of the war, internment camps for Axis nationals were set up in the center of each state. Those who were really active politically (such as the chief of the storm troopers and head of the Nazi Party) were interned on an island in the Bay of Rio.

Recife served as a fortified base for the North American fleet. This meant that my husband was not allowed to leave the city nor could he spend time around the harbor or the beach. As a result his life was limited even more than usual to his office and family, and we were especially pleased when Brazilian and American acquaintances would drop by from time to time. Their conversation brought a bit of excitement to our seclusion.

In particular, we learned a great deal about the Recife of the early decades of the twentieth century from Mr. and Mrs. Mean. They were the parents of John Gorden Mean, the American ambassador to Guatemala who was murdered by terrorists in 1968. They had been in Brazil since 1907 and had directed the Colegio Americano Batista from the time of its founding. At first they had to contend with all kinds of problems and they were limited at every turn by the dominant culture and by common prejudices.

For instance, physical labor was seen as something class related. The colonists' sons who had been to boarding school were quite embarrassed when they had to watch their teachers demonstrate the machinery in an agriculture course. Around the turn of the century it also seemed completely unnecessary to give girls an education. Many fathers were of the opinion that it was particularly dangerous for girls to be able to read. That would lead them to read novels and formulate romanticized or even revolutionary ideas about marriage.

Even in the way they led their own lives, female teachers had to show consideration for the prevailing attitudes. Mrs. Mean told us that a woman never went to the city unaccompanied. If her husband had to be away for some reason, then a son or, at the very least, the oldest daughter had to accompany the mother. In addition, a woman of rank would never go by foot. The two-horse carriage would stop in front of the store where she wanted to shop, and the salesmen would bring the goods out: it was improper for a lady not accompanied by her husband to spend time under the same roof as the salesmen.

It was surprising that Mrs. Mean herself still had had such experiences; to us they seemed more like something from a third-rate novel. By the 1940s things had changed considerably. Equal schooling for girls and boys was the norm, and many daughters of middle-class families had begun to have careers.

The war brought the decisive turn in the direction of equality between the sexes. Twenty thousand American troops were stationed in Recife, and many of the officers brought their families along. "The American way of life" soon began to rub off on the residents of Recife. American women not only went shopping unaccompanied, they even went to the movies alone or stopped to relax at a café where they could order some ice cream. Their only escort was a bag full of packages they carried home all by themselves.

The beautiful beach near the city no longer belonged exclusively to young men and the few lucky families that owned large houses there. Instead, bright-colored umbrellas and bathing suits lit up the sand on Sundays, and during the week the classrooms were

Wiedemann house in Terra Nova, Paraná.
Courtesy of Elisabeth Eckardt and Dorothea Wiedemann.

filled with suntanned young people. Pale elegance was no longer in fashion, having been quickly replaced by the athletic-looking tan.

The all-controlling "papai não deixa" [daddy won't allow it], a leitmotif of every daughter's existence, was heard less and less. Even on rainy days the classrooms were as full as usual, whereas before, daughters of the elite would have stayed home, rain being dangerous to a young lady's health. Eventually "faz mal" [that's bad for you] became as outmoded as "papai não deixa."

Since the beach was off limits to us enemy foreigners, we tried to become thoroughly acquainted with the city on our days off. There were many beautiful things to see here, too, such as churches and cloisters from the colonial period. There were also a few forts left over from the Dutch colonization, when Mouritz von Nassau had widened the harbor causing the sugar industry to boom in the interior of Pernambuco. The two rivers that flow through the city were at that time the major arteries for sugar transport. Even today many of the traditional middle-class houses in the city have docks on the river. Culturally, Recife never attained the same importance as Bahia, but a number of important men (such as Rui Barbosa, Castro Alves, and Joaquim Nabuco) did graduate from the city's university.

There were also a number of historical sights in the old city. In some parts of the business district you would think you were in Lisbon: there were rows of tall, narrow doorways with arches typical of the Iberian peninsula. Some of the four- and five-story houses were more reminiscent of old Amsterdam. Up until a few years ago, you could still find traces of each colonial period. Since then they have all given way to modern streets and high-rise buildings.

The outskirts of town had something quite different to offer. In contrast to the artistic business district and neighboring villa quarter, both of which were just above sea level, the huts of the working class were laid out on hills, in a broad half circle around the outside of the city. We Germans were accustomed to seeing the ruins of some knight's castle or at the very least some modern industrialist's villa on every hill. We were amazed to discover that the most beautiful view in a Brazilian city is often reserved for the poorest residents, who cannot take advantage of the location. The women have to drag the water up the hill from one of the wells built by the city government. The paths leading up and down are narrow and unpaved and they become annoyingly slippery when it rains. The huts, called *mocambos*, are tiny and are often built with a flimsy half-timber frame. They look as if one could just pick up a stick and put it right through the wall. But in contrast to the slums in many other cities, the *mocambo* hills in Recife are incredibly clean. Everyone cleans on Sunday, while groups of neatly dressed girls stand between the houses, and old ladies sitting in front of their doors in chairs, stools, or on crates, give a friendly nod to those passing by. You can hear radio music and children's laughter through the doors and windows.

Our children always enjoyed these walks and thanks to their blond hair and blue eyes they collected many friendly comments from the local residents. Even our youngest was enthusiastic about these outings, only one trip ended prematurely in a taxi. She stopped suddenly and said, "I'm so tired I can't even open my mouth to yawn."

The war took its course. We heard nothing from our friends in Germany, the U.S., England, or South Africa. When corresponding within Brazil we had to write in Portuguese, which really hampered communication between my sister (who lived in São Paulo) and myself. There were restrictions on my husband's work from all sides, and after a while he became depressed by the limitations on his freedom of movement.

These years of being isolated as foreigners and being ostracized by fellow Germans as anti-Nazis constituted the first really serious test of our marriage. It was a time of horrible inner desolation, full of worries and fear for our future, for the future of our homeland, and for everything that we felt united us.

I had a dream back then that has became a symbol of those years for me. I was hurrying along a straight, dusty road that passed through an empty plain and led to an industrial town on the horizon. To the right, the tree branches stretched their leafless arms into the gray sky, and to the left was an endless wooden partition. On the other side of the partition I heard the voices of enthusiastic soccer players, and I thought I recognized my husband's voice among them. I tried to look through the cracks in the partition. I called to the invisible players and I looked for a door. I raced forward in an endless search while knocking and calling.

In the dream I never did find the end of the partition, and even in later years it stood between Wilhelm and me once again, but in the final analysis I would have to agree with Thurber who wrote: "Marriage does not make one person out of two, it makes two people. It is sweeter that way—and simpler too."

The war was over. From the first photos of Hamburg, the first letters from Dresden, and the *Würzburger Chronik*, we began to hear not only about the terrible destruction but also about the horrendous death camps built to exterminate Jews. In addition to the sadness about what had been lost forever in cultural treasures, came the shock about the horrors, to which our people had let themselves be degraded. A people whom we had always loved as respectable and honest.

As the Brazilian detention camps were closed, most of the Germans we knew gradually began to return to Recife. We had expected to see them deeply shaken by the fall of Hitler's regime, which they had enthusiastically supported for twelve years. Instead we saw a different picture, similar to the one Fernau was later to describe in his book: *They Were Not Ashamed.* There we read: "On the contrary, we in Germany took off our wigs, hid them in the attic, and wrote each other declarations certifying that we had never been involved, and then those gentlefolk subscribed to the *ami du peuple*—for a few months, anyway."

In 1946, Wilhelm received an invitation to Dresden. He was being offered a good position in the Saxon Justice Department. It was not easy for my husband to pass up the chance to return to Germany and work once again at his old career. But he saw about as much of a future under a communist administration as he had under the Nazis. We therefore decided to stay in Brazil.

During the hard times that led up to the currency reform, we were at least in a position to help. For example, the Germans in Recife organized a drive to collect clothing, and more than 350 packages were shipped to Hamburg from Wilhelm's office. Later on the clothing was replaced by shipments of food.

The exchangeable value for the food we sent was a good indication of the urgency of Germany's predicament back then. For instance, in letters from Berlin we heard that one pound of coffee would get you 100–200 pounds of potatoes, or 1.5 pounds of bacon, or 3 pounds of dried milk, or 30 loaves of bread.

The first boatload of Germans returning to Recife arrived in February 1947. It was the *Santarém*, an ancient German steamship that Brazil acquired after the First World War, under a provision of the Treaty of Versailles. To accommodate all the passengers on this journey, the cargo rooms had been fitted with long rows of berths stacked in groups of three. The men had to be separated from the women and small children. As a result mothers had to suffer with a lack of help from their husbands. The overloading caused not only a lack of care but more critically a lack of water.

We were very happy to receive permission to go aboard the ship so that we could take some of the passengers home as our guests for as long as the ship remained in the harbor. They had spent the weeks before the *Santarém*'s departure in camps, where they were provided with little in the way of clothing and no foreign currency at all. It was moving to see the impression that normal city life made on them. The fabric shops in particular, with their large bundles full of material, brought tears to the women's eyes. And a little black boy drove the children into a frenzy of excitement when he opened a case full of toothbrushes to try and sell some. "Mommy, there are soooo many toothbrushes!" And then of course there was the childish delight and relief among the adults when they came to our house and finally had a chance to take a real bath or shower.

Letters and newspapers from back home also began to make it through to Recife. Commenting on the Swiss weekly *Die Weltwoche*, my husband wrote the following to an acquaintance of his: "for me one of the most important arguments for its distribution is that after so many years of being overfed with North American views, we need a European interpretation to European problems." In fact it was amazing to see the extent to which American newspapers, magazines, and books had come to dominate the Brazilian market right after the war.

Germans had exactly the opposite point of view. Johannes Funke, who would later became the main business manager for the Carl Duisberg Society, wrote to us that year, "I read American newspapers frequently now. After the isolation of the past years it seems as if someone has opened a window and let the fresh air in."

A passage in another of his letters reads: "We, too, are slowly beginning to take stock of the last few years. The destruction in the cities is far more widespread than even the worst rumors would have indicated." Later he writes: "because of the shortage of coal, so much wood is being cut that you can count the days until all German forests are gone. Erosion has become a real possibility in the near future."

Robert Tillmann, representative for the Christian Democrats and minister in Bonn, had earned his bread in the coal trade under the Nazis. In 1947 he wrote, "in spite of all the bitter and difficult experiences, we here in Berlin are once again beginning to build a life for ourselves, even though the land is in a grim state. Professionally, the outlook is also grim. For the time being I am coordinating the Lutheran Church's relief work in the Soviet Zone. I find this work satisfying despite the pains and difficulties involved. It does not pay to write about living conditions here. They are not pleasant."

One of the first letters that reached us came from the Eastern Zone in 1946. It was from our friend H. Krippendorff, who was writing from a small town near the Hartz: "In less than 20 minutes we lost everything we owned when the Americans bombed the center of the city (Halberstadt). It was only with great effort that we managed to save ourselves from the burning house as it fell apart. Now we are trying to build a new life. I have set up a shop to manufacture spare parts for farm machinery. We're still not sure if we will be able to maintain it in the face of all the political turmoil. After spending three months last autumn in a Russian detention camp, I hope that I have proven I am not a political threat. Expropriations are still occurring, however, and initiative is being stifled by uncertainty about one's safety. Just as you had to build a new home for yourselves back then, we, too, have to start over."

There were indeed similarities in our situation. For our friends, as for us, it was not just a matter of rebuilding a material existence, but of thinking about the more important question of our children's futures. Just as we moved from the country to the city seven years after our arrival in Brazil to guarantee our daughters a good education, the Krippendorffs decided to abandon the newly built machine shop in the east so that their children could take advantage of better educational opportunities and freedom of speech in the Western Zone.

We could not create the security of a middle-class life for our children, nor could we pass on to them their grandmother's cherry furniture. But it is satisfying to see that despite all the turbulence and distress we had to dodge constantly, we were able to smooth the way for our children, so that today they can live in freedom.

Translated by Matthew Kaplan

ALICE BRILL CZAPSKI

Born in 1920, Alice Brill Czapski was still a baby when her parents were divorced. She therefore had a close relationship with her mother, and saw her father only occasionally. At the age of twelve, Alice Brill became aware of her Jewish identity but could not yet understand the political implications. Shortly after the National Socialists seized power in 1933, she left school and traveled with her mother to southern Europe. This was the beginning of an odyssey that was to last many years. Alice joined her father Erich Brill, a professional artist, and sailed for Brazil in 1934.

In *Der Schmelztiegel* (The Melting Pot), an autobiographical novel about her wanderings between 1933–39, Alice's mother, Marthe Brill, introduces Erich as the painter Erich Schönberg. *Der Schmelztiegel* relates the story of Sylvia, who represents Marthe Brill, and her daughter Miriam, who represents Alice Brill, in the form of a *Schlüsselroman* (roman à clef). This was a popular genre in the 1930s, and allowed Marthe Brill to describe the people in her life without having to expose their true identities. Through the genre of literary fiction and by means of a third-person narrator, Marthe Brill safely distances herself from a difficult period in her life.

Alice Brill Czapski emphasizes her mother's interest in Hasidic culture and Jewish mysticism, and shows how this affected her own sense of identity. After the Nazis came to power, it became painfully obvious to German Jews that new laws regarding Jews would affect their children's education. The Law against Overcrowding of

146

German Schools and the resulting enrollment ceilings reduced the number of Jewish students in the German school system. Those who did stay in the same educational institution were taught Nazi racial doctrine. Many leaders in the Jewish community became alarmed that German Jews were no longer familiar with, or even aware of, Jewish culture and history.

Although many young Jews, such as Alice Brill, learned about Jewish culture from their parents, some Jewish leaders wanted to set up learning centers for young people. In May 1934, the *Mittelstelle für jüdische Erwachsenenbildung* (Jewish Center for Adult Education) was established under the leadership of Martin Buber. He coined the phrase *Rüstung zum Sein* (arming for existence), and used the slogan to describe the goal of the center, which was to provide spiritual sustenance to the Jews whose world was now disintegrating.[1] Seminars covering a variety of subjects were held in rural settings in various places in Germany. Buber was central in determining the themes for the meetings, taking inspiration from Hebrew Scripture. In this way, many young people who attended the meetings were instilled with Jewish consciousness in the tradition of humanism.

Baal Schem (1700–1760), whose name Marthe Brill held up to her daughter as a famous ancestor, was the founder of Hasidism. As a young man he had lived in the quiet of the forests, where he communed with God and discovered the healing powers of herbs. After moving back to a city, he became known as a healer, and was given the name "Baal Schem" or "master of the name." He began to preach that God was in all places and in all things in the universe. He also taught that in order to reach God, the sincerity of prayer was more important than sophisticated learning. Baal Schem emphasized devotion over learning, and that God could best be served through deep joy rather than intellectual ardor.[2]

MEMORIES FROM 1933–45

BY ALICE BRILL CZAPSKI

Born on December 13, 1920 I was the only daughter of German-Jewish intellectuals. My parents were of middle-class origin, and came from families that expected their sons to follow an academic career. This was a new privilege granted to Jewish students at the time. As eldest son, my father Erich Brill had to take a university degree in philosophy and economics to please his father and, in addition to this, had to obtain permission to study art on the side. But being a born artist, he never made use of his academic studies. My mother, Marthe Brill, lost her own mother, Bertha Leiser, in childhood. Bertha had been an outstanding female journalist quite exceptional for her time.

My mother was a woman of remarkable intelligence and personality, hardly to be expected in someone so small and rather frail. She chose to study literature with her mother's modest inheritance but, disappointed with the academic methods, decided to change her major to economics. She did not make much use of this profession, except in her youth during World War I, when she worked for the World Economics Institute to make a living. She told me that it was a fascinating job, where she organized a filing system based on daily news. All information had to be filed under several topics, allowing a great range of studies. She had this rare opportunity because there were no men available during wartime. When she was dismissed after the war, she mentioned proudly that three men had taken her place. Although she was not a devout Jew, she was proud of being Jewish, telling me that her family descended from the famous Rabbi Baal Schem. My mother was not brought up in a religious way, but was rather agnostic and liberal-minded with a socialist and cosmopolitan view of life, as was common among young intellectuals in her day. However, just like my father, she was very interested in all Jewish matters, even mysticism.

My parents were divorced when I was a baby, so I only had occasional contact with my father, who led a bohemian lifestyle devoted entirely to his artwork. As a passionate observer of life, he loved to study costumes, people, and contrasting landscapes in different countries. He traveled constantly, with short intervals in his studio in Hamburg to organize exhibits of his paintings. Although I was on good terms with my father's family, I was especially attached to my mother, as we enjoyed a close emotional and intellectual relationship.

Marthe Brill also loved to travel. As a writer, she was a collaborator of the tourist magazine of the Hamburg-Südamerika Shipping Company, where her journalistic contributions were paid in travelling credit. During the months when she went abroad every year, I usually stayed at my grandmother's villa. Sophie Brill was a strong person who managed her life alone since her husband had died rather young. She had three sons and one daughter, and my father was her favorite. Because the family had lost their fortune during the depression of the twenties, she rented rooms in her three-story mansion. When there was no help available, she did all the cooking and cleaning by herself. But when I was a child, she still had servants and she sent one of them, a very nice girl, to take care of me and help my mother. This girl, Annie, was my governess for many years and accompanied us to southern Italy, where we lived for a year in Positano when I was four.

When I just turned twelve years of age my mother planned for the first time to take me along on her trip to Spain. It happened to be March 1933, right after Hitler came to power. It was only at this time that I began to realize that I was Jewish. My mother was strongly antifascist and did not hide her feelings about what was happening in Germany. She also was a conscious feminist and held lectures on various topics over the radio. When Hitler took over all public communication channels in Hamburg, her lectures were immediately cancelled and her colleagues warned her to leave the country "for a while." As she had already booked our trip on a Hamburg-Süd ship, she decided to stay away as long as necessary. Our flat was left behind with all our belongings. Because we lived on her modest income as a writer, she did not know how we would survive. But she did not seem to worry too much. I left school at the beginning of the second year of the *Gymnasium*, which corresponds approximately to the sixth grade in the U.S. My class teacher was a Quaker woman, who later emigrated to England. She asked me to write reports for school on everything new I would be seeing: costumes, architecture, landscape, people and their behavior, flora and fauna. She said that she would read them to the class and grade my papers accordingly. In this way I could make up the schoolwork I would be missing, and could receive credit for the school year. I have kept these reports, and I use portions of them in this autobiography.

When our ship *Monte Rosa* left Hamburg on March 3, 1933, I suddenly saw a boat following us. It was full of children my age and as it came close I heard my name called—they were my schoolmates escorted by our beloved Miss Robinow, only the children of Nazi families were missing.

I was not really conscious of what was happening. Both of my parents had always traveled a lot by themselves, and it was my ardent wish to be allowed to go, too. This was what I had waited for, pure adventure, even more so as we had no idea if and when we would be able to return home. My diary of those days was still written in Gothic letters. I was amazed to discover that I can still read them. It is an accurate account of everyday life on ship and of all places we visited: Madeira, Tenerife, Tétouan, Ceuta, Casablanca, and the Spanish coast from Malaga to Barcelona, from where we crossed by boat to Majorca. From Palma we went to the interior of the island to rent a small *finca* with a farmer's cottage in the small village of Alcudia.

My first school report starts like this: "Dear Mrs. R. and class, I am sitting in the garden with a view of a large green field of grain and countless fig and almond trees. A little almond tree shades my table and if the fruit were already ripe, I only would have to stretch out my hand to pick a fig behind me and an almond just in front." After this I described our home and its rustic decoration, and the two cisterns, one for service, the other for drinking water, because there was no electricity, gas, or any other modern facility. I learned to live a primitive life without modern comfort. Fascinated, I watched our landlady cooking Spanish meals on a charcoal stove and wandered through the countryside by myself, observing everything from the smallest insect to human behavior. At the tiny port of Alcudia I remember sitting on the stones over the sea, with my legs in the water, to watch the sea life below. I observed the fishermen bring in their nets full of fish. Never had I been so free to do what I pleased in all my life, and I thoroughly enjoyed it.

My mother soon started a research project on the last Spanish Inquisition, which took place in Majorca. She was either working at the library or trying to interview members of older Jewish families, long converted Christians, whom she identified by name. She wrote her story (that was never published), but didn't succeed in making friends with the *marannos* or new Christians, who did not want to be reminded of their ancestors.

Thus, I was left alone to stroll about and watch the life around me. I studied the different culinary habits and wrote detailed accounts about meals and cooking, also about how people spent their time, about traditional crafts and costumes and much more. I also described a *noria*, a well linked to a big wheel, driven by donkeys to pull out the water. Once we wandered near swamps on a dark moonless night and saw the water lighten where a school of phosphorescent fish swam by. Suddenly, from May on, my handwriting changes to Latin writing. It describes our ten-day excursion through part of the island, including the places where the musician Chopin and his writer friend George Sand used to live, over a hundred years ago. Mother explained that George Sand was a woman of great talent, and that she used her pseudonym to be able to publish her writing. She also was perhaps the first woman to openly wear slacks and other masculine attire, causing scandal among the islanders.

Marthe Brill did not succeed in finding a job on the island. We managed to survive on $20.00 a month, which her brother Billy sent us from New York. But we had to find a place where she could make a living to build a new home for the two of us. After six months of wonderful country life in Majorca, news from Germany was still utterly discouraging, and there was no hope of a change for the better. So mother decided to leave our paradise, where life was easy and cheap but held no promise for the future, and to try her luck in Italy where she had lived years before.

We went by ship, arriving in Genoa at the end of September, 1933, just before the celebration of the Jewish New Year, Rosh Hashanah. My mother loved Italy and I was looking forward to seeing the wonderful sights and works of art she had been telling me about. We were poor emigrants and yet our search for a new home was a fascinating adventure to me. "Look, this is Italy," mother said as we arrived in Genoa. The first day of our arrival we left for Florence, travelling by bus along the beautiful Riviera.

An entry in my diary reads: "never was I so thrilled at the sight of mountains, forests and small villages as in this Alpine Italian landscape. People here just must be happy." Florence was like a fairy tale to me and I described everything I saw.

A few days later, our real situation began to dawn on me, I wrote: "This is the first time we celebrate our new year, Rosh Hashanah, as strangers, far away from the country which was home to us, I now feel what that means, here in Italy, where I don't speak the language. We went to the synagogue here. In spite of not understanding what was said, invisible threads tied us to those people. What a strange feeling: our people are everywhere, on both sides of frontiers, everywhere are similar synagogues, the same rituals, the same faith, chanting and horn blasting." I did not understand the Hebrew prayers, but I wept with emotion.

As strangers we were invited to a Jewish home for supper, as is the custom. Our host prayed intensely with his four-year-old son. The scene reminded me of the Wailing Wall in Jerusalem, where my father had painted a canvas. Suddenly I felt that these prayers must be full of hope, love, and confidence. After the blessing on bread and wine, the food was uncovered, full of age-old symbolism: the bread, in the middle of the table, had been formed like a hand, and its shape was supposed to reveal whether a happy year was ahead, while sweet dates were served to make the coming year a lucky one. The supper was illuminated by an old Sephardic oil lamp, inherited from generations of Sephardim (Spanish Jews.) The main dish was fish—"so that you may multiply and prosper like fish in the water."

This first meeting with Jewish faith and mysticism left a deep impression on me. I was filled with a sense of belonging. Ten days later we celebrated Yom Kippur (Day of Atonement), the most important Jewish festivity, and went to the main synagogue. It was overcrowded with families and small children, even though the service starts with the famous Kol Nidre, or chants for the dead, and the men are supposed to wear their mourning clothes. Again I was moved by the chanted prayers. I was honored as a stranger by being allowed to touch the Torah scroll and to put it back in its place. I felt again that I belonged here. I wrote: "This Yom Kippur, 1933, we felt reconciled with God, men and our destiny."

The only job my mother found was as a governess to an eight-year-old little girl of a rich family. As she did not know how to pay for all expenses on her small income, nor what to do with me, she accepted the offer of the Jewish Colony of Florence to intern me in the Jewish orphanage for girls. The four months I spent there I remember as the unhappiest period of my childhood. I was an exception in this institute, because I still had living parents. We had to wear long dark uniforms.

The other girls ignored me, and acted as if I had no right to be there. Everything was strange and different; I had never been confined like this before. I loved to learn, but we only had classes for girls such as sewing, which I hated. The only lesson I really liked was Hebrew.

Once a week I was allowed to see my mother. Both of us looked forward to this all week, but the poor orphans envied me and made me feel like a stranger among them. Mother and I would make the most of our time together, talking about our experiences while strolling through the lovely city. By this time she had rented a small room, but it was not heated and a cold winter was approaching. I remember that we went to the public post office to get warm because it was heated, but there were no seats to sit on. Money was sparse and we did not have enough winter clothes. Worst of all: there was no hope for a better future.

One day mother got a letter from the chief editor of the tourist magazine she used to work for in Germany. Dr. Lange wrote in a friendly fashion that he had learned of our difficult situation, and that he would like to help, offering us tickets to Brazil on one of the regular Hamburg-Süd tourist vessels. Many refugees were going to Brazil, he wrote, and they seemed to do alright. . . . This was a very courageous attitude in a country where an act of human solidarity to persecuted "outlaws" was considered high treason. Mother decided to follow his advice. We had to return to Hamburg, which would be our point of departure. By reading the newspaper we had some idea about the changes which had taken place in our country; even the language was no longer the same, patriotic and authoritative, sounding combative and intolerant. The idea of having to go back there, even for a short while, made us shiver.

We arrived in Hamburg in January 1934. The city had a strange look about it, young boys and girls marched in Nazi uniforms singing Nazi songs, and every wall was covered with slogans. Aggression was in the air and we avoided the streets when possible. And this was only the beginning! When my teacher had one of my compositions printed in the *Hamburger Anzeiger*, it was signed with a pseudonym.

My father came to see us off, but it was decided that I should stay with him and my uncle Fritz who lived in Amsterdam until my mother got settled in Brazil. We left for Amsterdam after a short visit at my grandmother's home. I was quite happy in Amsterdam, especially after recovering from an operation. It was there that I got my first bicycle; we did not separate for years to come and in Amsterdam I rode it to school every day. How wonderful to be back studying, learning Dutch and making new friends! Soon the strenuous German atmosphere was forgotten and I did not miss my father too much when he was travelling, as I had grown accustomed to his long absences.

It took my mother about half a year to get a job that suited her, as secretary to the newly founded Relief Committee for Jewish Immigrants. It was her task to find shelter and work for those people who had fled with a mere 10 German marks in their pockets. They were poor, utterly scared, few had a practical profession, and they did not know the language. It was a very difficult job indeed. My mother tried her best to help them. Some were inventive and

Marthe and Alice Brill in Hamburg, 1931.
Courtesy of Alice Brill Czapski.

Alice Brill in São Paulo, 1935.
Courtesy of Alice Brill Czapski.

managed to survive, especially the women. Take Mrs. Reichmann, for example. She was the wife of a scholar and mother of a ten-year-old boy. She decided to start a boarding house, rented a nice home, and began to cook, clean up, and wash clothes for her clients. My mother was her first lodger. She was glad to have a room for the two of us and not to have to worry about meals. Now that she had an income and a home, she sent for me.

My father decided to come along. He never had cash and always paid (even his tailor) with pictures. He went to an auction for the benefit of refugees and traded two paintings for two third-class tickets to Rio de Janeiro on a French ship. We embarked on the *Alcantara* in Le Havre in the beginning of August, 1934. It was a terrible journey. I was shocked by the situation of miserable immigrants lodged at the bottom of the ship, who had almost no belongings. Food was scarce and very poor and there were bugs in our small cabin. My father would have left the ship at the first harbor we stopped in, but I was determined to stick it out. I would have endured any hardship to be with my mother again. Yet I had to wait a little bit longer.

When we arrived, my father was completely fascinated by the beautiful scenery of Rio de Janeiro with its luminous colors and people of all shades. He found a little German *pension* for us on the island of Paquetá, just outside the city and easily accessible by boat. It was a perfect paradise, with its enchanting tropical atmosphere. In spite of being homesick for my mother, I enjoyed the time we spent there. My father went to Rio often to arrange for an exhibit in October at the Pro-Arte, a cultural Institute owned by a German, but we spent many days on the island painting together. He really was my first teacher and I will always remember his advice to follow no "ism," to just be myself and to learn from nature.

São Paulo was far away at that time, it took twelve hours by train to get there. When we finally arrived, I spent some days at the Hotel Astor in the center of the city with my father who, as usual, paid with pictures that were exhibited in the lobby. As soon as our new home was ready to move into, I joined my mother. We lived in a nice part of town, in the middle of beautiful gardens, where I loved to bicycle—the bike was the only treasure I had saved. I remember how shocked I was when boys whistled at me, because I was wearing sleeveless blouses in the intense heat. Things have changed radically since then.

Life with the Reichmanns was quite pleasant. I went to a Brazilian school with Herbert, who was two years my junior. We were in class with much younger children because of the Portuguese language. It was the "admission" class of the *Gymnasium* (approximately the fifth grade), and I picked up Portuguese quickly, along with Brazilian history and geography. At the beginning of 1935 we had to leave our new home because Dr. Reichmann found a job. At the same time my mother lost her position, because the foundation had no more funds. For quite some time we lived in sordid, cheap downtown *pensions*, quite a disagreeable experience. Mother looked for some type of employment, and tried everything from selling advertisements to teaching children privately. My father was not concerned with us, he was tired of São Paulo and bought an old car to drive around and see more of the country. He somehow survived but was annoyed by the lack of a cultural ambience and the impossibility of selling his modern paintings in a country where academic painting was dominant.

By this time, I was offered an *au-pair* position in the family of a school dean. He wanted someone to speak German with his children, who were my age. We had no choice and I accepted, glad to be able to support myself. I went to live in a typical old Brazilian kind of house, located near the school. It was furnished with the most necessary items, but to me it seemed bare and unattractive: the few little pictures were hung so high that one could barely see them. We took all meals at the school's mess hall and I had to get used to a monotonous diet of black beans, rice, or occasionally beef steaks and salad.

The family was friendly and tried to make me feel comfortable, but a girl was not allowed to go out by herself. I could ride my bicycle in the small inside yard only; I felt confined and unhappy. I tried to speak only German, but Mercedes and Nirmen, seventeen and thirteen, did not understand a single word. Dr. Freire did not allow me to teach his children, because he thought modern methods meant just speaking with no explanations. So I improved my Portuguese, but it did not work the other way around.

During the vacation we went to their farm so I could get acquainted with Brazilian farm life. I remember one little incident: I had never seen a mango fruit and was encouraged to try. I liked it and picked some more from the tree and ate quite a few, then I had a drink of milk. Dr. Freire came along and warned me never to eat mangos and drink milk afterwards. "What happens?" I asked, a lit-

156

tle scared. "Death, for sure!" he replied. Too bashful to admit I had already done it, I retired to an empty room with a crime story (which I hated to read under normal circumstances), and waited anxiously. Nothing happened, apparently the warning had a historical background: the masters of slaves invented such stories to discourage them from eating the fruit.

I finished the first year of the "admission" class while staying with the Freire family. After a while we parted as good friends, even though I had not succeeded in teaching them any German, and I joined my mother in a nice room she was renting. In the meantime, my Uncle Billy had visited us and urged my mother to send me to the São Paulo Graded School to learn English, so that I might study in the U.S. later on. He promised to help with the expenses. It was a great change for me, because I could dedicate all my time to studying and I worked hard to pick up the English language and all school subjects I had missed.

I was admitted to the sixth grade at the age of fifteen, and would be allowed to take examinations at the end of the year in order to jump to the tenth grade, the grade I should have been in according to my age. I loved to study and even succeeded in catching up in mathematics, which I had to learn by myself, because mother was a poor mathematician and we could not afford a teacher. She taught me history and Latin, however.

By the time I was admitted to the tenth grade, we moved to a one-room flat within walking distance from my school. We had no kitchen and cooked our simple meals on an electric heater in the bathroom. But we were quite happy; pigeons came to visit us and we fed them crumbs, I even had a little canary. Our small porch offered a nice view and we sat in the sun and watched the street market below.

At this time my father was back in São Paulo. He had made friends with other modern artists, Brazilians and Europeans, but he could not get used to a new country without the cultural tradition he was accustomed to, which was essential to his life. He even met some sophisticated art lovers and collectors who bought some paintings, but he dreamt restlessly of going home. My father was not politically aware like my mother and did not understand the necessity of patiently building up a new life in a strange and utterly different environment.

Finally he announced his departure, booked for January, 1936. Nothing could change his mind. Mother tried to convince him that things had become dangerous in Germany and that he should only go to Holland and maybe France, but not to Hamburg. She told him that returning refugees had recently been incarcerated and that he must avoid Germany. But he did not believe her. "The Germans are incapable of such behavior. It can't be true, they are a civilized people," he insisted. Nothing would stop him, and when she stated facts that could not be ignored he stated simply: "I trust my fate." He never stopped to think of me. I felt revolted, I was fifteen at the time.

I had been a tenth-grade student for some months when I was offered a job in an international book and art store belonging to a German refugee who had formerly been a lawyer. It was a small place not far from our flat and was almost hidden in a narrow passage linking two main streets. They sold foreign language books, art reproductions, and old maps. I was tempted to accept because I liked the idea, and went to talk it over with the principal of my school, Miss Moore, who had become a good friend of my mother's and later translated her autobiographical novel *Der Schmelztiegel* (The Melting Pot).

She advised me to do it: "You'll learn more than in school," she said "and you can take your final examinations with us whenever you are ready." I took the job, glad to work and help out with our expenses. It was fun: I attended customers, wrote letters, catalogued books, delivered purchases at home—something a young girl was not supposed to do—and read endlessly, often taking books home overnight. This job gave me the opportunity to meet all kinds of people, especially artists because they loved to look at art books. At the time there was not a single museum of modern art. (The first one was founded after 1947.)

I made friends with an architect/painter, whom my father knew. I asked Rossi if he would teach me painting, and after having seen some of my work he agreed. Now my days were quite full: I went to Rossi's studio early in the morning because I had to leave before 10:00 A.M. to go to work. He had studied in Italy. His apartment was on the fifth floor at the top of a building with a huge terrace full of plants. There he had built a kind of miniature tower for a studio. His wife was a musician and had a beautiful voice; although they had no children, they adored their cat. Rossi taught me in the academic fashion he himself had learned, but liked modern art and let me have my own way. He was very cultured and I learned much from him. He introduced me to other artists who worked as artisans

158

for a living; most of them were children of poor Italian immigrants, who still kept to the old ways eating their traditional cuisine and speaking in their original dialects. Mostly self-taught, they were serious and enthusiastic artists in their free hours, meeting for live sketching in the evening and for outdoor painting on weekends. Soon I joined them two or three evenings a week and on Sundays for the day.

After my father had left us we heard some good news from him: he had exhibited his Brazilian paintings in Amsterdam, and then traveled to several countries in Europe before returning to Hamburg, where his mother was still living. She had also warned him to leave, in vain. At first he was not bothered, he enjoyed months of freedom, travelling in Germany and painting wherever he went. But he defied his fate and could not escape it. I think that it must have finally dawned on him, for his last self-portrait, painted on New Year's Eve 1936 has a haunted feeling about it, reminding me of the picture of Dorian Gray. Soon afterwards he was imprisoned with the charge of *Rassenschande*, or race defilement. During the trial he said that he had ignored this new law, and was denounced for having an "Aryan" girlfriend. After a year in prison he was officially convicted to five years of forced labor.

I tried to renew his expired Brazilian entrance permit to keep a door open in case he could escape Germany at a later date, but under the profascist government of Getúlio Vargas no more Jews were allowed to enter the country. Until the war started, I kept up correspondence with my father, which was limited by prison regulations. To cheer him up I sent him some of my sketches. He replied that he could not comment on them, as they looked too much like his own early work.

Those were bitter years. We kept listening to the news over the radio in our spare time, frightened with the rising power of the fascist alliance and the threat of war as the only "hope" of delivering the world from such a menace. And then there was our own uncertain future and the struggle to survive, besides the tragedy of my father's hopeless situation.

After almost three years I decided to leave the bookstore. Under the strain of the political situation, my boss had become extremely neurotic and made me feel even more depressed. I also wanted to earn more money. I learned shorthand and typing and found a well-paid job as a bilingual secretary in an English firm. The former secretary was leaving in order to enter medical school.

She was a German refugee like myself, and introduced me to my work: we parted as friends for a lifetime. But I was employed there only for a short time, because the war was approaching and when it started I was dismissed as a German citizen! Even Brazil treated us like enemies, we were not allowed to visit the beach and other "strategic" places. Similarly, I was now an enemy for the English, although the Germans had cancelled our citizenship long ago. I felt betrayed and homeless.

Fortunately I soon found a job with the Dutch hormone laboratory Organon, which imported the products produced in Holland. When the containers arrived in Brazil I would get together with my bosses, an Austrian and a German immigrant, and we would work evenings to fill and label the bottles. My task was to organize and maintain a filing system of physicians who should be contacted. I was also responsible for the correspondence and translations of the treatment our specialist supplied upon request. Because hormone therapy was not well known at that time, many doctors asked for instructions on how to use it. I translated this and followed the cases and their development with interest.

All the time we were under pressure because of the political situation within our country and the war outside. We had to remain strong and hope for the best. We knew that our future depended on the outcome of the war, but there was nothing we could do about it. Life went on. I kept on painting in my spare time. On the streets it was forbidden to talk German or Italian, and all schools were obliged to teach only in Portuguese.

I loved my work, but like other import businesses Organon faced difficulties. I had to earn more than they could offer. I looked for another job and applied to Polobraz, a small trade company belonging to a Yugoslavian and a Polish immigrant. I was hired as a secretary to Mr. Czapski and his young son, who assisted him. I could not then foresee that we would get married years later. I did not like this job very much, as it required only routine correspondence concerning the trade of chemicals and countless other articles. My boss and future father-in-law was not a businessman by profession, in Poland he had run a huge farm specializing in thoroughbred cattle. I worked with him for almost three years, but the company was not doing so well. My friendship with Juljan tightened, and whenever possible we spent weekends outside the city and vacationed within Brazil. As a Polish citizen, Juljan did not suffer any kind of restrictions and we could go wherever we pleased.

But we lived under constant stress because the war was always on our mind, and we were always expecting the latest news. Business was difficult in those uncertain times and I lost my job when Polobraz had to close. The Czapski family had to find another way to make a living. Mr. Czapski returned to country life, running other people's farms. By this time I was tired of being a secretary, and I wanted to live from art or something close to it. I had a very close girlfriend who was in the same situation. We decided to take a part-time job in the same company for a regular income and dedicate all remaining free time to art work. We tried ceramics, painting tiles, and finally textile painting. It was great fun, but we never earned more than enough to pay our bills.

Fortunately the Nazis were defeated and the war came to a close. It is impossible to describe the emotional relief we experienced. My relatives began to search for my father; we had heard nothing from him throughout the entire war. My grandmother had left Hamburg just in time and found refuge in the home of her son Fritz in Amsterdam. But Fritz had been "repatriated" and killed during the Nazi invasion of Holland. His wife was an "Aryan" and very courageous, and she succeeded in hiding my grandmother until the end of the war. But Sophie Brill never recovered from the shock of losing her two sons. She joined her daughter Irma in New York, where I later visited, and she sent me all my father's paintings that had been saved. I saw her last on my way to Albuquerque, New Mexico, where I studied on a scholarship at the University of New Mexico in 1946 and 1947.

My aunt Irma was finally able to trace my father's fate. She received an answer to a request published in the German newspaper *Aufbau*, confirming that after his release from prison he was forced to join a transport to Riga, where he was interned in a concentration camp and executed among thousands on March 26, 1942. My grandmother was the one who had last heard from him. During the few days of freedom, she had received news from him! He had not given up hope. When he had to leave he asked permission to buy some painting materials to take along. It was granted and he departed quite confident . . .

Postscript

My studies in the United States during the years 1946–47 remained incomplete, because I was limited to two years of permanent residence in the U.S., owing to circumstances.[1] I still had no citizenship, because naturalization was not possible in Brazil during and soon after the war, and before the war I was too young. When I received the scholarship from the University of New Mexico, I traveled with a special one-page permit, testifying that I was entitled to permanent residence in Brazil. But this was only valid for two years. With a regular passport I could have gone to nearby Mexico to renew my permit at the Brazilian Consulate, and if I had had the money, I could have gone home during the vacation to revalidate my permit there. My unusual situation must have been responsible for my deportation to Ellis Island upon arrival in New York, which was never explained. I was released the same evening with the warning: "If you stay one day too long in this country you shall be arrested and deported."

I completed my studies much later, when my children were half grown, taking up philosophy and aesthetics at São Paulo University. I am conscious that not only the talent I inherited from my parents but also the fact that their life work was interrupted in early years urged me to carry on what they had begun. I tried to follow my mother's example of uncompromising integrity and uncommon farsightedness. It saved my life.

ANNELISE STRAUSS

Annelise Strauss (née Herzberg) was born in 1920 in Braunschweig, Germany, and grew up in a middle-class Jewish family. The war put an end to her happy childhood. Her memoir, "A Story of My Life," was written as a mature woman looking back on her life.[1] She stresses the importance of family and friends, and discloses her youthful awareness of being part of a rich Jewish tradition. Ties to this culture played a key role in her life, both before and after the Nazis came to power. With the help of the Hebrew Immigrant Aid Society (HIAS), Annelise immigrated to the United States.

HIAS was created in 1909 in New York when the Hebrew Immigrant Aid Society (1902) and the Hebrew Sheltering House Association (1884) merged. HIAS soon became a large national organization responding to the growing needs of Jewish immigrants from Eastern Europe. HIAS helped nearly a half million new arrivals to the United States with legal entry, employment, and subsistence. In 1927, the New York-based HIAS joined with the Paris-based Jewish Colonization Association (ICA), and the Berlin-based Emigdirect to form HICEM (an acronym of HIAS, ICA, and Emigdirect).[2]

Most of HICEM's work during the 1930s was devoted to funding emigration from Nazi Germany. The organization helped refugees from eastern and central Europe escape to other countries. After the Nazis invaded France, HICEM closed its European headquarters in Paris, and on June 26, 1940, reopened in Lisbon, Portugal. The neutral port of Lisbon was crucial for refugees traveling to

163

North and South America. HIAS continued to assist émigrés during World War II. In 1945, it dissolved its partnership with HICEM and later worked with the American Jewish Joint Distribution Committee.[3]

On a visit to Washington D.C., Annelise Herzberg met the Brazilian ambassador to the United States, Oswaldo Aranha. Although he publicly supported the Jewish community and was an advocate of the creation of the State of Israel, he wrote in a private letter that the Jews were driving the American government toward communism.[4] After living in Washington, his anti-Semitic views took on philo-Semitic overtones: he saw the Jews as a wealthy and industrious people who possessed the needed skills that could assist Brazil with it goals for expansion.[5] Annelise Herzberg became aware of this change of mind during her meeting with Ambassador Aranha.

The policy toward Jewish immigrants during the Estado Nôvo was inconsistent because of short-term political pressures.[6] The Vargas government had to reconcile two conflicting attitudes toward immigration. Many Brazilians, especially employers in the south, wanted more immigrants for the workforce. Others saw refugees as contributors to unemployment and wanted to stop all immigration in order to ameliorate their country's economic woes.[7]

Although visas were denied to those of "Semitic origin" in 1937, Jewish illegal aliens were not expelled. In January of 1938, the government was preparing to deport over one thousand Jews with expired tourist visas, most of whom were to be sent back to Germany. However, the United States put pressure on the government to allow them to stay.[8]

By September 1938, the Brazilian government's policy toward Jews became less restrictive, due in part to the philo-Semitic attitude of the minister of foreign relations, and former ambassador to the United States, Oswaldo Aranha, who had returned to Brazil in March 1938 and became the leading advocate for strong military and economic ties with the United States.[9] In late 1938, new visa categories were created for Jews who were professionally skilled, and for those with large amounts of capital.[10] Despite the anti-Semitic ambience of the Estado Nôvo and high profile deportations such as that of Olga Benario, immigration for Jews was possible before and during World War II. The scheming and volatile policies of the Vargas regime provide examples of how Jews were being manipulated for political gain.

Annelise Herzberg was able to join her family in São Paulo in the fall of 1938. A consequence of the anti-Semitism of the Estado Nôvo was the consolidation of the Jewish community, although to varying degrees, depending on geographic location. Major relief efforts were concentrated in Rio de Janeiro and São Paulo because of the large Jewish Populations residing there. Dr. Ludwig Lorch, president of the Congregação Israelita Paulista, helped German Jews in São Paulo. Under his leadership, the community thrived and provided refugees with employment, welfare services, medical centers, as well as language and trade schools.[11]

A STORY OF MY LIFE

BY ANNELISE STRAUSS

I was born into a middle-class Jewish family. As far back as we could trace our ancestry for four generations, our family had always lived in Germany. My grandfather, a widower, lived with his sister in Magdeburg and was an orthodox Jew. I remember him, sitting in his favorite armchair and reading his morning prayers near the window with the sun streaming in. I also remember the delicious kosher meals his sister used to prepare for us on our frequent visits. My parents belonged to the Jewish Congregation in Braunschweig, and my father participated in Jewish community work and belonged to the B'nai B'rith.[1] My brother Hans and I went regularly to Sunday School, and at Passover, Rosh Hashanah, and Yom Kippur, we went to synagogue with our parents. Afterwards we celebrated at home or with friends.

During World War I my father served in the German army and won the Iron Cross for courage in combat. While trying to save a comrade from enemy fire, his shoulder was pierced by a bullet, leaving his left arm permanently paralyzed. After the war he became a grain dealer. My mother was born in Leipzig. After her father's death, she moved to live with relatives in Hamburg, where she spent most of her adolescence. She became a teacher and taught in high school until she was married.

My mother adored music and literature and often went to concerts, to the opera, and to the theater with her friends and relatives. Her cousin, Edith Marcus, was a talented painter, some of whose paintings were saved and brought to the United States and Brazil

165

and recently rediscovered in the homes of several friends and relatives.

After my parents married, they settled in Braunschweig, then an old picturesque town of 150,000 inhabitants where my brother and I were born. At the age of six, I entered the *Volksschule* (grade school), where Fräulein Haun was our class teacher for four years. She was a wonderful person for whom I feel deep gratitude. Fräulein Haun taught us not only to read and write, but also to care for and to love all living creatures. I adored animals, gardening, music, swimming and our class excursions on bicycle into the Harz mountains, the Lüneburger Heide, and the beautiful forests near Braunschweig. I continued my studies at the *Städtische Oberlyzeum* (secondary school for girls).

My happy, carefree childhood ended abruptly in 1934, when the Nazis took over Germany. Many people from our Jewish community were rounded up by the Gestapo and taken to concentration camps. Most of them never returned and those who did come back were sick and totally broken, both physically and spiritually. However, a small group including my father miraculously escaped this terrible fate: they asked the local police for protection and hid from the Nazi fury in the city prison. My mother was permitted to visit my father in jail and bring him food and clothes. Friends sheltered my brother and me on a farm far from town.

Several weeks later, my father returned home, haggard and deeply depressed. What would be our destiny? We had no relatives outside of Germany who could help us. Then one day our rabbi, Dr. Gärtner, called on my parents and came up with a fantastic proposal: they could let their daughter join a group of Jewish children being sent with a "Children's Transport" to the United States.[2] My brother, three years younger than I, was considered too young. American Jews, led by Stephen Wise and Felix Warburger, had offered to save German-Jewish children from Nazi extermination by chartering a boat and bringing them to the United States, where they would be cared for as long as was necessary. The HIAS (Hebrew Immigrant Aid Society) and other Jewish organizations were deeply involved in this formidable task, providing all the professional resources. Considering our desperate situation, my parents were in favor of the proposal, but the final decision was up to me. I accepted immediately!

Preparations began at a feverish pace. My passport was made ready, and a visa for the United States was granted without delay, after the American authorities were informed that the HIAS guaranteed our stay in America. My report card and personal data, including a description of my hobbies and interests, were prepared for the HIAS Organizing Committee. My mother, sad but determined, packed a trunk full of clothes and, of course, a German-English dictionary. At school, I had studied English for only one year, but I could express myself fairly well in French. Suddenly, time seemed too short to learn all the things I should before my departure—the facts of life and how to survive on my own. Our relatives were shocked. How could my parents send me off alone at the tender age of fourteen?

On January 27, 1935, my courageous father took me to the ship anchored in the Hamburg harbor. We had decided on a brief farewell without tears, but all around us, parents were hugging their children tearfully and saying a last desperate farewell. Miss Karger, our guide, received us and prepared us for our overseas journey. The winter weather was stormy, and high waves flooded the deck. Although many of us were seasick and miserable, we soon made friends. After twelve days, excitement seized us when we sighted the Statue of Liberty in New York harbor, a famous welcoming symbol to a safe haven in the Promised Land for wary and persecuted travellers. We were overcome with emotion when we saw a huge crowd of people shouting, waving, and welcoming us at the pier. Reporters took our pictures.

Most children in our group were boarded temporarily in a shelter home in New York City until they were placed with an American family. I was very lucky: friends of my family invited me to stay with them temporarily. The Rosenhains had lived in Braunschweig, where Dr. Bruno Rosenhain was our family physician. Because Mrs. Rosenhain was an American citizen, their emigration to the United States was relatively easy. They had settled in Forest Hills, New York, where Dr. Rosenhain soon built up a thriving private practice. He was assisted by his wife, a warm-hearted person with a great gift for helping people with all sorts of difficulties.

The Rosenhains had three small children. Their home in Forest Hills was always full of recent arrivals—immigrants in need of help and advice. This family immediately made me feel welcome, although I must have been quite a burden in their crowded home. Adele, the oldest daughter, shared her bed with me because there was no space for another one in the apartment. I was sent to a public school in Queens where I got my first impressions of my new

American surroundings. It was a novel experience to be in a huge school with over 8,000 students and "one way" corridors. An understanding student counselor eased my initial anxiety by providing me with a pass that authorized me to go directly to her office in case I needed help.

Shortly after my arrival, I was called to HIAS headquarters for a lengthy interview with Mrs. Cecilia Rozowsky, the social worker who would be in charge of my case in the coming years. My first placement turned out to be a poor one. I just couldn't adjust! The committee then found me a temporary home with two elderly Dutch ladies, a translator and a seamstress, who also lived in Forest Hills. This allowed me to continue in the same school. Though both ladies worked very hard for a living, they received me with loving care, and I grew very fond of them, their pretty little daughter Gladys and their funny dog, Fluffy.

After several months, the social worker with whom I had been in touch regularly called to prepare me for another move. A home seemed now in sight, either for the coming summer vacation or, perhaps, for longer. I was invited to dinner at the home of Mr. and Mrs. Milton S. Erlanger at 117 East 64th Street in New York City. Mrs. Erlanger had contacted HIAS after reading a newspaper article about our group of 150 children, refugees from Nazi Germany who had recently arrived and needed to be placed in American homes. She asked if any children were still available. After careful consideration of the possible candidates, I was finally chosen. With special recommendations from my social worker, I was to present myself punctually and properly dressed at the Erlanger's residence.

I shall never forget the first evening in their lovely home and the rather formal dinner with the conversation going back and forth about books, concerts, dog shows, and the horse business. My English was still not sufficiently fluent to participate actively in the conversation. However, by this time I understood most of what was being said. Immediately I felt that this was truly a special family!

After dinner, the two daughters, Sally and Patsy, who were both a little younger than I, gave an impressive piano performance for the entire family. They later showed me their seventy-year-old gray African parrot, their Persian and Siamese cats, and their well-trained poodles. Finally we stopped in their bathroom, where they introduced me to their pet alligator, swimming leisurely in the bathtub! Would I pick him up? Of course! After being shown how to handle him, I stood there with an alligator in my hands. Won-

Annelise Herzberg, Braunschweig, 1934.
Courtesy of Annelise Strauss.

Annelise Strauss and family, São Paulo, 1955.
Courtesy of Annelise Strauss.

dering what to do next, I looked up and caught Patsy and Sally nodding to each other and smiling at me—I had just passed the test that decided whether I would fit in.

I stayed four wonderful years with the Erlangers, learned to adapt to another world, a dream world full of fascinating people whom I learned to love and admire. They taught me their way of life and how to handle and care for dogs, rabbits, mice, birds, and horses. I was frequently invited to concerts, to the opera, to the theater, and to such interesting events as horse and dog shows. Most importantly, I won a scholarship to the Dalton School, one of the most progressive, experimental senior high schools of New York, where in 1938 I graduated magna cum laude and valedictorian of my class.

The day of graduation was an unforgettably sad day for me. It was the last day I spent in this beloved school where I had acquired so much knowledge and skill and where I had found so many new friends among teachers and students. I remember repeating to myself the words of T. S. Eliot: "This is the way the world ends, Not with a bang but a whimper." What next?

In 1937, with the help of the Erlanger family, my parents and brother had received a visa to Brazil and had emigrated and settled in São Paulo. My parents had rented a small new house in Pacaembú, a new suburb at the outer limits of São Paulo. To make ends meet, they took in two boarders whom they provided with meals and laundry. My brother was enrolled in a professional school for boys, the *Instituto Profissional Masculino*, maintained by the Brazilian government. My father, after a difficult time adjusting professionally, finally found a job in the office of Moinho Santista, an international grain trading company, and worked there until he retired. My mother had taken up teaching languages again. She enjoyed her new activities and soon had an increasing circle of students and friends.

During my last year at Dalton School, the Erlangers offered me their generous help to complete my education after graduating from high school. I only had to decide whether I would want to stay in the United States and go to college or join my family in Brazil. I was torn between the two options. Finally, our resolute and practical high school principal, Miss Keefe, gave me a tip: "Make a list of all the advantages (+) and disadvantages (–) for Brazil and the United States; then count and see which option has the most (+)." In one night I had made my decision. I would go to Brazil.

Why? By this time my parents were already quite confident about Brazil, their new home, and its hospitable people. Also, I had made my own inquiries. During a school excursion to Washington, D.C., my school counselor had made an appointment for me at the Brazilian Embassy, where I was personally received by the Brazilian Ambassador, Dr. Oswaldo Aranha. He provided me with an impressive amount of information about Brazil and told me what to expect as a new immigrant. I felt greatly encouraged when he said how welcome immigrants were, in general, especially those of different educational and cultural backgrounds who had knowledge of several foreign languages. He said that I would probably have little difficulty, and that I would just have to learn Portuguese. Among a list of outstanding institutions, Dr. Aranha mentioned the fine Medical School of the University of São Paulo, which had been founded with the help of the Rockefeller Foundation and was considered the best in Latin America.

In the fall of 1938, leaving behind my fairy-tale family in New York accompanied by Spunky, my poodle, a farewell gift from Mrs. Erlanger, I set out to join my beloved parents and brother in Brazil.

Like hundreds of other new arrivals from Europe who fled Nazi persecution, we faced an exciting new phase of life in São Paulo. Many people helped us—Brazilians and older immigrants, of mostly Russian origin who had settled in Brazil in the first decades of the twentieth century. Also, we were received warmly at the Congregação Israelita Paulista, founded by the recent immigrants from Germany under the spiritual guidance of Dr. Fritz Pinkuss, a young and resourceful rabbi who had studied for the rabbinate at the Universities of Heidelberg and Berlin. By coincidence, Dr. Pinkuss had spent his youth in Magdeburg and still remembered my grandfather teaching him the first letters of the Hebrew alphabet in synagogue.

A group of qualified professionals, social workers, psychologists, and other volunteers at the Congregação Israelita Paulista worked with unlimited dedication to help us find our way in the new country. Among these wonderful professionals was Mrs. Rozowsky, the social worker who had assisted me in the U.S. and who continued her mission in Brazil, aiding new immigrants. Again, she was a guiding angel, helping us adapt to a new country, as she would help so many more refugees all over the world for many years to come.

I immediately started taking Portuguese lessons and soon found work teaching English and German to Brazilian children. Shortly after, I found a regular job as an executive secretary at Machine Cottons, a Scotch firm, thus putting to good use the training I had received at business school in New York.

Gradually I became aware of the numerous possibilities for young people in Brazil. This brought me to my final decision—I wanted, more than anything, to go into medicine. It seemed to offer opportunities not only in clinical work, but also in research and public health. I hoped that in this profession I would finally be on my way to becoming a useful member of society. Initially, however, I was discouraged by the director of the Medical School whom I had consulted. My Portuguese was not sufficiently fluent for taking the entrance examinations—there were only sixty vacancies for several hundred candidates. He thought that I didn't have a chance to pass and qualify for admittance.

During the following months, with the help of the best instructors I could find, among them Professors Napoleão Mendes de Almeida, and Paulo Décourt, I prepared for the revalidation of my American high school diploma. I passed the exams in Portuguese, Brazilian history and geography, and, later, the entrance examination to the Medical School of the University of São Paulo. In 1942, I finally entered the best Latin American medical school, the one that Ambassador Oswaldo Aranha had mentioned so proudly five years earlier.

Six years later, I graduated from medical school and qualified as a specialist in Pediatrics and Allergy. In 1955, I joined the staff of the Department of Allergy at the Hospital das Clinicas, the newly inaugurated hospital of the University of São Paulo, where I became Medical Assistant and also did teaching and research.

In 1958, I received a grant from the *Deutscher Akademischer Austauschdienst* (German Academic Exchange Service) and spent one year in the Children's Hospital of the University of Freiburg im Breisgau under the supervision of Professor Walter Keller. I also worked in the laboratory of H. Schubothe, Professor of Immunohematology. Later, I was a participant in many Brazilian and international seminars and visited research centers in Great Britain, Switzerland, and Germany. I also became acquainted with the Department of Immunology and Allergy run by Professor Ernest Witebsky and Dr. Carl Arbesman at the New York University at Buffalo. All these opportunities helped me greatly in my career.

In 1964 I defended my doctoral dissertation: "Allergy to Castor Beans: Cause of an Epidemic of Asthma due to Industrial Air Pollution by a Castor Bean Processing Plant." I published about 40 articles in Brazilian and foreign medical journals on childhood allergies, milk and food allergies, respiratory allergies, pulmonary function tests and the rehabilitation of asthmatics. For many years I served in the directorate of the *Sociedade Brasileira de Alergia e Imunopatologia* (Brazilian Society of Allergy and Immunology) where I collaborated in the organization of Brazilian and Latin American congresses. All of these activities fascinated me and kept me busy until my retirement in 1990.

Actually, I am still professionally involved as pediatrician in charge of the Lar das Crianças, a home for needy children maintained by the Congregação Israelita Paulista. I have been doing this gratifying volunteer work since 1952 and hope to continue it in the future.

At this point I am happy and thankful for the good fortune that miraculously saved me and my family from the Holocaust and enabled me, with the help and efforts of so many generous people, to start a new life in Brazil. I learned to love this country, where I now feel deeply rooted.

In 1943, I married Alfredo Strauss, also a German-Jewish immigrant. We have three sons, all married, and six grandchildren. Brazil has been a hospitable country for all of us, permitting us to grow and live a fulfilling existence.

KÄTE KAPHAN

When Käte and Heinrich Kaphan decided to flee Germany in the 1930s, they were still able to sell their property in Pomerania at a fair price. They immigrated to Brazil in 1936 with their three children, and eventually became coffee farmers near the town of Rolândia. "Immigration into the Brazilian Jungle" describes the tough, early period they endured in a primitive third-world environment. The Kaphans were brave enough to venture growing coffee, a crop which could be destroyed by frost. After eight laborious years, their efforts proved successful.

Their acquisition of farmland in Brazil was facilitated by Dr. Max Hermann Maier, who later became their partner and neighbor. Dr. Maier, a lawyer from Frankfurt, stayed in Germany long after it had become dangerous to do so, in order to give legal advice to Jews seeking emigration. He and his wife Mathilde fled the Nazis in 1938 and immigrated to Brazil, where they joined the Kaphans on their farm. While Max did the bookkeeping, Heinrich managed the land.[1]

Käte Kaphan still resides on a *fazenda* outside Rolândia in the state of Paraná. Her three children, Annemarie, Klaus, and Marianne, are married and also live in Brazil. Heinrich Kaphan died there in 1988.

IMMIGRATION INTO THE
BRAZILIAN JUNGLE

BY KÄTE KAPHAN

We gave our thanks to God that we had reached safe harbor with our three children when we landed in the Brazilian port of

174

Santos as emigrants from Nazi Germany in 1936. Whatever our fate brought, we wanted to forget the past, for now everything was up to us. We were blessed with determination and enough of a good sense of humor to meet the challenge.

After a short stay in São Paulo, we took a train to Paraná, a state located in southern Brazil. While still in Germany we had acquired land from a large English landownership; the actual site was selected after some weeks of searching and soil testing. But let me relate in chronological order.

From São Paulo we took the night train in a southwesterly direction toward the border between the states of São Paulo and Paraná, then traveled another ten hours on another track through the jungle. In the smaller towns, the train stopped for just as long as it pleased the conductor. We got off, drank a *cafezinho* (small cup of coffee) and bought a few oranges. Water and wood were loaded, then the train whistled and was on its way again quite unexpectedly. But it moved forward so slowly that we could catch up with it easily—going uphill, you could even get off and back on again without any difficulty. We arrived at our destination in the evening, dead tired and completely covered in dust.

Rolândia was the last stop on the line. The train was pitch black, the station dark, and someone took us to the "hotel" opposite the station, which—thank God—was also dark so that no one could see our dirty faces. We rented a small wooden house in the town square; in addition to ours there were perhaps twenty or thirty similar houses along the main street running parallel to the train tracks, but these were hidden in the jungle.

The entire family moved in right away. After we tilted our packing crates from a horizontal to a vertical position and called them "closets," we bought beds, borrowed a table, and transformed empty kerosene cans into benches by connecting them with wooden planks. Our furnishings, if not exactly comfortable, proved quite adequate.

The kerosene lamps were bright enough to illuminate more than one room through the gaps in the "wall." This light was all the more effective, because the wooden boards that separated the rooms only reached a certain height, which had an added advantage: we could hear the breathing of the children at night and the intercommunication from one room to the other was via the walls. "Mother I need a pair of socks," and over the wall they went with the greatest of ease . . .

Whenever it rained, it was very cozy. Pouring outside, the road was nothing but saturated red soft clay and your place was inside. The shutters were kept closed because of the nonexistent window panes—no house in the entire neighborhood had any. The kerosene lamp burned peacefully on the table. The rain did seep into the kitchen, which was situated somewhat lower, whenever we opened the door to get water that we drew from a well in the vicinity. We had to walk through the rain to reach the washroom and toilet.

At night, when it was dark, wet, and stormy, this would make the children break into tears. Oblivious to everything, they would ask: "Why couldn't we have stayed in Germany?" The children and I remained in our little house in the town square of Rolândia together with our good friend, Lore, whom we had brought with us from Germany as their teacher, while my husband selected the plot of land and started to cut down the jungle. After the earth had been cleared near a good spring, he immediately started building the house where we live today.

For seven months he resided in a tent in the woods in order to supervise the building and clearing of the land. Heinrich wanted to learn the language as soon as possible and get to know the Brazilians.

Seven months of adventure passed until the house was finished—a house lacking a great many things. We were not accustomed to the hard labor or to the foreign climate, but were full of satisfaction and looking forward to a modest but assured livelihood.

Finally, our home was completed. We moved out of our hut in the town square and into the house with the children. We thought the worst was now over. . . . But a few days later, my husband became very sick. We had to take him on the most impassable dirt road to the nearest hospital in Londrina, about nineteen miles from the farm. He had contracted a serious infection as a result of an insect bite in the foot. Heinrich had a high fever, and we carried him on a stretcher along a rugged path, stumbling over roots and tree stumps until we finally reached the street where a car was waiting.

During that terrible rainy night, it took seven hours for the driver to get into town. At the time the hospital consisted only of small barracks, but today it is a modern *Santa Casa* with several hundred beds. Even now I can still hear the incessant ay-yai-yai of the sick who were lying in the adjacent rooms. Luckily, the operation was successful.

Kaphan Kaphan

Today we can drive to Londrina, a modern, fast-growing city, on an asphalt road in less than an hour. Twenty years ago, it was just a small ugly locale with muddy roads in the rainy season, and countless dusty roads during the dry season.

When we first arrived in Brazil, we decided not to plant coffee. Who would want to run the risk of waiting five years for the first harvest, constantly fearing its ruin in a night frost? Nevertheless, just as the other settlers who gradually acclimatized themselves, we decided to take the chance. Trying just a little at first, then slowly gathering courage, we planted more and more each year. What we feared really did happen: everything was destroyed in one single night or better still, in one single hour on a gray frosty morning of –4 degrees centigrade. This threw us back two years. It happened after six years in Brazil, and so it took us eight years until our first harvest. What did we live on in the meantime? We planted cotton, rice, beans, and above all kept pigs because the soil was rich enough for corn and mandioca. We had bought two cows as soon as we arrived and during our first year we had cultivated a small pasture—an oasis in the wilderness.

Then slowly, the clearing of the forest began. In this process the woods are chopped down by experienced workers with axes, the tree stumps are left to rot, and the little lumber that is obtained is pulled away. After a few months of drying, the burning of the forest begins. This is indeed a tremendous spectacle.

As soon as the burning of the wood is over, the seed sowing begins, because the burning makes the virgin soil exceedingly fertile. With the help of small hand machines, corn and bean seeds are sown, and after a few months the harvest begins.

Coffee is also planted in virgin soil; the burnt wood is left to rot and thus serves as natural fertilizer. Because coffee is planted in spaces of twelve by twelve feet, the tree can grow there for about sixteen years, a process that continuously gives the plant new natural nutrition.

Although through the years almost 300 million coffee trees were planted in Paraná (as of 1956), each individual tree is still worked by hand. The plant needs constant attention and will only bear fruit if it receives careful handling.

All the workmen who found their home in the colonies are of varied ethnic origin. The native Indian long ago intermarried with Europeans, especially Spaniards, Portuguese, and Italians, or with the Africans who were brought into the country as slaves. The

177

Emancipation Proclamation of 1867 brought real freedom and even now our gardener relates, with horror and violent head shaking, how the slaveholders inflicted scars on his grandfather. Today there is no racial discrimination—man is judged by his moral standing and his achievements.

During our first years in Brazil, the worker was paid in the following manner: he signed a contract, then received a house, land, and payment for work that was two-thirds of the production of corn, rice, and beans. He signed a four- or five-year agreement for planting coffee, and would then clear the land, plant the coffee trees, and care for them for the duration of the contract. In return, the laborer received a small payment in cash, plus all the corn, rice, and beans that he planted between the rows of coffee trees; he also received the first and sometimes part of the second coffee harvest. After the contract expired, the worker gave back the well-nursed coffee trees. Usually he was already the owner of a small piece of land, and then planted more coffee—in this way he gradually acquired more land and money. Today quite a number of our former workers are themselves rich landowners.

RENÉE-MARIE CROOSE PARRY

After securing a Brazilian visa, Renée-Marie Hausenstein sailed for South America in March 1942. She became a foreign language tutor and earned enough money to provide for her livelihood and to save for the future. A vivid example of her political marginality in this South American country was her incarceration.

The author arrived in Brazil in 1942 during the dictatorship of Getúlio Vargas, the founder of the Estado Nôvo. Although she never discovered why she was arrested, one could say that the political situation in Brazil fostered injustice. Not only was she victimized by the regime because she was of German-Jewish origin, but also because she was a woman. What she had experienced in Nazi Germany seemed to haunt her again in Brazil.

Getúlio Vargas's success in seizing and maintaining power ultimately shaped the political and economic climate of Brazil in the 1930s and 1940s, a period when many Jews sought refuge there. However, the Estado Nôvo frequently attempted to exclude Jewish refugees, and Vargas often exploited immigration policies to meet his economic and military needs.

Anti-Semitism was widespread in the Estado Nôvo, particularly regarding refugee policy. "Not only were Jews of all nationalities barred access to Brazilian visas—an order disclosed apologetically afterward by Vargas's postwar Foreign Minister, João Neves da Fontoura—but refugees residing in Brazil continued to be harassed."[1] And in Rio de Janeiro, the police captain Dulcino Gonçalves followed a strongly anti-Semitic policy that angered both

Jews and moderates.[2] Such an atmosphere did not augur well for German-Jewish refugees such as Renée-Marie Hausenstein.

Croose Parry describes how Vargas profited politically from World War II. He and his collaborators, in their pursuit of power, were eager to build up the Brazilian military. Nazi Germany had been a ready source of weapons and a willing trade partner until 1937. After the coup in November of that year, pro-U.S. factions were stronger in the Brazilian armed forces and amongst the elite. Relations with Nazi Germany began to cool, even though high-ranking officials such as police chief Felinto Müller went to Berlin for talks with Heinrich Himmler, the head of the SS.

Although Brazil's economy improved, the Estado Nôvo had its sinister side. Security forces were given free reign, torture was routine, and censorship pervaded the media.[3] "Resident aliens (including German-Jewish refugees from Nazism) were harassed by the police after Brazil's entry into the war."[4] Vargas's *brasilidade* campaign, a patriotic movement extolling the virtues of Brazilian culture, encouraged unity within the country but restricted cultural expression by prohibiting foreign language clubs, schools, and newspapers.[5]

On August 22, 1942, Brazil declared war against Germany and Italy. The U.S. military and the State Department had at last succeeded in getting Brazil to join the Allies. Germany had failed to provide the expected armaments. This development, coupled with many other factors, induced Brazil to change sides. In his negotiations with the United States, Vargas promised to allow the use of Brazil's naval facilities and the establishment of several U.S. air and naval bases along the northeastern Atlantic coast, in return for the purchase of raw materials such as natural rubber and quartz.[6]

Croose Parry gives us a unique personal view of Brazil in the early 1940s. Being part of the Axis before entering the war on the side of the Allies, Brazil had become a refuge for both Nazi sympathizers and Jews. Through the filter of age and wisdom, she uses both metaphor and irony to recapture the ways in which she coped with racism and sexism under the Vargas dictatorship.

Gender and racial discrimination had created a fragile self-consciousness at a very young age. Having suffered social rejection and political eclipse, Croose Parry has never forgotten those experiences, which have imbued her entire life with heightened sociopolitical awareness.

After leaving Brazil for the United States in 1946, Renée-Marie Hausenstein became a naturalized citizen in 1952. She worked in New York for War Relief Services, and subsequently in Washington D.C. as the Special Assistant to the Director of the Office for Refugees, Migration and Voluntary Assistance. She then lived twenty-three years in London, where she and her husband Kenneth Croose Parry founded the Teilhard Centre, the ad hoc committee of People for a Non-Nuclear World, and the Parliamentary Liaison Group for Alternative Energy Strategies. They are now devoting their efforts to the Center for the Advancement of Human Cooperation, which they founded in 1984, and have been residents of Gainesville, Florida since 1985.

LIFE IN BRAZIL

BY RENÉE-MARIE CROOSE PARRY

First Encounters and Impressions

The vibrant activity in the ports of Recife and Bahía fascinated me. I had not anticipated seeing such overwhelming numbers of black, brown, and dusky people. The only human beings of color I had seen before were occasional natives of French Africa in Paris, black actors playing minor roles in American films, and the extraordinary sight in the thirties at the Munich *Oktoberfest*, where a whole village of plate-lipped Africans—their lower lips extended forward since childhood by the insertion of ever larger wooden disks—had been put *on show*. In Bahía, formerly the main port for the slave trade, we went ashore for the day. Even as a native of Bavaria, with its abundance of Baroque, I was struck by the sheer number of gilded churches. Many of their façades from colonial times reminded me, nostalgically, of Bavaria's curvilinear, luxuriant buildings of the eighteenth century, sacred and profane. Helmut claimed that there were as many churches in Bahía as there are days in the year. Little did I realize at the time the part played by the Catholic Church in the slave market, where millions of Africans were put through the ritual of baptism before being sold to the highest bidder. The tropical heat, the profuse vegetation in a myriad shades of green, the exotically scented air, the tall palm trees, their fronds reflecting the rays of the sun as they swayed in the wind, the people with their sharply differing builds, physiognomies, and complexions, the ups and downs as our taxi carried us through this city of hills—these were the rich, indelible impressions that I would take back to the ship at sundown.

The skyline of Rio de Janeiro took my breath away. But as we approached the harbor, my whole attention became focussed on the meeting I had feared for so many weeks. Helmut's parents stood by the dock with other members of his family. Of small stature and fair complexion, their undistinguished faces would not easily engrave themselves upon my memory. Their chauffeur seemed more personable, and had an empathetic, warm look in his eyes. After a round of greetings, a short man of slick, though slightly neglected, elegance was introduced to us. I thought I caught the name, Nonato Cruz. I discovered he was the family lawyer, charged to clear us as speedily as possible through customs and immigration, for which purpose he took away our passports. While I recounted to Helmut's mother the political and climatic impediments that had surrounded our departure from Germany, the joys of discovery in Lisbon, and our voyage on the high seas, Helmut took his father aside to explain that he would like to stay with me in Rio for a day or two, before coming home to São Paulo to provide a fuller explanation about his "gentleman's agreement." His father, of whose changing facial expressions I was able to catch a few discreet glimpses, grew solemn, and then quite angry, as one not used to being contradicted or disobeyed. Their conversation having come to an abrupt end, they walked toward us. Helmut's father told his wife, in a tone that preempted any further enquiry, and as if he had ordered so himself: "The children will stay in Rio for the next few days."

After a rushed goodbye, and before I knew what had happened to me, Helmut and I were sitting in a taxi, driving toward the center of the city. His father had clearly been unable to open his mind to Helmut's all too brief description of my family's plight in Germany, or to recognize his son's motivation in wishing to come to the rescue; concerns which it had been impossible to communicate through the mail without alerting the Gestapo, and jeopardizing our plans. Helmut had been given a few bank notes by his father to tide us over for two or three days. I felt deeply anxious, and sorry for Helmut, although he had anticipated that his parents would be unable to show sympathy or understanding for the decisions he had taken on my account. He chose the small but comfortable Hotel Suisso in the district of Flamengo, which lay near a sparkling bay on an avenue lined with large, shading trees, and within walking distance of shops and cinemas. We discussed the next step, and agreed it would be best for him to clear the air with his parents at the earliest moment, not least in view of the financial situation over which he had no control at the time. I urged him to travel to São Paulo immediately, while I acclimatized myself and studied the "help-wanted" columns. As we deliberated, the telephone rang to announce that the chauffeur had brought our luggage from the port. Having served the family since Helmut's childhood, he was very fond of him, and the two men were now able to engage in a heart-to-heart talk. The good chauffeur immediately offered to lend us money to cover the cost of my room and meals for several weeks. Greatly relieved, Helmut was able to leave with him to join his parents, having promised to keep in touch with me by telephone on a daily basis.

Now I was really on my own—in every sense of these words. Independence and freedom had seemed more appealing in the protective womb of the ship. I studied the city plan and the hotel's information leaflets. I could make sense of what I read! How pleased I was to have studied Portuguese so diligently on the boat: two to three hours every day, reading aloud, as well as written exercises. It was midafternoon and an enticing day. I could see from my window that buses stopped near my hotel. There would be no danger of getting lost if I could make a round trip. I told the concierge of my plan. He thought it might take two hours, or a little more, and said he would look out for me. To get out and not to brood, not to lose time, and to get a first grip on the city: it proved to be a wonderful idea! The bus ride was an ecstatic adventure. I had read that Rio de Janeiro was one of the jewel cities of the world. But it was more beautiful than anything I had imagined in my wildest dreams. The glories of Rio enveloped me, exhilarating the sensuous consciousness and love of beauty that had grown in me since early childhood: wandering in the Bavarian countryside, savoring the lingering aroma of incense and the extravagance of Baroque churches, learning to see through my father's ultrasensitive and penetrating vision, and not least through my studies of art and the history of architecture at university. It was late March, and the worst of the summer heat had passed. Suddenly, the heavens opened with a dramatic downpour. When it stopped, the asphalt, the many patches of earth and grass in between the roads, and the gardens behind the villas all began to steam under the sun. A bewildering fragrance caressed my nostrils as the windows were reopened. We traveled through a long, dark tunnel into the blinding light of Copacabana and Ipanema, where mountainous, translucent waves were breaking onto endless beaches. I wondered how I was ever going to swim in such a raging sea. . . Noting my enthusiasm and curiosity, some of the passengers wanted to know about me: where was I from? How long had I been in the country? I was proud to understand their questions and improvised my replies to their amusement and applause. It had been a thoroughly successful outing, and, after a thrifty supper at the hotel, I fell into a long and wholesome sleep.

The next morning I decided to venture out on foot in the direction of the city center. In Cinelandia I found a small drugstore where I could buy a new toothbrush. On the threshold I came face to face with a nun wearing the identical habit of the Missionary Benedictines of my convent school in Tutzing. The moment I laid eyes on her I remembered, as with a flash of lightening, something I had totally forgotten. The sister in charge of the boarding students had been assigned to Rio some years ago! Naively, I greeted the nun in German, and then in French. Alas, she spoke neither. I then articulated the name of the German nun: "Madre Theofóra— Conhece?" Did she know her? Again, her face remained blank. I repeated the name several times, when she suddenly gripped my arm and exclaimed with a big smile: "Madre Theófora!" No doubt it was the same uncommon name, though in Portuguese I should have stressed the first, and not the second "o". As was later explained to me: "Theo," the Greek word for God, and "fora," the Portuguese word for "out," would, in my pronunciation, have meant literally: "Out with God"; hardly the name for a nun! The sister wrote the address of her college on a small piece of paper, which I placed in a safe compartment of my handbag. We parted beaming over our linguistic victory!

I felt in my bones that this encounter had been nothing short of providential, that my Bavarian guardian angel must have crossed the Atlantic sitting on my shoulder, and that the solution of my immediate problems was at hand. If I were invited to stay at Collegio Santo Amaro in the *bairro* of Botafogo, I would not have to spend Helmut's money. He had done his share. I could hardly wait to get back to the hotel and the telephone. The college was on the line, but I knew from convent experience that it would take at least five minutes for Madre Theófora to walk the long polished parquet corridors from her cell. "Maria Hausenstein! Is it really you?" From the emotion underlying her voice, I could sense that she was deeply homesick and thrilled to hear me—a live messenger from home! I too could not wait to see her. I was no longer forlorn: I would receive a helping hand, and one I could trust absolutely. She asked me to visit her at 11 A.M. the following day, and gave me precise directions. The ever helpful concierge filled in the gaps. I left early the next morning, just in case I should get lost changing buses.

The college was situated in a residential part of Botafogo, with a decorative garden in front and playgrounds in the middle and to the rear of the buildings. The wrought iron gate buzzed open as soon as I had rung. When I entered the convent school I knew *I was home*. A young Brazilian sister led me to one of the small, immaculate reception rooms—it could have been in Tutzing! After an impatient half hour wait, Sister Theófora suddenly stood before me, and, with tears in her eyes, embraced me like a mother. I was moved all the more as she had been one of the most severe teachers and disciplinarians, whom most of us had respected, or even feared. Nostalgia had mellowed her and softened her features. Her first question was about my mother and father; were they alive? And then she listened to my story. I did not have to ask for help. How quickly could I pack and return in a taxi? I would have to tell Helmut when he phoned in the evening; I did not doubt his approval, or even his gratitude. I could be back by morning. With these questions out of the way, there was one more hurdle to overcome. Mother Superior would have to agree and give her blessing to the plan. Another anxious half hour passed, before sister Theófora entered the room with a relaxed smile: "Es ist alles in Ordnung, Marialein." Mother Superior was happy to come to the rescue, and welcome a former pupil from Tutzing, the Mother House of the Order.

Helmut agreed with audible relief, and promised to remain in touch. Unfortunately, his parents were continuing to cause him distress, a situation growing worse because of obvious differences in their appraisal of Hitler's Third Reich, and their apparent fears about my future intentions.

Time passed quickly with a strict regimen of prayers, study, meals, and leisure, according to the Benedictine motto, *ora et labora*. I was helped substantially with my Portuguese drills. Sister Theófora relished her chats with me in German about "the good old days" in Tutzing. After six or seven weeks, we agreed that for the first year at least it would be best for me to seek a living-in post as governess to Brazilian children, if possible with a requirement for French tuition. We drafted an advertisement: "GOVERNANTE— Jovem senhora recem-chegada da Europa, desejaria colocação em familia de alto tratamento para tomar conta de crianças. Ensinaria francês. Resposta, por favor, pelo tel. 42–4708."[1] I received several replies. The very first interview was successful: a medical doctor's family with two children, to whom I was to speak only in French, living in a villa in the outskirts of Rio near a lovely lake.

Getting Down to Work

The move was quickly accomplished. I had got my feet on the ground and felt relatively confident about my future in Rio. I was to take long walks and spend wonderful hours on the beach with the little girl, Eloisa, and her young brother, Roberto, whose names I remember because they appear under their photographs in an album from my Brazilian years. I discovered more and more of Rio and lived a very pleasing *Carióca* life,[2] continuing my studies of Portuguese every evening for two or three hours. I must have been in the country for over five months, when the children's mother, the daughter of a well-known judge, asked me whether I had registered with the Polícia d'Estrangeiros—the Police for Foreigners. I replied that a lawyer, who held my passport, would surely have seen that this was done. Being very sympathetic in her reaction to the circumstances in which I had fled Nazi Germany, she asked for the name of the lawyer with visible concern. When I replied that the man's name had sounded like "Nonato Cruz" and described his general appearance, she became quite agitated and told me to sit down and listen well. She warned that, considering the circumstances surrounding my arrival, it was quite possible that I might become the victim of foul play; that, after all these months, my passport should be in my personal possession, bearing the official stamp of residence from the Polícia d'Estrangeiros, as my only means of identification. The law, she said, required my expulsion from the country, if I did not register within six months of arrival, and she suggested that I take the matter into my own hands at once. She then instructed me how to proceed: I was to take a taxi the next day at 12:30 P.M., the fares of which she would gladly pay, and drive to the lawyer's office to arrive there after 1 P.M., when nearly everybody would be out for lunch. The taxi driver should be told to wait while I walked into the offices, where I should greet the receptionist with my kindest smile. I should then tell her that I needed urgently to look up information in my passport, and would she please let me see it for a moment. Once handed the document, I should make a dash for the door and run back to the taxi, which would then drive me to the Polícia d'Estrangeiros. Dona Xeres felt certain that I had not been registered, but suggested I thumb through my passport en route, so as not to take the long ride in vain. I thought it was a daring scheme, but what else was I to do? I admitted that I had been naive, and presumed that Helmut had failed to mention this requirement to me, because he was unfamiliar with regulations as they pertained to foreigners. We spent the evening hypothesizing about the motives that could have led Helmut's parents to ask their lawyer to keep my passport, and not to warn me of the need for timely registration.

The next morning Dona Xeres ordered the taxi herself, and gave the driver the two addresses with strict instructions. She saw me off with a warm, encouraging *abraço*, and said she would be home when I returned. I did exactly as she had said. When we reached the lawyer's office, the taxi made two rounds to find a propitious spot to wait. The secretary looked puzzled and a bit hesitant at first, but the decisiveness of my voice, or perhaps my smile, disarmed her. She may have thought that foreigners are given to making unusual requests. I did not see her expression as I ran off, but do remember her calling out several times: "Senhora, Senhora!" as she pursued me down the stairs. But I made it into the cab, and we sped off as she appeared at the door of the building. As Dona Xeres had suspected, there was no stamp of residence in the passport. When the official looked at the date of my arrival, he merely remarked that I had left it very late, while waving to a little boy in a white cotton uniform to offer me a *cafezinho* from his tray.

That evening we played music and celebrated my new legality. When the children had gone to bed, it was their mother's turn to confide in me. She said that she was in a celebratory mood herself for yet another reason: she had made the very hard decision to request a legal separation from her philandering husband, whom I must have been surprised to see so little of. His practice in gynecology had put too much temptation in his way, she added, tears welling up and rolling down her cheeks. She warned me of Brazilian men's double standard, which, for many women, made it all too often more desirable to be "kept" than to be married. A mistress, she said, lived in a luxurious apartment, with a *dame de compagnie* to watch over her, and to ensure her complete fidelity—the mistress being the "prized possession," a macho status symbol to be flaunted in the company of peers. Lavish jewelry, servants, elegant parties, and grand holidays were showered on the mistress; the responsibility of raising children, of running the "official" household, of looking after relatives—these were the wife's "prerogatives"! She warned me not to marry a Brazilian, especially one from the big cities. But even more importantly for me, she described the finer points of her impending *"Desquite Amigável"*—a formal, amicable separation, there being no divorce in Brazil at the time—and suggested I follow the same course to obtain proper alimony, which, she feared, my in-laws would do everything to prevent. I explained to her that I could not dream of taking another penny from Helmut or his family; that by bringing me to safety he had kept his side of the bargain, while still paying a heavy price in terms of strained family relations. This, Dona Xeres was reluctant to accept. She urged me to reconsider, pointing out that my in-laws were wealthy and had already played a dirty trick on me. She suspected them of anti-Semitism, of being involved with the "Fifth Column," and of harboring the fear that I might encroach upon their fortune if I remained in the country. And then she added with a kindly tap on my cheek: "Thank God, the judge who deals with your legal separation will insist that you think of your financial future, especially as you are under 21!" It would take many months, and many more crises, for me to digest what I had heard and experienced on this one day.

Dona Xeres, the children, and I now moved to an apartment in Copacabana. Though she was no longer able to afford a governess, she invited me to stay on until I could find new, remunerated work. I accepted this arrangement with gratitude. I had saved practically all my earnings, and felt less destitute. I was very pleased to live in this more populated, affluent neighborhood, where, I thought, I might begin to earn my living by teaching French privately. One afternoon, having taken the children to a matinée at the luxurious local cinema, we passed a boutique, not far from the Copacabana Palace Hotel, with a very elegant display of dresses, and a discreet notice in the corner of the window: "Sales Assistant required. Apply within." I visited the shop the following day, imagining that I could work for a fixed salary by selling clothes, while slowly building up my teaching on the side. The Abramovichs, whom I guessed to be in their late forties, and who had fled from eastern Europe some years earlier, appeared to be doing extremely well. They engaged

188

me on the spot at an agreed salary, to be paid at the end of each month. Prior sales experience, I was told, was not necessary. When I explained my plans, Dona Xeres suggested that I had better remain with her for the first month or two, before seeking quarters of my own. In return, I would help in the house and keep an eye on the children when she was out.

From the first day of my new job I was surprised at the small number of customers coming into the shop, especially considering its splendid location. I had few opportunities to sell anything, and was repeatedly directed to stand near to, and face, the window, and to appear gracious and welcoming. . . Dona Xeres and I came to the conclusion that I had been taken on to attract customers, and to allow the owners more free time to follow other, unknown pursuits. At the end of the first month I was given only half the agreed amount. I was shocked to be treated in this manner by fellow refugees, and resigned immediately.

I had already been giving some lessons in the evenings and on weekends, and now decided to launch myself into full-time teaching. A notice offering tutorials in French and German was placed on the board of Livraria Kosmos, by courtesy of Walter Geyerhahn, one of the two owners. Thanks to the advertising in this busy bookshop, and word-of-mouth recommendations, I soon had enough students to keep afloat. I managed to arrange a discount for my books and for those of my pupils. I taught in their homes all over the city, which gave me an added insight into the life of *Carióca* families. My youngest pupil was eight years old, and my oldest in his seventies.

My contact with Livraria Kosmos also led me to rediscover Susanne Bach.[3] I had known her in my late teens in Munich, where she had been one of the favorite students of Professor Karl Vossler —the eminent chairman of the Romance Languages and Literatures Department, and one time president of Munich University— whose work my father held in high esteem. Susanne was the only other German, besides Madre Theófora, whom I had known in Bavaria and would meet in Brazil.

The time had come to take my grateful leave from Dona Xeres, although I would visit her regularly from my new room in the apartment of an Italian family just around the corner, only half a block from Copacabana beach. I was soon able to save half of the fees I received for teaching, and began to give more and more thought to the future. From my contacts with students and their families, who never talked to me as a person on the same social, or even human, level, I could see that, as a working woman, I would find it hard to form a community of Brazilian friends through my teaching activity. I therefore concentrated wholly on my work, and built up the fullest schedule possible to increase my earnings, and to provide for greater freedom of action later.

On Sundays I would recuperate from my labors by swimming and sunning myself on the beach. One day, in a chance encounter, I made the acquaintance of Andrée Koller, a member of the Swiss Embassy. Thanks to her I found myself quite suddenly immersed in a new circle of beach companions from Europe and the United States. We were enjoying the Brazilian summer months of late 1942 to early 1943. More and more Americans appeared on the scene, particularly in Copacabana, the charms of which attracted newcomers like magnets. Getúlio Vargas, Brazil's dictator president, had made the belated decision to switch from the Axis to the Allied cause, after Hitler's offensive against the Soviet Union had received a severe setback, due to the early onset of snow and freezing temperatures during the march on Moscow in the autumn of 1941. Vargas had not wished to risk being left standing on the losing side, and was therefore drawn quite easily into the alliance, a step made more palatable through the economic incentives offered by the United States. Although I had experienced the first reverberations of the Brazilian shift in policy as I was fleeing Germany, the implications of the new relationship with the United States were only now becoming evident to me.

A U.S. aircraft carrier, the SS *Roosevelt*, if I remember the name rightly, docked in Rio harbor on a goodwill tour. It was to bring my first tangible experience of American military power, and my first encounter, in the person of a young ensign, with what I imagined a true American to be. He invited me on a tour of his imposing warship. The absence, in a mundane sense, of all sophistication, the simplicity and natural intelligence that underlay the straightforwardness of my clean-cut ensign host, impressed me. I infinitely preferred the paradox of his respectful, shy, and yet robust, manner, to the suave Latino polish of the Brazilian men I had met. However, I was soon to be saved from any naive tendency to generalize my experience with the U.S. Navy, upon meeting other Americans stationed with the Embassy, or with American companies. One ensign, I discovered, does not a nation make! My recollection of the ship's anatomy and crew, of the tea and music aboard, is far less vivid in my memory today than the spectacle I would enjoy when he treated me to dinner afterwards at the Casino Atlantico, well known for its flamboyant floor shows. Never in later years, not even in Paris, would I see a display of such exquisite taste. Lavish costumes, perfect color combinations, and brilliant choreography combined to rivet our attention. We learned from the maître d'hôtel that the show had been created by a refugee stage director from Vienna. After fifty years, I can still remember a hunting scene: young, svelte ballet dancers wearing the shortest imaginable velvet frocks in rich deep bottle green, secured in front with mink covered buttons, and at the neck with snug mink collars, leaving bare their shapely backs to well below the waist. Matching little bell-shaped hats, dressed with mink tails at the back, accentuated the coquette allure of their pretty faces. They looked adorable, danced impeccably, and the crowd was ecstatic. My young ensign could not believe his eyes.

As my teaching revenue increased, I was able to look for a small, affordable apartment of my own in the same neighborhood. I quickly found the ideal two-room flat with a minuscule kitchen and bath on the second floor of a newly built four-storied apartment house, half-way up a hill from Rua Barata Ribeiro. My short, steep street bore the rather pompous name of Rua General Azevedo Pimentel, and led up to a hilltop, from whence I could descend on a stone staircase to Avenida Copacabana, one block from the sea. I furnished the apartment sparsely, carefully weighing the absolute necessities, among which was a first bookcase for my growing library. Although it was a modest beginning, I felt proud and, for the first time, almost at home. On the other hand, part of me had already begun to realize that I was not likely to make my life in Brazil. Despite my love affair with the unparalleled beauty of nature in and around Rio, which provided me with consolation and inspiration on a daily basis, I could not visualize my individual evolution, nor any serious involvement, in Brazil; at least not on the level I had been taught by the example of my parents, their friends, and the nuns at school. Although I was not familiar with the writings of Stefan Zweig at the time, I could not help but wonder about his and his wife's joint suicide in the summer retreat of Petropolis above Rio— a tragedy I learned about from Susanne Bach. It had happened as I was flying from Munich to Lisbon. Reading about their life and death in *Morte no Paraíso*[4] decades later, revived memories of my own reactions to the country that Zweig had called "paradise."

191

My contacts with Brazilians—with very few exceptions—remained superficial, and rarely went beyond matters connected with my teaching. The members of the various embassies I knew through my friend Andrée adopted an analytical, detached attitude to the country, and a transient one to human relationships. Most of the European refugees whom I met socially were engrossed in sustaining their own lives. No community, or community of interests, existed, to which I could relate and belong. Nor were the laws then governing Brazilian naturalization an inducement to pursuing early, participatory citizenship. Applications required twelve years prior residence in the country, which, at the age of twenty, seemed like an eternity. And thus I, too, became a transient, creating my own personal and temporary spheres.

Brazil entered the war on the allied side in August 1942, having already lost two vessels to the torpedoes of Nazi submarines, one of which was sunk on the west coast of the United States. Roosevelt had put pressure on Getúlio Vargas to declare war on Germany— not without having added further considerable economic incentives. The airports of Pernambuco and Natal, the nearest points of the entire American continent to Africa, were opened to the U.S. Air Force for transfers to North Africa, and the battles against Rommel. The security of these bases was looked after by the Brazilian military. It was only at the start of 1944, that Brazil actually sent an expeditionary force to join the U.S. Fifth Army in the Italian theater of war, where it remained until the end. Five hundred men were never to return.[5]

During our last conversations in Tutzing, I had agreed with my parents that the only hope for us to remain in touch over the long term would be through a friend living in a neutral country such as Spain. Maria Caballero in Madrid, whom my parents befriended in the twenties when her husband represented Spain in the Bavarian capital, was chosen to become the recipient of our letters, which she would forward in new envelopes with Spanish stamps to Germany and Brazil respectively. But the first anxiously awaited letter from Europe reached me only in November of 1942, written by H. G. Pauls in Zürich,[6] who had evidently agreed to act as a go-between, and who acknowledged my parents' receipt of two of my letters, the first sent from Portugal in March 1942 and intended for my father's sixtieth birthday on June 17. Miraculously it came into his hands on that very day! My frequent moves had made it difficult to receive mail, and Hans Pauls's first letter never found its way to me. It was balm for my soul to read that some thirty of my parents' friends had come to Tutzing to celebrate this birthday; among them my god-father, Benno Reifenberg, Dolf Sternberger, Max von Brück, Uhde-Bernays, and the painter Max Unold. My parents' health, Pauls assured me, was satisfactory. Several weeks later, the first letter in my mother's own hand, of October 25, arrived safely, thanking me again for my twelve-page missive:

" [. . .] plusieurs très émouvantes allocutions ont fêté ses soixante ans. Une atmosphère d'affection, de respect lui ont prouvé combien il est aimé et apprécié."[7]

A radiant, warm autumn had allowed my parents to spend a restful interlude at a guesthouse owned by a peasant family in the mountains, where I had often vacationed with them as a child. The letter mentioned harmless subjects: they were reading *The Odyssey* again, which I so enjoyed having read to me by my mother when I was nine. My father had added a few lines, though some words were illegible because the censor had put what looked like water marks diagonally through the pages of the flimsy airmail paper, probably in search of secret communications in invisible ink! This letter from my mother was the first to be received via Maria Caballero: our plan was working at last. The next letter to arrive had a whole line and several words cut out of it. Although I had mustered the courage to destroy the sinister card, slipped to me at Munich airport, by throwing it to the winds as I crossed the Atlantic, the fear of repercussions upon my parents' safety continued to haunt me. Holding those fragile sheets of paper in my hands, I would scrutinize the writing to detect the slightest change, tremor, or weakness in the strokes of their pens. It took great discipline to remember at all times not to mention anything concerning the climate, or nature—I was living in a land of different seasons, flora, and fauna to Spain— or my work and relaxation: Maria Caballero did not teach languages, and was not living by the sea; in other words, I could not mention anything that was not applicable to Madrid and our friend. It was easier for my parents to put across meaningful messages to one so intimately familiar with their life and surroundings, than it was for me, living in circumstances totally unknown to them.

My new apartment was a joy. As I spent most of my days away teaching long hours, I engaged the help of Ambrosina, an eighteen-year-old with skin as black as ebony, to do my shopping, washing, and cooking, besides keeping my flat immaculately clean. She was one of the many children of those poor families living in makeshift shelters on the hills of Rio—shantytowns, known as *favelas* in Brazil. The more I learned about the lack of sanitation, fresh water, or the most rudimentary hygiene, and the ever present danger to their precarious existence from landslides during the frequent torrential rains, the more I wondered about the role of the mighty Catholic Church and the professed piety of many Brazilian Catholics. I admired Ambrosina's uncanny talent to keep herself clean and groomed in such dismal surroundings. Although she looked and dressed like a child, with her frizzy hair in neatly braided pigtails, and was barely able to read and write, she was possessed of a more developed practical intelligence and philosophical insight into the causes of her and her family's condition, than I could have mustered in Germany when I was her age. Indeed, she was ahead of me in common sense and in her earthy wisdom. It was her lucidity and outspokenness over the years, that opened my eyes to the consequences of economic and social injustice for those who actually suffer it; a recognition that would influence my sociopolitical orientation and my choice of work in later life.

Brazil was then a country of between 50 and 55 million people of whom the vast majority lived in abject poverty. The church still acted as an ally of the government and of the rich elite. Ambrosina told me how a priest, who regularly visited her district, had collected the equivalent of a week's wage from her neighbor to baptize her tenth child, a fee the mother paid obediently in fear of the "eternal hell-fire" that would otherwise await her baby after its likely death. Many children were dying of milk tuberculosis for lack of sanitary controls, and because of the profitable practice of milk adulteration in the shopping areas of the poor.

Ambrosina did not cease to amaze me. I had been suffering for many months from what looked like urticaria or hives, small itchy bumps covering my body. I had seen a series of doctors, who, invariably, prescribed newer and better lotions, pills and ointments, at considerable cost, none of which relieved my agony, let alone dealt with the underlying cause. During our conversations—we both enjoyed talking to one another—Ambrosina asked me a thousand questions about Europe, about my family, every detail of how we lived, and, her favorite, my voyage to Brazil. One day I told her how hard it was to concentrate during my lessons due to this awful itch. With the seriousness of a seasoned nurse, she replied that it was a frequent complaint among the foreigners she had served, and that I would certainly be cured if I asked the pharmacist at the corner below the hill to administer *uma injeção de calcio na veia*. One of her previous employers had found it the only remedy that helped. Ten minutes later, I interviewed the apothecary, who was quite willing to give me a series of shots without a special fee. But now I had to choose the brand of calcium among the boxes he put before me. Luckily, one brand name was immediately familiar: Merck & Co! It so happened that my godmother, née Elisabeth Merck, was a member of the founding family in Darmstadt. The pharmacist dispensed the injection very slowly, with obvious experience, so that the hot flush it caused was quite bearable. To my amazement, the bumps disappeared within a day or two, never to return. As an "insurance," I took the few remaining shots over the following weeks.

One morning, not having heard from Helmut for a considerable time, I received a telephone call from the family chauffeur. He asked with a grave voice whether I could meet him the same day, as he was only passing through Rio. He refused to discuss the matter on the telephone, obviously afraid of wire taps, a form of surveillance that, as I learned later, had been widely practiced at least since 1935.[8] I postponed one or two tutorials to meet with him at once. He had, in fact, come to tell me that Helmut had been arrested in São Paulo, and that he could not foresee a quick end to his detention. Although he did not mention it with a single word, his eyes conveyed a clear message: the hope that I might help secure Helmut's release. Again, I was impressed by the man's personal loyalty. He remained discreetly noncommittal when I suggested that his employers' direct or indirect involvement in the activities of the Fifth Column could have been the reason for Helmut's imprisonment. He assured me that he had come entirely on his own volition. I felt enraged that someone, who had recognized the Nazi regime for what it was, and had, at considerable personal sacrifice and emotional pain to himself, brought a young woman to safety in Brazil, should now be jailed. I promised I would go to São Paulo the next day, and asked him for the address of the prison. He warned me about the wartime regulation—of which I was unaware—that nationals of the Axis powers, the Germans, Italians, and Japanese, could not travel without a special permit from the police. Fortunately, he knew where I should go to obtain it.

Back home I rang a lawyer friend, whom I had met through Dona Xeres, to seek his advice. He thought my plan was very dangerous, and that I should not meddle with this case. When he realized I was determined, he insisted on coming with me, saying that there was other business to which he could attend in São Paulo. As we left the train, I was suddenly seized by two plainclothesmen, pushed into a waiting car, and driven off to the prison in which Helmut was being held. My lawyer friend caught up with me later, but it seemed that there was little he could do. I was made to walk down endless corridors, and, when I was finally given a chair in a dingy office, there followed interminable questions about names and situations I knew nothing about. In the end I had to insist on telling *my own* story: where Helmut and I had met; why, in 1941, he had reached the decision to leave Nazi Germany—even against his parents' wishes, as conveyed to him in an outspoken telegram; and that various other people might well be imprisoned, but most certainly not Helmut, whose thoughtful and chivalrous help had won my lasting gratitude. I then asked to see him. I remember waiting a long time and reminding the functionaries around me that I had lessons scheduled in Rio the next day. After several hours, I was asked to sign my deposition. It was many pages long. I scrutinized the wording carefully and corrected errors. I then put my signature to the document with a mixture of satisfaction and foreboding. A few moments later Helmut stood before me, unsmiling and in his shirt sleeves, with trousers that seemed too large, as he had certainly lost weight. His clean-shaven face looked pale and weary. The question on how he was being treated was on the tip of my tongue, but the forbidding expression of the man behind him tightened my throat. I made a step forward to take hold of his hand, but, as if to discourage me, he moved slightly back, leaving me to stammer a few helpless words about coming to São Paulo of my own free will to make known the truth of his valiant efforts to save my life; that I felt certain my deposition would help convince the authorities of the nobility and integrity of his purpose. The very faintest trace of a smile came over his face, before we were told: "That's enough." It was the last time I should see him. There was nothing more I could do. The police dismissed me without a word of explanation.

Arrest and Imprisonment

After the traumatic experience of my abduction in São Paulo, I could hardly wait to find the addresses of my parents' friends in the United States. The U.S. Embassy seemed unable, or unwilling, to provide them, nor was anyone else I asked of help in the matter. I therefore took a chance and posted an airmail letter to Professor Curt von Faber du Faur at Yale University; but months passed without a reply. It was on the way to the post office around this time that I first became aware of being followed in the street by two men. I found this particularly disconcerting when I came out of my pupils' homes: there they were, standing on the other side of the street watching the doorway in which I was to reappear. Heaven knows what they may have told the concierges! I soon realized that I was being watched around the clock. This spurred me to send even more letters to other addressees, hoping to locate the second potential sponsor for my immigration to the United States: Kurt Wolff, my godmother Elisabeth Merck's first husband, who, in 1921, published the very first book on Paul Klee, written by my father[9]—as well as other titles from his pen. Weeks passed without an answer to any of my letters. As there was absolutely nothing I could do to stop my being shadowed day and night, I began to joke with my trackers, sticking the envelopes I was posting under their noses, describing their contents and telling them that I wished to escape this oppressive country by emigrating to the United States! Sometimes, when I taught double lessons, I suggested they go off and relax over a beer or a *cafezinho*, in the naive expectation that honesty and friendliness would pay in the end.

As Carnival approached, I was often invited to dinners and dances by the embassy crowd or by resident Americans, through my Swiss friend Andrée. Occasionally, we would go on to see the shows at the Casino Atlantico or the Urca, where I first heard the famous Carmen Miranda, then at the height of her career and popularity. I found her coarse and unattractive, and the best I could say of her was that she had unbounded energy and an insuppressible elan. I could never understand the extent of her success, especially in Hollywood.

One evening in early March of 1943, I had gone out in the company of four Americans, one of whom vaunted his role with the Lockheed Corporation. This left me quite unimpressed as I had never heard of it before. The other two were military officers, whose immediate reasons for being in Brazil escaped me. A lady friend of theirs made up the party. The new sambas of the Carnival season had put us all in a swinging mood. I wore a black moiré dress with a deep neckline and upright collar at the back, with short puffed sleeves and a wide swirling skirt that I had sewn myself at the fashion school in Munich. I remember being asked for the next

dance, and trying to get up from my chair, when a strong hand
gripped my shoulder firmly from behind. I turned around and saw
two men, one of whom took me by the arm and ordered me in a
quiet, insistent tone of voice to come along immediately, and without fuss. Fortunately, I had the presence of mind to grab my handbag from the chair. My companions looked startled. Two of them
followed me out onto the street, and tried to argue with my captors.
But, as in São Paulo, I was shoved into a car and driven off. A thousand thoughts raced through my mind, and I could not help wondering why my companions had not acted more forcefully on my
behalf.

After a long drive we stopped before a large house, which
looked more like a neglected villa than a place of detention. Apparently, it was an office of the Polícia d'Estrangeiros. It must have
been nearly midnight when I was handed over to a guard in civilian
clothes, who answered to the name of Paulo, and who seemed to be
expecting me. He was a serious looking man in his late thirties or
early forties. He led me to an unfurnished room on one of the upper floors. I was made to sit down on the only chair and told to wait
till morning. He left the light on and the door wide open, so he
could see me from his desk in the corridor. He had taken my handbag and locked it in one of his drawers. I did not sleep that night on
the hard wooden chair. I doubted that my American acquaintances
would make any attempt to extricate me from the clutches of the
police. I even began to suspect them of complicity. I worried about
my students who would be dumbfounded, as I had never been late
or absent without a prior call. Ambrosina would be beside herself. If
any one of them called the police, what good would it do, and what
lies might they be told? It was a nightmare! I tried to remain calm
by telling myself that, having done nothing wrong, nothing unto-
ward could happen to me. But then I thought of Helmut. As far as I
knew, he had done nothing wrong either—and yet he was in prison.
I spent the night trying to understand what was happening to me,
until I was too tired to think. The sun rose and showed up the unkempt condition of the place, and the lines in Paulo's face that gave
it character and strength. It was the tenth of March, and still quite
hot. I asked if I could use the bathroom. He replied that he had orders: no sleeping, no washing; but that he would allow me to use
the toilet. He spoke in an embarrassed, almost human way, and
then handed me a pin, pointing at my plunging neckline. I could
feel that he was ill at ease with his young prisoner in a party dress,

198

Renée-Marie Hausenstein
(age twenty-two) in Rio de Janeiro, 1944.
Courtesy of Renée-Marie Croose Parry.

Margot Hausenstein with her husband, Wilhelm
Hausenstein, late 1945, after a two-month stay in a
sanatorium. Courtesy of Renée-Marie Croose Parry.

even though I had removed my glamorous pendant earrings—my father's engagement present to my mother in 1918, which she had
wanted me to take along on my journey, as a remembrance.

Around nine in the morning, I was taken downstairs and confronted with two interrogators, called Neumann and Baumann.
Ironically, the latter bore the maiden name of my paternal grandmother from Hornberg in the Black Forest. The moment they
opened their mouths, I suspected that they both belonged to the
Nazi remnants in Getúlio Vargas's government, and wondered why
they had not been purged. Couched amongst a host of questions
about circumstances, names, and places totally unknown to me,
they interposed veiled queries on why I felt such a dislike of my par-
ents-in-law, and had such harsh things to say about them in São
Paulo. They gave no reply when I reminded them that my in-laws
would have succeeded in getting me expelled from the country, had
my Brazilian employer not alerted me in time. Throughout their
interrogations, which went on for three days, I gained the impression that they were angling desperately for any straw with which to
construct a case against me to justify my imprisonment. Was this to
be a punitive retribution on behalf of Helmut's family? Some of
Baumann's, or Neumann's, remarks confirmed that he was still in a
São Paulo jail. Was this why they were persecuting me? There was
no way in which I could anticipate what they intended to do to me.
The only point on which they might have scored, if what they
claimed was in fact true, concerned my apparent contravention of a
wartime regulation with regard to aliens, when I went out at night
to a public place. For the moment I was being held incommuni-
cado. Having grown up in Hitler's Germany, the idea never came
to my mind to ask for the presence of a lawyer. Had I done so, I
suspect they would have laughed at my request.

To this day, I have tried in vain to unravel the web of internal
rivalries and contradictions between the various police departments,
following Getúlio Vargas's major switch in policy when he joined
the Allies. It is possible that my interrogators had been retained for
a paradoxical double purpose: on the one hand for their intimate
acquaintance with Nazi operations through their bonds with the
Fifth Column, and on the other for the knowledge they had acquired through their investigations of the Communist Party, and
the persecution and imprisonment of its members since the thirties.
After all, their boss—until his replacement—had been Filinto
Strubling Müller, the chief of police in charge of Greater Rio de

Janeiro,[10] a notorious fascist strongman and anti-Semite, under whose reign the worst imaginable tortures of communists and socialists had taken place. Could it have been that one of my two questioners had been the unscrupulous Jõao Guilherme Neumann, the very man Filinto Müller ordered in 1936 to be the plainclothes escort of Olga Benario Prestes, the Jewish wife of the imprisoned Communist leader, Luís Carlos Prestes, during her unconstitutional extradition and delivery into the hands of the Gestapo in Hamburg harbor in the eighth month of her pregnancy?[11]

As I think back, I can hypothesize, but am still unable to identify the reason for my arrest. Could it be that I had become the victim of ambiguities within the police? Perhaps the Polícia Paulista had been so thoroughly purged that they were actually pursuing the Fifth Column. Could it have been that both Helmut and I were being held because his parents, or other members of his family, were under suspicion of Nazi collaboration? Perhaps I was suspected on my own account, having arrived with the last group of refugees from Europe, rumored to have included spies—or because I was attractive and spoke fluent French and German, and had learned Portuguese so quickly. Or, perhaps, Helmut was being held because of me.

At the end of each day's relentless questioning, I was taken upstairs toward evening, exhausted from lack of sleep, food, and drink. After the offices were closed, and everybody else had left, the remaining guard turned me over to Paulo, when he arrived for the night shift. Having made sure that we were now alone in the house, he would unpack an enormous beef sandwich, for which he must have paid with his own money, and pour me a glass of water. I don't remember when anything tasted so good. He admonished me not to breathe a word, and to remain looking weak and despondent. He refused my offer to pay for the food, which worried me. Opposite his desk there was a second room with a bed and bare mattress, on which he rested when not watching over detainees. On the second day, at about midnight, Paulo took pity upon me, fearing I might fall off the chair, as my head swayed from one side to the other. Rousing me from my stupor, he suggested that I lie down on his mattress. I was too weary to think whether this was a wise thing to do. I fell asleep instantly. When I woke at dawn, Paulo was sitting on a chair a few yards away, watching me. I felt terribly uneasy in my party dress, and wished its snug bodice was less revealing of my contours. But then he allayed my anxiety by saying the totally unexpected: "If only I were a sculptor, I would immortalize your body!" He spoke these words with Latin flair, and yet with gravity. After all the brutalities, of which I had heard rumors, I was being guarded by a *gentle*man. I thought back to Germany, to Ellen Bühler, and tears filled my eyes. Showing me to the bathroom, Paulo instructed me not to straighten out my hair, nor to wash my face. He then shared his coffee and milk with me.

At dusk of the third day, and before I could express my gratitude to Paulo, I was whisked away in the same black car that had brought me. We drove through more densely populated districts before stopping in front of a large building: the Polícia Central. As night had fallen, and the feeble lightbulbs hung high in the corridors, it was hard to distinguish where I was being taken. I vaguely remember several stories of curving open galleries. The guard murmured to himself as he led me around one of these interminable inner balconies above the central courtyard. Finally, he knocked at a metal door, behind which another guard signed a receipt on his chaotic desk to the effect that I had been delivered. When the door fell closed behind me I burst into tears. The guard avoided looking into my eyes while he took my handbag and the fine moiré belt, still tied in a creased, slept-on bow around my waist. With his eagle's eye he even spotted the tiny pin which Paulo had given me to close the V-line of my décolleté. He then led me around the corner of a dark narrow corridor, opened another, heavier metal door with an iron key, and switched on the miserable light that hung from the ceiling. As he locked the door, he opened the small grille through which I could be kept under observation by the male guard on duty.

I cried and cried in a state of utter despair, such as I had never known before. What I was able to discern in the dim light through the stream of my tears was not reassuring: six bunks on metal frames with worn mattresses, two on top of each other against three of the walls; on the fourth, facing the door, a small chipped basin with one tap for cold water, and on the left of it, taking up the corner, two dark, five foot high partitions forming an enclosure, with a half door opening onto a toilet bowl, from whence the odor of a creosote-based disinfectant permeated the cell. High up above the basin a rectangular opening in the wall, secured with iron bars, enabled me to see the bleak reflection of the light in the guard's anteroom, upon the corridor walls beyond. I lay down weeping on the lower bunk to the left of the door. I did not look up when somebody put a plate of food beside my head, the smell of which repulsed me, though I was desperately hungry. When my tears ebbed for a moment, I took a spoonful of the black beans and of the rice underneath. There was a substance in it that felt like grit between my teeth, and the once white enamel plate was nearly black from so many chips. The guard looked through the grille and scolded me for not eating. I broke into tears again, and must have cried myself to sleep. I woke frequently. The scratchy brown blanket at my feet stank, and so did the stuffing in the pillow. Dawn was barely discernible, as the corridor windows to the courtyard were too distant to provide daylight through the crossbars high above the basin. The first day passed with more weeping, and without any answers to the questions I would ask the guards.

I think it was the following night, after I had slept for only a few hours, that a rude push brought me back to my anguished reality. I should follow the guard. It was past midnight on the clock with the big black hands behind the warder's desk. We had walked along the galleries for some time, when the guard knocked on a large double door. "Entra!" said a tired male voice. The guard saluted the uniformed officer, whom I could hardly see behind the huge stacks of faded, fingered, musty folders to either side of his desk. He opened the file in front of him, and asked me to sit down under the strong light overhead. He seemed to be in his early to mid fifties, with banal features, intent on making a correct impression. I could hardly see out of my swollen eyes, and the front of my dress was stained and wet for lack of a handkerchief. Once again, I was asked questions about names and places I had never heard before, some of which were German or English. At intervals I tried to interject comments on my family's precarious situation in Germany, on that of my grandmother and uncle in Belgium, and our relatives in Holland; and on my gratitude to have been able to emigrate to Brazil, and especially to Helmut who had made it possible. Again and again, I asked why I was being held in detention. I described how I had just begun to build a life for myself as a tutor of languages. Surely, it could not be his intention to destroy this fragile start. Though he was taking notes, he never reacted to my comments or questions. When the guard took me back to my cell, I heard him address the officer as "colonel."

These eerie interrogations were repeated once or twice a week during the next four weeks—mysteriously, always at night. At one time the colonel left the room, and a man who seemed to be American took up the questioning. If I have little recollection of what I was asked, it is because I was totally unfamiliar with the matters raised. As I learned later, the FBI and the British Secret Service co-operated with the Vargas dictatorship, both before and after the latter's conversion to the Allied cause, the difference being that all of them were now trying in unison to dismantle the remainders of Nazi and Fascist operations in the country. One question, I do remember, concerned the Lockheed Corporation. Did I know what it produced? And did I know anyone connected with it? My answer was: no, I had no idea what it produced; and, yes, I knew a man by the name of Duke Robertson, who was present at the party when I was arrested, and who had seemed very eager to tell me he worked for Lockheed.

I never was allowed to leave my cell and walk in the courtyard to get air and sun; nor did I see or hear any other detainees. By the end of the first week the skin under my lower eyelids had turned into patches of reddish crusts, chafed from the continuous wiping of my salty flood of tears. I had nothing to read, nor anything with which to write. The guards, worried by my low intake of food, agreed to buy me sandwiches upon my promise that I would pay for them later.

After about a week, my solitary routine was to be altered drastically by the arrival of five women, brought in to occupy the remaining bunks. From what I understood them to say, and *not* to say, they had been rounded up, following a campaign by the new chief of police to improve morality in Rio—which I interpreted as meaning the closure of certain establishments in Latin America's renowned capital of brothels. "From now on," one woman exclaimed, throwing her fist angrily into the air, "let no couple be found without a marriage certificate hanging over their bed!" I wondered whether brothels might have been used to hide agents the police wanted to get hold of? But if they were to close them all, what would they do with the thousands of women? The new arrivals in my cell were between thirty and forty years of age, looking thin and indifferent, and wearing plain, modest dresses. They were anxious to know my history, and seemed intrigued by my party dress—or what was left of its once glamorous appearance. Two or three of them hung their rosaries on the posts of their bunks. Every night, I could hear them pray in the dark, especially to the Virgin Mary. Some expressed deep concern about their children, and who might be looking after them. Hearing their troubles, I found myself crying less, and my

204

predicament seemed more bearable. A night guard had taken to bringing me white rolls and bananas. I shared them as best I could.

Ten days must have passed when, suddenly, I heard a familiar voice arguing loudly with the warden outside, mentioning my name. I could not believe my ears—someone had found me! I was not totally forgotten. It was Stefan Wertheimer, a member of a small group of émigrés I had met a few months earlier. Once alerted to his presence, and hearing every word through the wall between us, I realized that it was not an argument at all. He had raised his voice in the hope of alerting me that he was there, and had brought some clothing. He asked repeatedly to be allowed to hand me the small case in person. To my great distress, the guard would not permit him to see me. Stefan had done some thoughtful packing, probably with the help of Ambrosina: a freshly washed and pressed housedress and underclothes, plain shoes, some fruit and money; but, alas, no letter.

Stefan Wertheimer, a very tall, lean, reddish-blond, German-Jewish refugee, had arrived in Brazil long before me, and was building up an import/export business in Rio. From the day we met, he had always been attentive and kind to me. True to his character, he was the only person who would expose himself to the likely stigma of knowing and aiding a suspect. From that day onward, I breathed more easily. A true friend now knew where I had been taken. The word might spread, and it would be that much more difficult to make me "disappear."

More women were arriving. That night we heard heartrending screams rise from below. My imagination ran riot. I felt the same terror as on the first night upon arrival at the Polícia Central. During the past few days, and owing to my experience with the guards and the colonel, I had begun to feel safer from physical mistreatment. Now, the same dreadful panic overcame me. My cell mates took to their rosaries and prayed. Then, a frightful commotion started in our corridor. A screaming woman was being taken past our door. A few seconds later a metal door slammed shut, sending a tremor through our cell. One of the women exclaimed: "Coitada! Foi posta na solitaria."—"The poor thing! She has been put in solitary confinement." The women explained to me that we were not really "in prison," but only in a detention cell at the headquarters of Rio's Central Police. As long as we were here, they tried to reassure me, there was light at the end of the tunnel; once transferred to prison, it could take years to get out.

After twenty-one days—I had made a scratch on the wall every morning—I felt the urge to act, to do something *decisive*. I was gaining weight from all the bread, rice, and bananas I was eating. In the absence of fresh air, sun, and exercise, my menstrual cycle had come to a halt. I felt I was deteriorating. I asked the guard for pen and paper to write an appeal to the Chief of Police. Fearing to make mistakes in Portuguese, I wrote in French, then the second language of most educated Brazilians. I also hoped my plea might thereby be given more attention. It was nothing more than a simple statement of facts: first, who my parents were, and their threatened existence in Nazi Germany; second, about myself: I had been held for over three weeks, I had not been accused of any crime, my health was suffering, my work base was being destroyed, rental and other bills were lying unattended, I was being held with five women in a small airless cell, the interrogations at night were meaningless as I knew nothing about which I was being asked; and, lastly, and most gravely, I could not write to my parents, who, if they were still alive, would be worrying about me. For all these very serious reasons, I begged to be set free. Alas, I was never to know whether this letter had ever gone beyond the desk of my interrogator . . .

Another week elapsed before I was pulled out again to be brought before the colonel. This time he asked no questions. In an almost friendly tone he admitted that I had been in detention long enough—and not in the best company. My God, I thought, I shall be freed! But then he went on to say it was high time that I be able to take regular walks in the open air, and get better food and medical attention, and that he had made arrangements for my transfer to a less confining place, where my health would improve. My hopes collapsed. "I shall be forgotten there," I sobbed through a stream of tears, pointing at the stacks of folders on his desk. To this he answered with an encouraging smile: "Don't worry, I won't let your folder get to the bottom of the pile. I know what I've decided is best for you." I was ushered out before I could ask why I was not being released. When I told the women that I was being transferred, they looked rather solemn. "Vamos rezar para você"—"We will pray for you," they said. Indeed, I believed I would need all their prayers. I remembered to count the tiny scratches on the wall. Allowing for the time spent at the Polícia d'Estrangeiros, it was now thirty-three days since my arrest.

I was fetched toward evening. The women gave me hearty Latino hugs and many words of encouragement. Once again in possession of my purse, I paid my debts to the guards. This time I was transferred in a Black Maria, gripping the little case I owed to Stefan's kindness. I remember nothing of the drive, being unable to see outside, and consumed with the fear that no one, not even Stefan, would find me now. I was handed over to a short, friendly looking guard in a light khaki uniform. A bunch of gigantic keys, hooked to the right side of his belt, clattered to the rhythm of his gait as he led me into a dark courtyard. I began to hear the sound of women's voices, and then of shouts and raucous guffaws as we drew nearer. Turning the corner, an enormous enclosure appeared on the left, fronted by iron bars from floor to ceiling. I saw what seemed to be hundreds of women huddled together, sitting on the stone floor or standing in groups, growing more quiet as the clatter of keys announced our coming. Some of them reached out to grab my arm, and asked questions I did not understand. Others hissed and jeered. More prostitutes, I thought. The guard urged me to walk faster.

We approached a massive, sparsely lit building, where the guard picked one of his largest keys, some seven inches long, to open the first iron door. As it clanked shut behind us my panic soared. Climbing up the old, spiral stone staircase in the center of the building, I realized I was now in an ancient prison, which, judging from the thickness of the walls and the size of the grating locks, must have dated from the early eighteenth century. On the landing of the second floor an endless corridor stretched away to the left behind a high grid of iron bars. Scores of wretched looking men in striped prison garb thronged the corridor, some clasping the bars and pressing their faces between them to get a better look at me. Others managed a smile at the rare sight of a young woman passing in the night, or made approving signs with dexterous fingers—a macho commonplace in Brazil, which used to embarrass me when I would have to pass a group of men chatting at the corner of a street. Yet others whistled to catch my eye and give expression to their deprived desires.

The guard hurried me on, up to the third, fourth and last floor. He unlocked the screeching iron bar partition on the right of the landing, making me enter a corridor with a high vaulted ceiling, so long I could not see its end in the gloom. The reverberation of our steps on the massive stone floor produced a haunting sound. Along each wall, at regular intervals, low arched iron gates with heavy locks held back the unknown in the dark beyond. Everything conspired to induce the fear that here I had reached the end of my road. The guard shoved me on, farther and farther down the dark corridor. There, at the end of it, two ghostly silhouettes were moving toward us, their shadows preceding them, cast by a diffuse light coming from the left. I stood in terror, paralyzed. I could neither cry, speak, nor move. Moments later, I felt a warm arm around my shoulder. I stood stiff and immobile. A woman with an Italian accent whispered in my ear: "Tomorrow morning, when the sun shines into the corridor, and our cells are light, you will feel much better. It's not such a bad place." The second woman, with a distinct, clipped German accent, spoke to the warden, who agreed to lock us in an hour later than usual. He opened one of the "black holes" with a smaller, four-inch key, and turned on the light. This was to be my cell. The walls were whitewashed, and the worn, light wooden floor planks scrubbed clean. After the ordeal I had just experienced, it seemed almost friendly. The metal bedstead was an improvement on the bunks, and beside it stood a wooden chair. The window sill was at least one meter deep, and the iron bars spanned an opening about two feet square, through which I could see distant lights.

My new fellow inmates wanted to show me their "living room"; a corner cell with window openings on both walls, a table, two benches, some plates, glasses, and cutlery, all of which made me think they had been there for some time. They offered me an apple as we sat down to talk. The older woman, in her early fifties, looked Saxonian, with stringy dark blond hair gathered at the back. She seemed skeptical and worn, whereas the woman with the Italian accent, probably in her early forties, spoke and acted with vigor, self-assurance, and a trace of warmth. I imagined that both had been active in the Fifth Column. I said as little as possible, mentioning no names and watching my every word. The last thing I wanted to do was to provoke their animosity. The less I asked, the less I hoped I would be asked. The German woman too was very secretive; perhaps because I had revealed my own German origin. I never learned anything about her history. I think the name of the black-haired Italian was Maria Cavalcanti. I remember her saying that she was known as "the mascot of the L.A.T.I.," the Italian Airline! Perhaps she had been a courier between Getúlio Vargas and Mussolini, and knew too much. The guard interrupted our talk to lock us up in our individual cells. After the nervous strain of this terror-laden day and my utter emotional exhaustion, I managed to sleep most of the night.

I woke when I heard the clink clunk of keys and the noise of a metal trolley being pushed along on the stone floor outside. A key turned in the lock of my cell, and in came a giant black prisoner, at least six foot five inches tall, causing me a dreadful fright as he bent over my bedside to put a metal mug with coffee and some bread on the chair next to my pillow. As I discovered, he was the inmate in charge of delivering food from the prison kitchen. I made sure the following night to place the chair behind my bed nearer the entrance, and to put my underclothes at the foot of my bed. As the women had promised, the cells looked almost cheerful in daylight. Gone were the many "black holes." Warm breezes traveled down the corridor and through the many cell window bars. I shuddered to think how cold it would be in winter, if I should still be there. Our breakfast giant, the women said, had been convicted of murder when he was very young, and had already served a twenty-year sentence. He had grown satisfied with prison life where he had found secure shelter, work, nourishment, and clothing—much of which he had missed as a free man. The guard had told them that he seemed unable to face being released into the world outside, and that he had become more and more restless, difficult, and morose, as the end of his sentence approached. A week or two before he was to go—or so the story went—he murdered a fellow inmate, a man he had always disliked, hoping to earn a life sentence. This he was granted! Serenity returned to the hardworking, friendly, model prisoner, to everybody's benefit—even ours, as he would also bring the noonday and evening rations, sometimes sneaking in additional bits of fruit in his pockets. I did not know whether to believe the story; his kindly smile made me wonder . . .

One afternoon, on the way to our daily recreation in the courtyard, Maria pointed out a slender man, leaning against the iron bar partition on the second floor, and looking past us with distant, sad, intelligent, and deeply pensive eyes. "That's Luís Carlos Prestes, the Communist leader," Maria whispered in my ear. "Filinto Müller caught and imprisoned him in 1935!" I had never heard Prestes's name before, and knew little about Brazilian politics. I read an account of the aborted revolution and his personal tragedy years later, when I participated in the Christian-Marxist dialogue in Europe. His fate was both of historic and of personal interest to me. In 1989, a friend in Munich sent me a biography of his wife, Olga Benario, a fellow native of Munich, though born fourteen years before me, on February 12, 1908. A Jewess and activist fired by communist ideals, the Brazilian police under Filinto Müller did not rest until they had caught and incarcerated her. Although I had read a great deal about the Holocaust, and though my mother's brother and other relatives had been killed by the Nazis, or had committed suicide to escape a worse fate, Olga's biography by Fernando Morais, the minister of culture of the State of São Paulo, moved me at the deepest level, especially in relation to my acute awareness of so many desperate contemporary ills. Reading fifty years later of such individual human courage and endurance vis-à-vis the government's corrupt and heartless sociopolitical agenda, I felt anguished not only about Olga's cruel fate, but also about the tragic irredeemability of politics in the last decades of this century. Olga's photograph on the first page of the book portrays a countenance of such nobility, empathy, and beauty, that one can find but one word to describe her being—diaphanous. Looking into these eyes, I grasped all that has been wrong with humanity to this very day. Olga was put to death in the gas chamber of Bernburg, one hundred kilometers southwest of Berlin, in early 1942, while I was on my way to Brazil.[12]

As we descended the spiral staircase, Maria had only slighting things to say about Luís Carlos Prestes—of course. Years would pass before I learned to relativize and objectify my own thinking on world politics, with its fateful and merciless impact upon human affairs.

I had now spent eight days at the Casa de Correção. I had almost settled in, making a conscious effort not to be despondent, and trying to be as casual as my two women companions. Determined to utilize this period of forced leisure to perfect my knowledge of Portuguese, I assembled pieces of old newspaper, which had been cut up in squares for our use as toilet paper. Once I had memorized all the new words, which the women enjoyed translating and explaining to me, I returned the precious pieces to their place of intended use . . .

Periodically, torrential rainstorms bombarded the old tiles on the roof above with a deafening noise. The first evening it happened—we had just been locked in for the night—a swarm of gigantic cockroaches invaded my cell from the window, flying in freely through the iron bars, crawling over the deep sill, racing along the edges of the floor, settling on walls, and even on my blanket and chair. Some measured four or five inches in length. They completely destroyed my night. I could not turn out the light for fear they might land on me, and was too afraid and disgusted to start killing them. Their erratic behavior kept me alert till dawn. A few moved on to the corridor, while others chased rapidly across the sill, back out into the open. I had always adored animals, and was fascinated by the intricate beauty of insects. But I could not help having an almost irrational revulsion against these shiny, brown, winged creatures with their long, probing feelers. Although I had learned to expect them since my first encounter on the *Siqueira Campos*, I had never come face to face with such monsters, or such numbers; they struck me as a totally different breed. I imagined how this prison without windows must have functioned over the centuries as an ideal refuge from tropical downpours for innumerable generations of roaches. But why *my* cell, with the scores of unlit, uninhabited cells all around me? When I complained to the guard about my sleepless night, he brought me several thick newspapers and a few stones with which to weigh them down on the sill. What a relief! I could now study the papers during the day, and cover the iron bars to keep the roaches out at night.

On the ninth day I was told to ready myself for another move. The news caused me great alarm. It terminated most cruelly what little mental equilibrium I had been able to attain in the less stressful environment of the Casa de Correção. However, my two fellow prisoners believed that the move was a good sign: it showed that someone was working on my case. The guard volunteered that it would be a better and friendlier place. For one thing I had certainly learned to be grateful, especially with my memories of Hitler's Germany: the prison personnel—all men—though short on words, were always helpful and protective. I had not suffered a single indiscretion, nor witnessed any vis-à-vis my cell mates, with the one horrible exception: the screams at the Polícia Central—an experience I was never to shake off. It remained deep within my psyche, whence it would rise whenever I was to read later in the journals of Amnesty International, or in the press, about this torture-inflicting and torture-perfecting world. If I brought myself to read the biography of Olga Benario Prestes from cover to cover, it was to overcome my own cowardice, to honor Olga. If she could suffer such extreme agonies with her head high, while giving solace to others, *I should suffer knowing it:* to be an informed witness to her life, courage, and idealism, and to the bestiality of her colluding killers.

The Black Maria was waiting. We left in daylight, and I could look out through a glass-covered grill in the bolted back door. I remained quite calm and collected as long as we drove through the *bairros* of Rio. But this transfer was to take much longer. We appeared to be going in a northerly direction. We passed factories and then reached open spaces, fields, and trees. The farther and faster we went, the more restless I became. To appease my fears, I tried to rationalize that my third transfer could not possibly be worse than the previous two. Finally, the driver stopped in front of an enormous complex, unbolted the door, and helped me down with my little case. I was startled at what I saw. I stood before a large rectangular enclosure with twelve foot walls, painted in fresh, friendly ochre, the dark rich yellow with which I was so well acquainted from Baroque architecture in Bavaria and Austria. There were no black iron bars in sight. To my complete amazement the doorbell was answered by a nun, who immediately took charge of me with a reassuring smile. I asked her whether I was in a convent now, to which she replied laughing: "I'm afraid not. This is the women's prison of Bangú. But we sisters are in charge." I was first taken to a curtained room with a dozen or more beds, immaculately clean as in a convent school or hospital. She placed my case on "my bed," and allotted me my own washbasin in the shower room, which was lined to the ceiling with snow white tiles. Most of the inner walls and surfaces were white, and the premises could easily have been taken for a well-run sanatorium. An inmate told me that the building was an exact copy of a modern correctional facility for women in the U.S. state of Pennsylvania.

I was not given a prison uniform, and told I could keep on the housecoat I was wearing, though the sister suggested that I had better wash it. The women with whom I shared the bedroom and shower room wore dark blue dresses with white collars, while the vast majority, whom I met in the dining and recreational facilities, were dressed in neat, light beige prison clothes. I was told that most of them were serving time for petty theft and other minor offenses; though some were common criminals, or serving life sentences for murder. My anxious mind was soon to draw the positive conclusion that I would not remain here for too long, for otherwise I would surely have been put in a blue uniform. My roommates seemed more middle-class, and strangely silent about the reasons for their imprisonment. I remember only one foreigner among them; I think she was Hungarian.

Early the next morning we were called to chapel for mass with all the sisters and their superior. I cannot remember whether participation was obligatory, though many prisoners had come. It was a Latin mass, and, as had happened before at Collegio Santo Amaro, the familiar recitation of the words, the sisters' choir and their angelic chant, transported me back to my school days in Tutzing and Garmisch. I drew a deep and consoling strength from the quasi-universal Latin of the Catholic liturgy, from the communion of words and music, and the healing it catalyzed—at least for a while. But there was more to it: I could sing again. How long had I not sung! The same day one of the nuns came up to me with a few sheets of music for mass on Easter Sunday. It appeared the nuns had been impressed with my voice and my knowledge of the Latin texts. They hoped I would agree to sing the solo part, for which I would be free to practice in the chapel as long as I wished. As an added inducement, they held out the promise that all the sisters would pray for my release right *after* Easter, and that, with so much prayer power, my chances should be very good indeed! I was flattered, but, above all, and for the first time since I had left Collegio Santo Amaro, I felt the balm of care.

From a brief conversation I had with the sister-receptionist upon arrival, the word spread among her colleagues that I had been educated in two convent schools, and had spent time with the Missionary Benedictines in the capital. No one could ever have been made to feel more at home in a prison, than I was in Bangú! I practiced every day, and with great pleasure, for the chapel's acoustics were excellent. During these days I reflected frequently on how my voice would have developed, had I been able to work with Erna Morena in Munich. For the first time since leaving Bavaria, I felt the full impact of what it meant to have been forced to let my greatest talent fall by the wayside.

All aspects of prison life, including the quality of food, were much better in Bangú. In good weather, we spent long breaks before the evening meal in the tree-shaded courtyard where I could mingle with, and talk to, anyone I wanted. I was curious to discover the particular reasons for some of the women's imprisonment, to hear their stories and how long they would have to stay in Bangú. I did not know then to what extent Brazilian women were—and still are today in many instances—underdogs before the law. I sat down on the sun-warm tiles of the walkway skirting the building, beside a mixed group of younger and older women. I found it hard to follow their rapid exchanges, because of their accents and manner of speech. Having answered their most immediate questions, I decided to ask a few myself. Nothing could have prepared me for their replies. Of about seven in our circle, one had killed, and one had castrated her husband—drunkards and rapists, who had beaten and abused their children. The women were quite eager to describe in minute detail what had been done to them, and how they had gone about disposing of their men: lots of drink, followed by a hammer on the head for a first knockout; the size and razor sharpness of the knife with which one of the women had cut off her husband's penis, and why and how this was a very difficult thing to do. I did not wish to appear squeamish or lacking in sympathy for their suffering; so, for a while, I stopped asking questions. What insufferable violence, I thought, must these women have endured, to lust for such bloody, fiendish acts of vengeance, and to be able to tell and retell the gruelling stories with glowing eyes, and almost euphoric satisfaction. Or did I misread their motivation? I was too young to judge. Thinking back, it may well have been a question of survival, of retaining their sanity, to exteriorize the dreadful burden of poverty and cruelty weighing down their minds, in order to face life another day. One of the storytellers, quite self-possessed only minutes before, broke into tears as she related the abject humiliations she had endured in her conjugal relationship.

That night I recalled my long conversation with Dona Xeres on the painful double standard and domination to which Brazilian women were subjected. I now discerned that this was true for the rich, *and* for the poor—never mind the niceties of costly legal separations versus violence and murder. I found it very difficult to fall asleep, and not only on account of the graphic stories I had heard. One of the nuns, who had seen me sitting with the group, took me aside after supper to talk to me. In a protective, well-meaning manner she admonished me not to associate with these women. "Nothing good will come of this," she said. "You ought not to expose your mind to their sinful world." Somewhere, deep down, her words left me with an obscure feeling of guilt: not for having listened to the women's sordid tales, but, rather, for receiving so much of the sisters' personal and preferential attention, when, in fact, it was those convicted of crimes with long sentences who had the greatest need for the sisters' understanding and affection. After this experience, my rehearsals lacked the innocent joy and enthusiasm with which I had first undertaken them. I had begun to share a few of the invisible burdens my fellow inmates carried behind their pale, usually impassive faces. Providence alone knew how many tragedies remained untold within these walls, and how much suppressed, harmful suffering was left unarticulated in the absence of an existential, authentically Christian approach to these ravaged women.

It was Good Friday. I had lived in Bangú for almost a week. The sisters were joking about my release on Monday or Tuesday, after the Easter Mass. But it was to be otherwise. A telephone call from the Polícia Central asked for my return to the *detenção*, which the nuns interpreted as a good omen. "Things are moving!" they exclaimed. "You will be set free! It can only be a matter of days now." As I said goodbye, the Mother Superior in charge of the prison came to embrace and bless me. The sister who directed the choir wiped a tear of regret from her eye. The guard with the Black Maria looked on in astonishment as four of the nuns accompanied me beyond the prison threshold.

Arriving at dusk, the dim lights and fearful shadows in the galleries and corridors of the Polícia Central forced me back into the darkest night. There were new faces in the old cell, but I was grateful for anybody's company to save me from my solitary woes—the brooding and weeping, and the crusts under my eyes, suffered during the first week in this inhospitable place. The colonel was to see me another four times; once during the first week to ask more questions about a new assortment of names and situations unknown to me, and, again, in the presence of English and American agents. I then saw him twice in the following three weeks to lay the ground for my release. During our last encounter, he asked me at what time of day I wanted to be driven home. In my excitement I never enquired about the availability of my apartment, and concluded afterwards that he knew the owners of the building had not evicted me for my failure to pay the rent. I replied that I would like to leave at night, and as late as possible, in order to escape the eyes of my neighbors, what with the Black Maria and my dreadful, slovenly appearance. The colonel promised I would be driven by his chauffeur in his own car, and as late as I wished. I was too nervous to take exception to what was clearly a most informal, personal approach to my release. He then picked up a blank sealed envelope from his desk. He handed it to me with a tinge of embarrassment, and with the throwaway remark: "Não è nada—è uma pequena ajuda para vôcé."—"It's nothing; it's just something to help you along." In a similar vein, he added that he felt sorry about the whole affair, and encouraged me to telephone if there was anything he could do to help. He took a pencil and wrote down his office number on a blank slip of paper. He expressed the hope that all would go well for me from now on. Back in the cell I recapitulated what had happened. Curious about the envelope, I went behind the toilet partition to open it as quietly as I could, flushing the bowl at the same time. It contained a few bank notes, but the light was too dim for me to read the amounts. I placed the envelope carefully into the pocket of my housecoat. The colonel's cavalier manner in dispatching me into the outside world caused me considerable apprehension. The greatest, most joyous news in over two and a half months did not feel so liberating and uplifting anymore. Something was fishy. I did not like it at all. But as hard as I would think about the alternatives—handing back the envelope; insisting on a taxi for which I would pay with what was left in my purse—anything I would say or do now might jeopardize my release; and besides, had not every step in the various stages of my detention been totally arbitrary and "informal" . . .

In Search of Freedom

It came almost as a surprise, when, after days of anxious waiting, I was ordered to get ready for my release toward midnight. I shook hands with the women I would leave behind, and paid the guards for the rolls and fruit they had brought me—this time without my having asked. After a last nocturnal walk through the obscure passages, I was politely ushered into a limousine by a chauffeur in uniform. I sat back in the large car with my handbag and small case, feeling quite forlorn. I could not believe it would all be over in half an hour. I felt an eerie disconnectedness as I looked out onto the streets, and watched people walking home, or chatting in cafes. The bright displays in the shop windows belonged to another world. I asked the chauffeur for the name of his boss. I think I heard him say Colonel Olindo Deniz. Now I recognized my own district, up Rua Barata Ribeiro, and then left into my little street leading up the hill. There were people on the sidewalk. I asked the driver to stop a few yards before the entrance door of my building. An awesome sensation came over me as I took my first, unrestricted steps in the breezy night air of Copacabana. I had to think of the giant black inmate at the Casa de Correção, who brought me "breakfast," and who had murdered an inmate rather than face the outside world again. I was terrified lest I meet anyone—with my

216

puffed eyes and limbs, unkempt and overweight, and in a grimy
housecoat I had not been able to wash for a whole month. But I was
lucky.

The simple act of unlocking the door to my apartment, to
which I would not have given a second thought before my imprisonment, now marked the beginning of my transition from captivity
to freedom. I did not switch on the lights. I needed to adjust slowly.
I was afraid of the shock. The street lamps cast their glow upon the
walls, as I walked to the bathroom to shed my soiled clothes. I bun-
dled them away tightly so they would not contaminate the clean
smelling air. I showered and soaped, and showered again, and found
myself humming a tune. I washed my hair. Dried and turbaned I
danced across the rooms. I cried and laughed, and behaved quite in-
sanely. The joys and fears of being free came over me like tidal
waves. I took a dressing gown from my wardrobe, and then sought
the tiny key to my mailbox, which I found in the usual place. There
might be letters from my parents! Bills! I raced downstairs in my
slippers, but the box was empty. Stefan Wertheimer, I thought, may

Renée-Marie Hausenstein and U.S. ensign at the Casino
Atlantico, Copacabana Palace Hotel, Rio de Janeiro, ca.
1942. Courtesy of Renée-Marie Croose Parry.

have taken the mail for safekeeping. Back in my flat, I locked the door behind me, and turned on the lights, one by one. I relished each act as if for the first time. Everything was clean; Ambrosina had not given up on me completely. There were no dead roaches in the kitchen. However, the papers on my table were not stacked the way I had left them, and some seemed to be missing. My books were not in the same order. I wanted to ring Stefan, but I would surely wake him. Oh my God—the telephone! Would it work? I picked up the receiver; it gave the normal dial tone. Who could have paid the bills? At last, I braced myself, and looked into the bathroom mirror. I stepped back aghast. My face appeared several years older, bloated and vulgar. I could only cry. It would be weeks before I dared show myself on the beach—after much exercise and a strict diet. As I scrutinized the kitchen, my brain snapped when my eyes caught sight of the calendar on the wall. No one had torn off the pages—it still read March 9, 1943! What day was it now? May 25, or 26? I left the calendar with its fateful date intact. I would have to wait for morning, and besides what did it matter now—I was free! I opened all the windows. The gentle, mellow breeze brought life to my heavy limbs and dried my tears.

I felt like running; running by the sea! I put on my beach shoes, and a blouse and shorts freshly washed and ironed by Ambrosina. What a luxury! I took my key and flew down the stairs, up the hill, down the steep stone staircase, over Avenida Copacabana, into Rua Fernando Mendez, across Avenida Atlantica—and on to the sand. I took off my shoes and began to run at the water's edge. I was soon out of breath and had to slow down. The sea was unusually calm. White foamy wavelets washed around my ankles. I was intoxicated by the wide open spaces and the salt-laden air. I cleansed my lungs of creosote disinfectant and all the other prison odors, and of the dust and grime breathed at the Polícia Central. I savored the taste of salt on my lips. I drew in the air with my mouth wide open. Filling my lungs with air was like filling them with hope. My personal will, immobilized for weeks on end, grew stronger with every breath. I would straighten out the mess, pay my debts, and leave for the United States as soon as I could find my sponsors and earn my passage!

Ambrosina had been forced to take other work, but she still found time to come and help me. It was a great reunion, as if with an old and tested friend. Some of my adult students accepted my explanation: that the police had made a mistake, a fact which could be verified by ringing Colonel Olindo Deniz. But the parents of my younger pupils were quite curt with their replies. They did not wish their children to have anything to do with me—and that was that. I thus had to rebuild my teaching base from scratch. The money in the envelope was far from sufficient to cover my debts: all the rent and utilities that friends had paid while I was in prison. I decided that the only way I could repay them quickly was to sublet my apartment, and become a lodger as I had been before. With the literal invasion of Rio de Janeiro by more and more Americans, most of whom wanted to live in Copacabana near the beach, rents were rising dramatically, and I could not have chosen a better moment to find a tenant. Saxby, an American friend who lived on the top floor of my building, introduced a newly arrived member of the U.S. Embassy to me, who was delighted with the flat, and willing to take it for one year, while accepting my condition of employing Ambrosina for longer hours and at a better wage than I could have afforded. This arrangement took care of my livelihood, and allowed me to pay back my friends within six months. I could begin to save again with the proceeds from my teaching. The humbling sacrifice of giving up the freedom and amenities of my fledgling home had not been in vain.

Some thirty years later, I was to be reminded of Sam Papich, my friendly, clean, promptly paying tenant, when I read his name in an article about the CIA . . . But the agency did not exist in those days: it was still the FBI and the OSS, and other intermediaries working undercover—and with regard to such matters, I was still a babe in the woods.

Although I had taught French almost exclusively, Brazil's new orientation toward the United States and the Allied cause soon made English the most desired second language. Having learned the rudiments in school, I could now practice it on weekends while playing bridge with American and Puerto Rican acquaintances. Soon I was able to teach English to beginners, and in the evenings often went to see the films of Bette Davis, who was much in vogue at the time. I found her diction to be superlative, the best of any American film star I had ever seen on the screen. In the dark, with a note pad on my lap, I would scribble down words and phrases I wanted to memorize. As I already spoke Portuguese much better than English, the subtitles helped my understanding. I saw her films again and again—three, four, and even more times, until I recognized every word. And, since I had learned so much of my Portuguese vocabulary in the translated novels of Daphne du Maurier, I now turned to her English originals, trying to speed up the learning process.

After my release from prison—or, more accurately, from my multiple detentions—my days were filled with so many demands requiring immediate effort, that there was little time to reflect upon, and digest, what I had suffered. My émigré friends, Susanne Bach, Stefan Wertheimer, Georg Wassermann,[13] Wolfgang Hoffmann-Harnisch, and others, were quite naturally preoccupied with carrying forward their own lives in difficult new circumstances, and were unable to provide me with opportunities for a meaningful, verbal catharsis. Our gatherings were usually lighthearted, with Wassermann often playing the piano to entertain us. In our conversations, my prison experience was generally treated as "one of those unfortunate occurrences in times of war." I was reminded of my good luck in not having been arrested while still in Germany, where I might now be dead! Although common sense told me that this was true, prison had nevertheless left me confused about a host of things. I knew, if only subconsciously, that I would have to come to terms with many of my intangible emotions, learn to digest them, and eventually perhaps even derive benefit from those fateful months. To put it another way: my mind felt like a plowed field, whose furrows remained gaping and painfully empty.

I don't remember how *The Prose of Oscar Wilde* came to stand on my bookshelf. Somebody must have lent it to me, or left it behind. One night, when my lessons were over and I had finished supper, I was drawn by the book's red linen cover and began to thumb through its pages. I found it very difficult reading. My attention was caught by the titles "Letters from Reading Prison" and "De Profundis." Some of the short, lapidary sentences immediately spoke to my condition:

> Behind joy and laughter there may be a temperament, coarse, hard, and callous. But behind sorrow there is always sorrow. Pain, unlike pleasure, wears no mask. [...]
>
> Clergymen and people who use phrases without wisdom sometimes talk of suffering as a mystery. It is really a revelation. One discerns things one never discerned before. One approaches the whole of history from a different standpoint. [...]
>
> To regret one's own experiences is to arrest one's own development. To deny one's own experiences is to put a lie into the lips of one's own life. It is no less than a denial of the soul.

I was deeply moved by Oscar Wilde's insights. Though I had to read many sentences over and over again, and even then did not understand them completely despite the help of my dictionary, I struggled on until I had worked through all the seventy-three pages of "De Profundis." Absorbing these soul-baring thoughts at that moment in time reconciled me with the fears and humiliations of my experience, while simultaneously helping me to transpose them on to another plane: "At every single moment of one's life one is what one is going to be no less than what one has been."

I was touched by his remembrance of these lines from Goethe:

Who never ate his bread in sorrow,
Who never spent the midnight hours
Weeping and waiting for the morrow,—
He knows you not, ye heavenly powers.

Although I had suffered less than three months imprisonment, reading a great and tragically tested writer helped me to integrate my prison experience with my feelings about the past, with my awareness in the present, and into a more balanced approach to the future.

> I have had a year longer of imprisonment, but humanity has been in the prison along with us all, and now when I go out, I shall always re-member great kindnesses that I have received here from almost every-body, and on the day of my release I shall give many thanks to many people, and ask to be remembered by them in turn.
>
> The prison style is absolutely and entirely wrong. I would give any-thing to be able to alter it when I go out. I intend to try. But there is nothing in the world so wrong but that the spirit of humanity, which is the spirit of love, the spirit of the Christ who is not in churches, may make it, if not right, at least possible to be borne without too much bit-terness of heart.[14]

I was now in my twenty-second year. During this long night of reading, literature had entered my life as a potent source for judg-ment and reconciliation, and as a yardstick with which to begin to measure the value of events and people. Oscar Wilde's stirring tes-timony to the evolution of creative human endurance—to the emergence of an informed, constructive humility through a process of sublimation—opened my young eyes to the possibility of genuine transformation through a religious spirit uncluttered by dogmas and judgmental thought: an imploding reality that has its roots in sorrow and suffering.

That night I crossed my first intellectual threshold, taking an independent step no longer directed by parental omniscience. It marked the beginning of a fateful pattern that has accompanied my better self, in which I would find the right book or the right human being whenever it was critical for my rescue, or development as a person.

The next day I went to buy the most beautiful tie I could find. I wrapped it with a note of gratitude to Paulo, my thoughtful guard at the Polícia d'Estrangeiros.

After months of anxious waiting, a letter arrived from my parents, confirming that they were alive and still at the *Buchenhaus*, though I sensed something had happened that they felt unable to communicate. As I would learn much later: while I was in prison my father had been dismissed from the *Frankfurter Zeitung* upon the order of Joseph Goebbels, together with Benno Reifenberg and Dolf Sternberger, depriving them of their livelihoods.[15]

My teaching flourished once again as I found all the work I could handle. Also, my third and fourth languages, Portuguese and English, became more fluent with each passing day. My friendship with Saxby grew more tender. I learned to play a fair hand of bridge, and to prepare deep dish apple pie and pancakes for my American acquaintances. We made exotic excursions to the outskirts of Rio, admiring the breathtaking views of the hills and high ocean breakers along Avenida Niemeyer—and on to Joá; and to the magnificent Botanical Garden, with its palms reaching high into the heavens, often in avenues resembling the naves of Gothic cathedrals. I had worn a light summer dress and sandals, not knowing of the treacherous bites that would be inflicted by *borrachudos*, a special breed of vicious, long-legged mosquitos. Although their stings were barely noticeable at first, my legs swelled up into huge, rigid cylinders over night, preventing me from moving either knees or ankles, and keeping me prostrate for several days under the care of my new landlady. She loved to chat. Relishing her captive audience, she indulged in telling me macabre stories about the *Macumba* fetishes of her religious sect, whose ceremonies seemed to be an amalgam of African and Christian rituals. I had rented a small room from her with a splendid view over Avenida Atlantica, the beach and the sea beyond, in an apartment on one of the upper floors of Edificio Egypto, only a few minutes from my own apartment. It was an exhilarating outlook, but the ocean air gnawed away at the furniture, destroyed mirrors, and attacked my clothes and books, most of which, fortunately, I had left in my flat under the watchful eyes of Ambrosina.

Upon this busy and relatively carefree life, a new menace was to encroach. My widowed landlady, as punctilious as she was nosy, and thus a most reliable transmitter of messages—very helpful if prospective pupils rang, or students wished to change the hour of their lessons—had left an ominous note on my dresser. A call had been received from Colonel Olindo Deniz, who asked me to telephone him at his office as soon as possible. I tried to quell my all too vivid imagination. Yet, no matter how great my apprehension, I realized it would be foolish not to return his call. I did so the next morning. At first it appeared to be no more than a friendly enquiry on his part. How was it going? Was I working? And so on. But then came the question that I had feared. Would I meet him for lunch at a certain restaurant behind Cinelandia, any day that week? Evasive replies flashed through my mind: "Yes, as soon as I have less work," or, "Might I call you back when I have more time?" But I was too fearful to refuse. After all that had taken place, I would only be left in a state of constant worry about his intentions. I preferred to face him and clear the air—if I could. I switched two weekday lessons from lunchtime over to Saturday. I rarely stopped for lunch, munching sandwiches instead as I went to and fro on the bus.

Two days later I was on my way, wearing a sober, tailored dress, in good time to arrive punctually at the appointed place. The restaurant was around the corner from a hairdresser, where I had once experienced the fright of my life: an encounter with a truly gigantic, woolly bodied spider, which, apparently, was so dangerous that everybody present climbed onto their chairs, while the brave proprietor tried to kill it. I hoped that incident would not prove to be an omen! It was the first time I saw the colonel in bright daylight and in civilian clothes. He looked less imposing without his epaulettes, and considerably older. The menu was Portuguese, and he insisted on ordering a fortifying *bife a cavalo*—a steak mounted by a fried egg, and my favorite desert, *creme de abacate com sorvete de creme*—avocado whipped with ice cream. I tried several times to guide the conversation toward the reasons for my imprisonment and its long duration. He eventually blamed it upon the confusion that had followed the drastic changes taking place in the new political climate: while the Polícia Central had already been restaffed under a new Chief of Police, other sections had not—with me caught in the middle. That is why it had taken time, though he had tried his best to set me free.

Toward the end of the meal, during which the colonel asked many questions relating to my work and earnings, he suggested that we take coffee at his apartment—a few steps away—to discuss a very important matter. Why I did not immediately reply: "Can't we discuss it here?" is hard to understand. Looking back, I must assume that the fears I lived with in Nazi Germany, which had been reinforced in Brazil through Helmut's imprisonment, and my own arbitrary arrest, had succeeded in subjugating my will, and in conditioning me not to oppose persons in authority. After all, I had experienced the colonel as one wielding absolute power over me for more than two and a half months. I tried to escape my forebodings by telling myself it could well be his home, and that I might even meet members of his family. But I was quickly disabused of such illusions.

We entered a narrow, tall building with a claustrophobic little elevator. I could see there were at least two or three apartments on each floor, suggesting small size flats. The lift stopped on one of the higher landings. As the colonel unlocked and opened the door, I was able to take in the whole scenario in one split second: the studio apartment was a space-saving feat, with oblique walls and a small, mysterious corridor leading off on one side; the heavy maroon curtains were half drawn over opaque, dingy blinds; a small sofa and two armchairs covered with cheap upholstery surrounded a tiny coffee table on which stood a vase with dust-laden, artificial flowers; facing the window, a huge bed took up every inch of the remaining space, the wooden bed-head repeating touches of the crude art nouveau designs of the lamps and furniture elsewhere in the room. A large, maroon, ersatz-damask bedcover, its valances resting on the polished wooden floor, covered the vast expanse of the bed. In the center sat a huge Spanish doll, with black locks falling on her shoulders and curling up her cheeks; her full yellow skirt neatly draped in a circle, and her stuffed flesh-colored cotton arms opened wide, ever ready to embrace.

My throat tightened as the door closed behind us. I knew I had to act promptly and decisively. "Colonel," I said, looking straight into his eyes, "I suppose you have a daughter?" "Yes, I have two girls." "Am I not the age of your daughters?" I asked. "More or less," he nodded. "Would you want your daughters to be in my situation?" At this question he grew extremely embarrassed, and after an anxious pause said with an assumed calm, "Sit down, please. I have a serious proposition to make to you." I sat down in an armchair, with the length of the coffee table between us. "You don't earn much money with your teaching, and you could do much better," he said. "I would like to suggest that you come to work for us in a special capacity, which would provide a good salary for investigative tasks you may find very interesting." I intuited that my refusal might not have serious repercussions, and even suspected that the offer could have been an improvised retreat from an awkward situation. I tried to find polite, determined words to explain why such activities would be against my very nature. "After so many interrogations, you know this to be true, Colonel, don't you!" He pondered my reply, and hesitated for a moment before rising from his chair. We skirted the width of the bed in the direction of the door. A stone fell off my chest as we left this miserable place. Once in the lift, I put my hand on his arm, and said: "You were always correct towards me, Colonel, and, under the circumstances, perhaps even thoughtful. I shall always be grateful to you for that." A tired smile passed over his face as we shook hands, before going our separate ways. It had been a delicious, but very trying lunch . . . I would not hear from the colonel again.

As my teaching activity expanded, I was able to save more and more for the realization of my dream: to emigrate to the United States. I had at last established contact with the von Faber du Faurs, and with Kurt and Helen Wolff, who, I discovered, had founded a new publishing house in New York from their apartment in Greenwich Village.[16]

My friend Saxby helped smooth the way for me at the American Embassy. I completed the never ending forms, and submitted to the fingerprinting required for immigration, so that everything would be ready once the war in Europe had ended. No one explained to me that owing to the war the German quota was totally undersubscribed, and that, with reputable sponsors, there could be no plausible reason for a U.S. visa to be denied. I thus lived with this uncertainty for a very long time. Yet, the experience added to the growing mystique that I was already absorbing with every new issue of *Time* and *Life*—obligatory reading among my friends from the United States. I was flattered and proud at the time, when a large spread about Rio de Janeiro in *Life* magazine, covering a penthouse party to which I had been invited, showed us, cocktails in hand, looking down upon the crescent beach and the foaming breakers beyond.

As the months and years passed, I began to realize that the swelling American presence in Rio was not simply confined to business interests and military strategy, but that most of the people with whom I happened to become acquainted were linked to U.S. intelligence. Although Saxby's official employment was with the R.K.O. movie company, it soon became apparent that he had been detailed to Brazil by the FBI. I had great difficulty understanding how a Christian Scientist, a thoroughly likable and honest man, deeply devoted to his parents and sister—a reporter for the widely known and respected *Christian Science Monitor*—could choose to work "undercover." But after my own encounters with the Vargas regime, and my trials and tribulations caused by the Fifth Column and the Brazilian police, I was more than willing to give the United States every benefit of the doubt. My total ignorance of the more complex issues in world politics allowed me to believe what I was being told by all my U.S. friends: that the United States of America was the most just, the most democratic, the most sympathetic and benign nation on earth. Besides, America had joined the war against Hitler and was likely to contribute to the liberation of my mortally endangered parents—if indeed they would still be alive.

Concomitant with these beliefs, I fell easy victim to the view that appearances, material abundance, and moralistic code words— not to mention the ubiquitous influence of the men in snow white, gold-braided uniforms—were *proof* of the great qualities of the United States. With European civilization on its knees, and the Catholic Church in Brazil so discredited in my eyes through its collusion with temporal power, what new parameters, what credible, countervailing influences were there to hold me back from confusing appearance with substance, or "economic development" with social justice—especially when vaunted in the name of freedom and liberty?

The war in Europe came to an end on May 8, 1945. The last letter received from Madrid was of November 19, 1944, written by Maria Caballero herself. When I saw the envelope, I feared the worst. Some sentences had been rendered illegible by the censor. Although she conveyed in veiled language that her daughters, Lolita and Charito, saw my parents often, and that my father and mother were in good health and sent their love, the fact that they did not write themselves raised my fears for them to new heights.

Something, I suspected, must have happened to prevent their writing in the last months of the war, during which Hitler had made such insane attempts to hold out at all cost and by all means. The last letter in my parents' own hands was of February 1944. It had included the request that I try to obtain word from my mother's mother Gabrielle, and from her brother Alfred, in Brussels, as my parents were without news of them, and desperately worried. I had already written several times to my grandmother Gabrielle without receiving a response, and shared my parents' grave anxiety.

With the Allied victory in Europe, my plans for immigration to the United States took on a new momentum. I was eager to straighten out my personal affairs, and took steps to obtain a *Desquite Amigável*—a lawful, amicable separation. During these proceedings an elderly judge proposed several times, and with considerable insistence, that I demand alimony to guarantee my livelihood. When I explained why this would be anathema to my way of thinking, he warned me that I might be very sorry when I grew older or infirm, or if illness should prevent me from working. With the good health and insouciant optimism of my twenty-three years, I reasserted that I would be able to manage by myself, and abrogated my rights to any part of Helmut's fortune. Finally, and although I was advised that the validity of a Mexican divorce—not recognized in Brazil—might be disputed in other countries, I nevertheless instructed a lawyer to obtain it for me. The document was executed in Cuernavaca in the State of Morelos, with a variety of imposing stamps and seals.

A whole year would pass before my visa was issued and I could buy my air ticket to the United States. Happily, I was able to spend the last few months in the comfort of my own apartment. On weekends I made certain to visit all the landmarks in and around Rio that I had not yet seen. These included such "tourist musts" as the Corcovado, where, most spectacularly, upon a rock 2,300 feet above the bay of Rio, a giant Christ figure had been erected in 1931, standing 98 feet high. With arms stretched out dramatically, this gigantic monument was to remind the world that love is the essence of Christ's teaching. But I knew in my heart that these arms could not encompass all the misery crying to high heaven from the *favelas* of Rio de Janeiro. Fifty years later Christ's towering presence above Rio still remains more an attraction for tourists, than a spur to the conscience of Brazil's rich and powerful to design a system of social justice for the now more than doubled, and ever growing, masses of the poor—including the seven million homeless children, roaming the streets and combing garbage dumps in the big cities.

On the other side of Rio, beyond the seaside districts of Copacabana, Ipanema, and Leblon, lay a magnificent winding road leading up to glorious vantage points, more breathtaking than the *corniches* on the Côte d'Azur. The intensity of the sun reflecting from the ocean and from the luscious greens of the abundant tropical vegetation, the luminescent, exhilarating atmosphere—everything conspired to highlight nature and the people moving in it, as I had never seen before.

During my last days I discovered the work of a Brazilian architect, whose discreet, light hand enabled him to design buildings that stood up to the challenge of this ebullient nature, not by competing with it, but by blending into and being enhanced by their natural surroundings. I am speaking of the world renowned Oscar Niemeyer, who contributed so much to Brazilian architectural culture, in Rio and elsewhere. Although I know the following only from pictures, his Island Restaurant built in 1942, and his Church of St. Francis, completed in 1943, both in Pampulha in the state of Minas Gerais, are typical examples of the grace and curvaceous flow, the cooling use of light and shade, so characteristic of his creations. Coming from Hitler's Germany, I had never seen modern architecture less monumental or aggressive, exuding such empathy and respect for nature, even in the construction of ministries and other public buildings.

On a different, more intimate scale, the display windows of Rio's jewelers rivalled the radiant splendor and brilliancy of this city's place in nature. As I passed their shops I would find myself glued to the ground, admiring the raw nuggets and iridescent gems, delicately mounted rings, bracelets and broaches, as one would contemplate great works of art. I had long dreamed of bringing my mother a translucent amethyst ring set in gold, to wear with her antique necklace of sculpted opaque amethysts. I also yearned to own such a ring myself, with a matching pair of ear clips. I learned much later that amethyst is the talismanic stone of Aquarians, and wondered whether my love for such deep lustrous violet was not more than a coincidence! A friend helped me find two large, and two small, perfect stones and an imaginative, but reasonable, jeweler, who mounted the stones to designs we collaborated to produce. The outcome gave me a thrillingly creative satisfaction. I also bought my first wristwatch on a slender bracelet of Brazilian eighteen-karat, warm reddish gold, and a ring I had flirted with for well over a year. When I found it still sitting in the corner of the window, I quieted my conscience by telling myself that, besides being a good investment, it was obviously meant for me: an auburn, radiant, burnt topaz, set against five, tiny, scintillating diamonds. It fitted perfectly on my left little finger. I also fell for a gorgeous handbag, crafted with the finest crocodile from the beast's underbelly, glossy rust, set in a heavy frame of highly polished brass. Such was the quality of merchandise in those days, that the bag remains unchanged after almost fifty years; although, as a concerned environmentalist, I would not have purchased it today. . . Finally, I chose a handsome wallet and belt in black tinted crocodile for my father.

I realized that I was racing ahead of myself in gathering these presents, but either my subconscious knew that I would find my parents alive, or my love for them and my nostalgia made me believe that if I pretended hard enough the miracle would happen. Indeed, their first, long, personal postwar letter, written immediately after liberation in May 1945, arrived in the autumn confirming that they had survived the terror. Subsequent letters also reached me with many months delay. Strangely, it was much harder to correspond after the end of the war, under U.S. occupation, than it had been previously via Spain. In his second letter, my father asked me to get in touch with José António Quelho Benton, president of the Academia Goetheana in São Paulo, who, a few years later, would invite him to become a Corresponding Member, honoring the publication of his book, *Zwiegespräch über den Don Quichote*.[17] My father suggested I enquire whether, with Benton's help and intervention, he might be able to build a life in Brazil that would accord with his intellectual interests in the literature, art, and general history of Europe, whilst also allowing time for both my father and mother to recuperate from the semistarvation they had endured, and for my father to treat his heart ailment that had worsened significantly during the twelve years of Hitler's rule. Quelho Benton confirmed my apprehension, and agreed that there existed little prospect for a positive, mutually satisfying solution in Brazil. I remembered only too well the difficulties and disillusionment surrounding Stefan Zweig's immigration, and also feared that my parents would not be able to endure the extreme summer heat. Unfortunately, because of the inhuman delays of correspondence with the U.S. Zone of Occupation in Bavaria, my parents had not yet received the letter in which I had explained in considerable detail my intended move to the United

States. In fact, I was growing more and more anxious to leave for the U.S., from where I hoped it would be safer and more expeditious to send medicine and food, of which my parents were now in dire need. I also thought at the time that the United States might prove to be a more propitious country in which to start a new life, should their wish to emigrate persist.

When my father was forced to leave the *Frankfurter Zeitung* in the beginning of 1943, he lost his last possibility of working and being published as a writer. My parents only survived the last two years of the war through the generosity of friends, and by borrowing money from them—as well as through the sale of their dining-room furniture, which had been custom-made for them in Munich in the late twenties. During this period my father worked on several books, the completed manuscripts of which he would place in a drawer of his desk in the hope of being able to publish after Hitler's defeat: in particular, the first volume of his autobiography, *Lux Perpetua*; a monograph on Charles Baudelaire with translations of his poems; and a further volume of translations of French poetry from Chénier to Mallarmé. My parents' postwar desire to leave Germany, in seeming contradiction of their earlier determination to stay on, was a reaction to the catastrophic bombing to which German cities had been subjected, and their inability to visualize the resuscitation of the country within their lifetime. Their health too had been severely undermined by having lived in constant fear and anxiety for twelve years, and with too little food and medicine during the war. My father's heart ailment had grown much worse, and my mother was suffering atrocious pains from pernicious gallstones, brought on by so much worry, and not least by the news that her brother had been killed in a concentration camp, as had several other relatives—if they had not committed suicide.

It was June 1946, and only six weeks until my flight to Miami. I began to wind down my lessons, and to pay my last visits to the few friends who had made a real difference to my life—especially at the Collegio Santo Amaro. The U.S. Embassy now required a paper from the police certifying that I had not been accused or convicted of any crime. This was obtained after considerable struggle with the Brazilian bureaucracy. American friends provided the necessary references. The final heap of documents was at least one and a half inches thick, and I was forced to buy a special handbag, large enough to carry this enormous dossier. I was also given a host of addresses by my friends, and especially that of Saxby's family, whom I hoped to meet if ever I traveled to Washington, D.C.

A small group of friends came to see me off, and admired my trio of pigskin-covered suitcases, which I now rued to have bought—so ostentatious in their pristine splendor! I boarded the PAA twin-engine, propeller-driven plane bound for Belém do Pará on the north coast, east of the Amazon delta, where we were to spend the night. As I flew out over the ocean, I thought of Ambrosina, wondering how she would fare in life. I had grown very fond of her, and had given her most of my household possessions. I had also provided her with the names of well-paying American families in need of reliable assistance. Although her state of functional illiteracy would inhibit her from trying to write to me, I did not doubt that she would make her way.

My departure from Rio caused me no regrets; neither did I feel bitterness. I was alive and well. Whatever could have happened to me in Nazi Germany would have been infinitely worse. I had learned a great deal, not least to fend for myself in difficult circumstances, and had acquired the solid knowledge of two more languages. I was more self-confident than when I first arrived in Rio, less than four and a half years earlier. I would certainly not miss the macho double standard; the disdain for working women that classed them unfit for admission to "society"; nor the constant and painful irritation about my own impotence vis-à-vis the obscene disparity between the rich and the poor, and the deplorable role of the Catholic Church, then standing silent, if not colluding in the persecution of those involved with progressive initiatives.

During my journey north, I befriended an intelligent and helpful woman from eastern Europe, who was probably in her early forties, and had often traveled between Brazil and the United States. Not only was the flight more instructive and reassuring at her side, but she cleverly arranged for a special favor from the crew, so that I was allowed to sit in the cockpit during the overflight of the eastern Amazon region, both before our Belém landing, and, more importantly, the following morning. As far as the eye could see, the earth was covered with dense virgin forest—an undulating carpet of multishaded green crowns. Intermittent clearings drew my attention to neat circles of small round huts, roofed with Chinese looking hats of reed. I have forgotten the name of the Indian tribe the captain mentioned. He explained that except for overflights such as ours, these native Brazilians still lived quite out of touch with the world.

We arrived in the late afternoon, and saw little of Belém. For the first time I slept under a mosquito net, in a spotlessly clean guesthouse with shining hardwood floors. The flight across the breadth of the Amazon delta, during the forenoon of the next day, was a powerful experience. The only body of water I would see in later life, flowing as massively and relentlessly, and with a similar color of light muddy clay, was the mighty Yangtze in China. But the thick jungle and virgin forests, stretching away from the banks of the Amazon, gave the river a much richer and more mysterious appearance. I can only shudder with despair at the thought of the destruction of lands and native peoples that has been wrought there since. Although I saw but a minuscule part of the enormous territory surrounding the Amazon—forty percent of Brazil's landmass— I readily believe the claim that in its former, pristine state this great basin provided the planet earth with fifty percent of all land-emanating oxygen.

ONE DAY IN MIAMI

We landed at Miami airport before midnight in the last days of July 1946. I was thrilled and excited to have brought the project, begun in Rio de Janeiro three years earlier, to a successful conclusion. My travel companion insisted on staying at my side. She had been a refugee and an immigrant, and knew those accelerated heartbeats from personal experience. . . She would take no chances with her adopted protégée. The inspector at the immigration desk was perplexed at the sight of so much paperwork, when I handed over the large envelope. He disappeared with it and left us waiting for two hours. I don't know whether he thought he should seek advice, or whether he found the documents irresistible reading; but it must have been 2 A.M. by the time we left the airport. I felt sorry for my friend, although she remained unflustered and took it all in her stride.

Rooms had been reserved for us by Pan American Airways in a Miami hotel, and the two of us took a taxi with a friendly driver, who made admiring remarks about the quality of our Brazilian luggage. It was nearly three o'clock in the morning when we registered at the reception desk. My friend filled in the card and was given her key, while I struggled to complete mine. The receptionist watched as I applied my signature at the bottom, and having looked at it said without a muscle moving in his face: "Sorry, the lady here took our last room," pointing at my friend. I reminded him that Pan American Airways had made reservations for all passengers in transit, and suggested that he must be mistaken. But he was adamant that there was no room for me. Suddenly, as if she had remembered something of which she had not thought before, my companion threw her room key on the desk, tore up her registration card which was still lying on the counter, and declared indignantly: "I know what's going on here. I will have no part of it!" She took me by the arm, called the bell-boy, who had been watching over the trolley with our luggage, and, seeing new arrivals coming through the revolving door, exclaimed in a clear voice: "No decent person should stay at this hotel!" Having reached the sidewalk she led me to a plaque on the wall, where I read in relatively small script, under the large letters giving the name of the hotel, the word: RESTRICTED. "What on earth does this mean?" I asked innocently. "Let's get away from here," she said, "I'll explain in the taxi." We drove to another hotel which she knew from previous years. On the way she tried to convey to me as tactfully as possible the cause of what we had just experienced. "Your name," she pointed out, "ends in 'stein.' In the United States it is quite automatically assumed that any name with this ending must be Jewish. There are quite a few hotels in Miami that refuse to receive Jews." I looked at her in utter disbelief. "Yes, all is not perfect here, as you will soon find out. It was bad luck that it had to be your first impression." When I begged her to explain the reason for this discrimination, she circumvented my question as delicately as she could, and said that I would come to understand, though never to excuse the practice, if I lived in New York for any length of time. I realized I had asked an awkward question, and though I was dying to understand, I did not want her to lose more sleep on my account as her connecting flight was leaving in the morning. When we said goodbye to each other, I could not help but joke about the irony of the receptionist's conclusion, since my father's family name had been traced back to wayward aristocrats in the thirteenth century—among them robbing knights on the highways of the Holy Roman Empire. We both had a good laugh, and I was glad that we could part on this light note. What would I have done without this thoughtful fellow passenger on my first night in the United States!

Alone in my room, I travailed over the implications of what had just happened to me on my first visit to an American hotel. Since my mother had never imparted Jewish religiosity to me, beyond her innate Jewish Belgian culture, my Bavarian, rural, Catholic environment and schooling, and the intensity of my father's Christian humanism, had been the main determinants of my personal identity. Although the receptionist had indeed been mistaken in the literal sense, he had, unknowingly, been right in a Jewish interpretation of my descendance, in which the *mother* is the decisive factor in denominating a person's racial and religious lineage. The hotel employee had, in fact, applied the yardstick of Hitler's law, by judging my racial descent, albeit erroneously, according to my father's name. Although this rejection conjured up memories I had so wanted to forget, the belief I had formed in the ideals of American democracy allowed me to fall asleep still clinging to my hopes for the future.

I was booked to take a plane in the afternoon for New York, from where I would catch a train to New Haven, Connecticut, the university town in which Curt and Emma von Faber du Faur had made their home. Professor von Faber du Faur had sold his huge, fabulous library of Baroque literature to Yale, where he now taught and worked amongst his books. After a restless night I woke early. There were several hours to spare before the flight. As I had done on my first day in Rio, I enquired at the desk whether there was a bus stop near by. I wanted to make a partial tour of the city and be back in time to drive to the airport. I boarded a bus through the middle door, and took a seat right there near the steps. I could feel the eyes of my neighbor looking at me, and turned towards her. She seemed aghast. I self-consciously checked the buttons of my blouse, my skirt—everything was in order. I glanced into my little hand mirror, and could see no makeup smudges on my face. I held my purse ready to pay the fare. The bus attendant walked toward me from the front of the bus, and with a heavy southern drawl said something that sounded like "You've got to move Ma'am; up there in front where you belong." As I could not understand why I should move, and assumed I had misunderstood him, I said: "I am perfectly comfortable and like sitting near the door. How much do I owe you to the end of the line and back to where I got on?" Instead of giving me a civil answer, he threatened in a loud voice that he would have the bus halted and order me off. At this point the black lady to my right, and a black man sitting behind me, both urged me to comply. "Do as he says Ma'am!" "Please don't make trouble Ma'am!" Looking back to the rear of the bus, I now noticed that there were only

234

black people sitting there. I could not believe what was happening to me. None of my U.S. friends in Brazil, none of the books I had read, had warned me of racial segregation in the United States. As I could feel the atmosphere growing more and more tense, and did not want to cause an uproar on my first day in the country, I decided to move. I turned to my neighbor and apologized, and then said loudly, so everyone around me could hear: "I'm sorry to be so ignorant. I've just arrived from Brazil where people of all colors sit just where they please!" I took a seat in front and asked my white neighbor whether this separation of blacks and whites was practiced everywhere in the United States. He shrugged his shoulders with an impish smile, and gave no reply.

As I flew north that afternoon, I wondered how I would come to terms with the experiences I had met with in Miami. If this was democracy, how would I live with it?

PART 4

RESTITUTION

TRUDI LANDAU

In her analysis of war restitution, Trudi Landau relates how the Federal Republic tried to compensate her and her mother for tangibles, such as the loss of their property, and intangibles, such as the loss of their freedom. It was not until 1945 that the world realized how much six years of war had devastated human life and property. Although the Federal Republic of Germany paid official indemnification to the state of Israel and to the Jewish people from 1953 to 1965, the proceedings for restitution began long before. Chaim Weizmann, on behalf of the Jewish Agency, presented the first official claims for restitution of property on September 20, 1945, to the governments of the Soviet Union, France, Britain, and the United States.[1]

After Israel became a state in 1948, it became clear that both the new Jewish state and the world Jewish organizations were the most appropriate parties to make restitution claims on behalf of the Jewish people. The government of Israel submitted a note to the four occupying powers on January 16, 1951, demanding that the existing legislation be expanded, that the Federal Republic of Germany share the financial responsibility for indemnification, and that the process of restoring and transferring property and funds to claimants living outside of Germany be accelerated.[2]

On March 12, 1951, Israel sent a second note to the Allied powers, which eventually became the cornerstone of negotiations for reparations.[3] For the first time, the demand for collective indemnification was explained in great detail. It called for compensation of the 500,000 Jews who had been the victims of Nazi persecution, and who had emigrated to the *Yishuv* (the Jewish community in Palestine before the state of Israel was established) and later to Israel. The cost per person was estimated at $3,000, adding up to a total of $1.5 billion. Israel asked for $500 million from East Germany and $1 billion from West Germany. The note also emphasized that there could be no form of restitution for the crime of genocide, hence no atonement by material means.[4] The claimants were known collectively as the Claims Conference—the conference on Jewish Material Claims against Germany. The claims were made on behalf of the victims of Nazism, the Jewish people, the State of Israel, and the half-million victims who were now living in the newly formed state.

West Germany agreed to pay reparations even though it was not bound to do so by international law. Much of the credit for Germany's actions at this time is due Chancellor Konrad Adenauer, who was deeply aware of Germany' moral responsibility toward the Jews. He admitted Germany's guilt and did not wait for the West to pressure him into action.

Although the note of March 1951 was not addressed to West Germany, Adenauer responded to it in a positive manner. On September 27, 1951, at a meeting of the Bundestag, he declared that reparations to the Jewish people and restitution for Jewish property be made. He stated that Germany was obligated to make material and moral amends for the horrible crimes that it had committed against the Jewish people. With this declaration the Federal Republic of Germany assumed responsibility for Nazi war crimes.[5]

Despite heated debate, Israel's parliament, the Knesset, voted to enter into negotiations with West Germany in January of 1952. On September 10 of the same year, Israeli Foreign Minister Moshe Sharett and West German Chancellor Konrad Adenauer met in Luxembourg to sign the Reparations Agreement between Israel and the Federal Republic of Germany. The final agreements between the Federal Republic and the Claims Conference were not approved until March 1953. In the agreement with Israel, West Germany promised to pay Israel $845 million over a period of twelve to fourteen years in the form of goods. Israel would give $110 million of this to the Claims Conference, whose funds were used to assist Jewish organizations, institutions, and communities in thirty-nine countries. The Federal Republic of Germany honored all its obligations.[6]

The Bundestag passed a law regarding restitution that went into effect for all parts of the Federal Republic of Germany and West Berlin on October 1, 1953. Unlike reparations, restitution was made to individuals to compensate them for loss of education and opportunity, loss of property, and other suffering incurred during the Nazi period. The Restitution Law was fully observed, just as the Reparations Agreement was. Since 1956, as a result of negotiations between the Federal Republic and the Claims Conference, the scope of restitution has been increased far beyond what was originally planned. The former West German government estimated in 1978 that a sum of 85 billion German marks will have been paid to the victims of Nazism by the year 2000. In contrast, the former government of the German Democratic Republic never recognized the Jewish people's right to indemnification and restitution.[7]

WIEDERGUTMACHUNG — A PERSONAL VIEW

BY TRUDI LANDAU

This is the word the German authorities used to describe the legal proceedings begun in the fifties, that were to determine how much money Jews should receive, who, rich or poor, had been robbed, persecuted, humiliated, or driven insane. Restitution was due to Jews whose families were killed, whose lives were destroyed or otherwise damaged by the Nazi regime for the unique reason that they were Jews, no matter how long they had been German citizens or what their contribution to German society had been. The government also gave lifetime pensions to the widows of men killed by the Nazis—pensions that widows and orphans of dead soldiers are entitled to.

I think the word *Wiedergutmachung* (restitution) is inappropriate, as it means literally "make good again." How can one make up for murdering a family and for destroying a young person's chance to study, work, or choose a career? Nevertheless, the German government did do something toward making up for the atrocities of the Nazi regime. I know of no other government in Europe that would have done the same. Those French, Polish, Yugoslavian, Lithuanian, Russian, and other collaborators who helped the Nazis deport and kill Jews never really admitted their deeds and the new governments refused to take any responsibility for what had happened.

In Brazil I have lived during a period when the military dictatorship killed hundreds of young idealists only for having said or written something in opposition to the political status quo; killed in the insane rage that reigns everywhere as soon as absolute rule is established. There has not been one case in which the government would even consider help or financial compensation. And what has Argentina done in the case of those *desaparecidos* (missing persons) whose mothers are still wondering what happened to them?

For my mother to receive either a lifelong pension from Germany or compensation for specific losses or damages, she had to fill out forms, describe situations, furnish testimonies, and spend a few years waiting, while a lawyer or some other knowledgeable person handled the claims. Some Jews worked directly with attorneys in Germany, others handled it through intermediaries who became specialized in these kinds of legal procedures.

I have kept hundreds of letters and am today aware of how difficult it is to deal with the German bureaucracy. The various items were treated separately, such as *Gesundheitsschaden* (damage to health); *Schaden an beruflichem Fortkommen* (damage to professional career); *Ausbildungsschaden* (damage to education), or impossibility of studying because of Nazi restrictions and persecutions; *Vermögensschaden* (damage to belongings); and *Schaden an Freiheit* (damage to liberty).

At first, I took no initiative because I had no information on how to proceed. My mother, who was living with her second husband in Petropolis, State of Rio, had already filed restitution claims in her name as well as mine, because we were my father's heiresses. Both of us were entitled to compensation for unemployment, expenses, and family possessions left behind including Nazi confiscation of jewelry and silver. Correspondence concerning this matter began at the end of 1955 and was handled by Mr. H. Utecht in Essen, Germany, who had been recommended to my mother.

Many agencies had been created for the sole purpose of confirming eligibility and furnishing proof of injury or loss for restitution claims. The first compensation of this type was finally made in July, 1960, when mother and I received a sum totalling DM 5,700.00.

We also had a right to compensation for the windows that were broken during the *Kristallnacht*, for house and store furniture we were forced to sell, and for the loss of our business. Because of the boycotts and Nazi propaganda, Germans were, of course, afraid to buy at our shop and we had to sell it. This last item, in German, is called: *Verlust des Goodwills der Firma Albert Joseph.*

I filed many claims. The first loss suffered was the loss of my educational opportunities, called *Ausbildungsschaden,* or damage to education. For this, Mr. Utecht received a copy of my report card from my old school in Opladen, the *Marienschule Armer Dienstmägde Jesu Christi.* The copy of the original of April 1937 was dated June 13, 1956. I look upon it today with a smile. I was only satisfactory in music, sewing and handwriting (and this continues today), but I was good in all the other subjects and very good in German. I find this very ironic since Hitler had declared me foreign rabble.

My mother served as a second witness who, of course, confirmed what a clever and dedicated pupil I had always been—even though she was never aware of the sense of humor I had had as a child. Adults were always keen to talk to me and laughed a lot when they heard my opinions and analyses. I had charm.

It took Mr. Utecht five typewritten pages to substantiate my claim. Nearly six years later, in January 1962, he told me that I had finally received DM 5,000.00 as compensation for the loss of educational opportunities, which would have changed my life. Four years later, in March 1966, I received an additional DM 5,000.00, because I had been entitled to DM 10,000.00.

Another damage was to my career. This claim was filed in June 1956 and remained unsettled for years. On January 1, 1939, I was fired from my job when the firm Stierstadt and Co. in Cologne was "aryanized." Mr. Utecht had to get proof of my employment from people in Germany by tracing them. I still remembered a few names of the people with whom I had worked at that time. I was a foreign language secretary.

Alfred Stierstadt, the Jewish owner, and the other Jewish employees could not be found. If they had not left Germany in time, they were probably murdered. The man who had taken over, Kurt Sindern, had gone bankrupt in 1951, as Mr. Utecht later discovered. But then he had the good fortune to find the former executive secretary Arthur von Beckerath, whose address he got through the *Einwohnermeldeamt* in Cologne. Beckerath confirmed my statement. Under the circumstances, in 1939, I could not have found another job in Germany and also had no other means of earning money.

I also had been unable to work while in Belgium and France, because I had to live *incognita* during the war. When I arrived in Brazil in 1946, I did not speak the language nor did I know anything about the laws and customs. I had to learn Portuguese and wasn't able to work until 1949. Mr. Utecht asked me for statements of my earnings where I had worked, and in late 1962 I received DM 10,292.00 as *Wiedergutmachung* for damage to my career.

I was also compensated for the personal things I had left behind in Cologne and Brussels. My "fortune" had consisted of a bicycle and an Erika typewriter. As for the required list of other items, I intimated that it was impossible for me, in 1956, to remember how many skirts, blouses, shoes, dresses, and underwear I had had, especially considering how much had happened since then. The fact was that I had practically nothing, save a suitcase.

To my surprise, Mr. Utecht traced the sparse savings I had abandoned at the bank in Cologne-Ehrenfeld in 1939, money that had been devaluated because the old Reichsmark had been converted to the Deutschmark. Mr. Utecht figured that there was DM 27,84 left in my account.

I have a separate file on "loss of liberty," a thing which is difficult to calculate in monetary terms. How can one compensate a person for the loss of liberty? The correspondence goes back and forth from 1956 to 1964, containing my testimony and explanations required by the German authorities along with their arguments justifying the sum they were willing to pay. This amount of money was their estimate of how badly I was affected by the loss of liberty. In the end, Mr. Utecht persuaded me to accept their proposal.

The specific periods during which I was imprisoned or illegally detained are as follows:

Prison in Brussel-Forest	Oct. 16–Nov. 13, 1939
Camp de Rassemble	May 18–May 28, 1940
Camp de Gurs	May 29–Aug. 13, 1940
Nice, illegal residency	Aug. 2–Oct. 1, 1942
Nice, women's prison	Oct. 2, 1942–Jan. 2, 1943
Southern France, illegal residency	Feb. 1943–Aug. 8, 1944

Those periods covered the days, months, and years during which I was effectively imprisoned and/or was in a situation where I was in danger of being imprisoned or deported. As a matter of fact, I was once arrested for carrying false papers, which led to a three-month prison sentence in Nice. I had been caught with a false identity card that bore the name Madeleine Thomas. After I left prison, the French Resistance provided me again with a new identity, this time that of a Madeleine Lafarge. Madeleine was a person I liked very much (the wife of cousin Otto Weil) and Lafarge had been one of the officials who had been in the army with my husband, Jeannot. This was the inspiration for this name.

After I filled out questionnaires, Mr. Utecht had to find women who could confirm my testimony and then had to solicit declarations from them. These girls had been in France with me, but had since moved to other countries. They were all in distant lands, one living in Perpignan, France, the second in the U.S.A., and the third in Ottawa, Canada. These three girls, who had all since married, were asked to send declarations to Utecht to testify that I was real and not a figment of my imagination, as one might have thought I was.

For my loss of liberty and all the horrible years I spent hiding, running, and suffering, I received less than I had received for my interrupted education. They gave me DM 3,450.00.

The Rio de Janeiro morning paper *O Globo* published an article about the *Wiedergutmachung* on November 11, 1979. An entire page was devoted to the article, which contained interviews with Jews in Brazil who were receiving or had received money from the German government through the program. I was one of the ones interviewed and gave them a considerable amount of information. A friend of ours, a lawyer in Rio who had taken care of many such cases, called me on the telephone and insulted me for having made certain details public. I told him to go to hell and said that I saw no reason to keep any of it secret.

I know that many Jews did not discuss the *Wiedergutmachung* with outsiders for their own reasons. Maybe they felt ashamed of having accepted money which, in my opinion, we certainly deserved. One reason for concealing this information was probably the fact that they did not change the money into local currency at banks at the current rate of exchange, which was always below the black market rate. Another reason was that the recipients often didn't declare the money for income tax purposes. Because I wanted to avoid complications, I declared it from the beginning as "Money, free of taxes, received in 1962 and in following years from the German government for material and moral damage suffered under the Nazi regime."

NOTES

All notes are the editor's, unless otherwise noted.

Introduction

1. Fernando Morais, *Olga*, trans. Ellen Watson (New York: Grove Press, 1990). Ruth Werner, *Olga Benario: Die Geschichte eines tapferen Lebens* (Berlin: Verlag Neues Leben, 1961).

2. Marion A. Kaplan, *The Making of the Jewish Middle Class: Women, Family, and Identity in Imperial Germany* (New York: Oxford University Press, 1991). Claudia Koonz, *Mothers in the Fatherland* (New York: St. Martin's Press, 1987). Renate Bridenthal, Atina Grossmann, and Marion Kaplan, eds., *When Biology Became Destiny* (New York: Monthly Review Press, 1984).

3. Sidonie Smith, *A Poetics of Women's Autobiography* (Bloomington: Indiana University Press, 1988), 16. Smith describes these as *aute* (sense of identity), *bios* (experience), and *graphia* (textuality). See also Elaine Martin, ed., *Gender, Patriarchy, and Fascism in the Third Reich: The Response of Women Writers* (Detroit: Wayne State University Press, 1993), 169–200.

4. Bella Brodzki and Celeste Schenk, eds., *Life/Lines: Theorizing Women's Autobiography* (Ithaca: Cornell University Press, 1988), 8.

5. Elizabeth W. Bruss, *Autobiographical Acts: The Changing Situation of a Literary Genre* (Baltimore: Johns Hopkins University Press, 1976), 33–92. See also Smith, *Women's Autobiography*, 46.

6. Telephone conversation with Renée-Marie Croose Parry, March 1994.

7. Carolyn G. Heilbrun, *Writing a Woman's Life* (New York: Ballantine Books, 1988).

8. Annelise Strauss, "A Story of My Life" (manuscript, private collection, São Paulo, Brazil, 1991), 6.

9. Hertha Spier, "Das Leben in Auschwitz und Bergen-Belsen" (manuscript, private collection, Porto Alegre, Brazil, 1957), 2.

10. Esther Katz and Joan Miriam Ringelheim, eds., *Proceedings of the Conference on Women Surviving the Holocaust* (New York: Institute for Research in History, 1983), 17–19.

11. Eva Hirschberg, "Als die Männer im Lager waren" (manuscript, private collection, São Paulo, Brazil, 1975), 6.

12. Trudi Landau, "My Life Story" (manuscript, private collection, São Paulo, Brazil, 1990), 19.

13. Landau, "My Life Story," 20.

14. Ilza Czapska, "Unser Weg von Obra nach Brasilien: 25 Jahre in Brasilien" (manuscript, private collection, São Paulo, Brazil, 1982), 6.

15. Renée-Marie Croose Parry, "Escape, Hope, and Disillusionment" (manuscript, private collection, Gainesville, Florida, 1992), 18–19.

16. Croose Parry, "Escape, Hope," 58.

17. Hilde Wiedemann, "Der Weg ist das Ziel" (manuscript, EB autogr. 328, Deutsche Bibliothek, Deutsches Exilarchiv, 1933–45, Frankfurt am Main), ch. 1.

18. Ethel Volfzon Kosminksy, "Rolandia, a terra prometida: Judeus refugiados do nazismo no Norte do Paraná." (São Paulo: Faculdade de Filosofia, Letras, e Ciências Humanas/Centro de Estudoes Judaicos-USP, 1985).

19. Israel Gutman, ed., *Encyclopedia of the Holocaust* (New York: Macmillan, 1990), vol. 4, 1258.

20. Brodzki and Schenck, eds., *Life/Lines*, 322.

21. Wiedemann, "Der Weg ist das Ziel," ch. 46.

22. Alice Brill Czapski, "Memories from 1933–1945" (manuscript, private collection, São Paulo, Brazil, 1991), 3.

23. Czapska, "Unser Weg," 1.

Trudi Landau, Introduction

1. Raul Hilberg, *The Destruction of the European Jews* (New York: Holmes and Meier, 1985), vol. 1, 16–17.

2. Ibid., 17–19.

3. Ibid., 18.

4. Ibid., 21–22.

5. Karl A. Schleunes, *The Twisted Road to Auschwitz* (Chicago: University of Illinois Press, 1990), 21–22.

6. Ibid., 29.

7. Monika Richarz, ed., *Jewish Life in Germany: Memoirs from Three Centuries* (Bloomington: Indiana University Press, 1991), 1.

8. Hilberg, *European Jews*, vol. 1, 98.

9. Claudia Koonz, *Mothers in the Fatherland* (New York: St. Martin's Press, 1987), 354.

10. Hilberg, *European Jews*, vol. 1, 100.

11. Landau, "My Life Story," (manuscript, private collection, São Paulo, Brazil, 1990), 6.

12. Albert Joseph's fate is documented in Serge Klarsfeld, *Le Mémorial de la Déportation des Juifs de France* (New York: B. Klarsfeld Foundation, 1978).

13. See Trudi Landau, *Vlado Herzog—O que faltava contar* (Petrópolis, Rio de Janeiro: Vozes, 1986).

Notes

Trudi Landau, Essay

1. This phrase was coined by the Wilhelminian historian Heinrich von Treitschke. See the introduction to Landau's essay.

Ilza Czapska, Introduction

1. Nazi terms in German: *germanische Herrenrasse, jüdisch-bolschewistische Führungsschicht.*

2. *Raul Hilberg, The Destruction of the European Jews,* (New York: Holmes and Meier, 1985), vol. 1, 188.

3. Ibid., vol. 1, 191.

4. Ibid.

5. Ibid., vol. 1, 205.

6. Ibid., vol. 1, 206.

7. Israel Gutman, ed., *Encyclopedia of the Holocaust* (New York: Macmillan, 1990), vol. 4, 1633–35.

8. Ibid., 1634.

9. Ibid., 1635.

Ilza Czapska, Essay

1. Obra was the name of the village and estate located in the province of Poznan. The estate had been the property of the Czapski family for more than 100 years. At the time the story takes place in 1939, Juljan (Julek), the oldest son, is fourteen; Genia, the daughter, is thirteen; Janek, the youngest son, is three; and Evunja, the niece, is two.

2. Stare Wies is located approximately thirty kilometers from Warsaw.

3. Oo is the grandmother's nickname, mother-in-law of Ilza and Roma's aunt. She had a house on the farm and was the only member of the family who had not been baptized. Dyba was the driver of the family and on friendly terms with everyone.

4. Dobrzyca was an internment camp in western Poland between Breslau and Poznan.

5. They were discharged east of the Vistula (Weichsel) River about fifty kilometers away from Stare Wies, out in the country near Lublin.

Käte Kaphan, Introduction

1. Cited in Marion A. Kaplan, *The Making of the Jewish Middle Class, Women, Family, and Identity in Imperial Germany* (New York: Oxford University Press, 1991), 53. Rahel Straus, *Wir lebten in Deutschland: Erinnerungen einer deutschen Jüdin* (Stuttgart: Deutsche Verlaganstalt, 1962), 142.

2. Raul Hilberg, *The Destruction of the European Jews* (New York: Holmes and Meier, 1985), vol. 1, 166.

3. Karl A. Schleunes, *The Twisted Road to Auschwitz* (Chicago: University of Illinois Press, 1990), 106–7.

4. Ibid., 107–8.

5. Hilberg, *European Jews*, vol. 1, 166.

6. Ernst M. Manasse, "The Jewish Graveyard," *Southern Review* 22 (1986): 296–307.

Käte Kaphan, Essay

1. January 30, 1933 was the day of the *Machtergreifung*, or Hitler's seizure of power as Chancellor of the Third Reich.

Renée-Marie Croose Parry, Introduction

1. Christian Zentner and Friedemann Bedürftig, eds., *The Encyclopedia of the Third Reich* (New York: Macmillan, 1991), 531.
2. Claudia Koonz, *Mothers in the Fatherland* (New York: St. Martin's Press, 1987), 196.
3. Harold Osborne, ed., *The Oxford Companion to Twentieth-Century Art* (New York: Oxford University Press, 1981), 149.
4. Zentner and Bedürftig, *Encyclopedia of the Third Reich*, 185, 187.
5. Osborne, *Oxford Companion*, 149.

Renée-Marie Croose Parry, Essay

All notes in this essay are the author's.

1. As a writer for *Münchner Neueste Nachrichten*, my father Wilhelm Hausenstein had been informed from Switzerland that two of his colleagues, Erwein Freiherr von Aretin, the editor for home affairs, and Mr. Cossmann had been arrested in the course of a sudden purge of the paper, and sent to the concentration camp in Dachau, where they were held for many months.
2. As we learned recently, Rabbi Isaak Rülf intervened on behalf of these refugees by addressing an appeal to Bismarck. See letter, dated Memel, 2 September 1885, to Sr. Durchlaucht, dem Reichskanzler Fürsten Bismarck, from Rabbiner Dr. I. Rülf. (A copy of this letter is in the possession of Dr. Ingeborg Willke, professor in Comparative Education, Institute of Education, Ruhr-University at Bochum, who is writing a study on the life and work of Isaak Rülf.) In this letter, the Rabbi tried to persuade Bismarck to rescind the expulsion order of over two thirds of his Jewish community from Prussia.
3. Isaak Rülf, *Metaphysik*, vol. 1, *Wissenschaft des Weltgedankens*; vol. 2, *Wissenschaft der Gedankenwelt*; vol. 3, *Wissenschaft der Krafteinheit (Dynamo-Monismus)*; vol. 4, *Wissenschaft der Geisteseinheit (Pneumato-Monismus)*; vol. 5, *Wissenschaft der Gotteseinheit (Theo-Monismus)* (Leipzig: Hermann Haacke, ca. 1897–1904).
4. Wilhelm Hausenstein, *Kunstgeschichte* (Berlin: Deutsche Buch-Gemeinschaft, 1928).
5. *Reichsschriftumskammer.*
6. Thea Lethmair, "Die Frauenbeilage der 'Frankfurter Zeitung': Ihre Struktur—ihre geistigen Grundlagen" (The Woman's Supplement of the 'Frankfurter Zeitung': Its Structure—Its Intellectual Foundations), Ph.D. diss., University of Munich, 1956.
7. Fred Hepp, "Der Geistige Widerstand im Kulturteil der 'Frankfurter Zeitung' gegen die Diktatur des totalen Staates 1933–1943" (The Spiritual Resistance in the Cultural Coverage of the Frankfurter Zeitung Against the Dictatorship of the Totalitarian State, 1933–1943), Ph.D. diss., University of Munich, 1949.
8. In *Herbstlaub*, by Johann Armbruster, 16 (Fulda: Parzeller and Co., 1947). (Johann Armbruster was one of Wilhelm Hausenstein's many pseudonyms adopted during the Nazi regime.) A revised version of the essay appeared in *Der Traum vom Zwerg*, by Wilhelm Hausenstein, 5 (München: R. Piper and Co., 1957).
9. A film was made of these executions, and it has been reported that Hitler demanded to view this macabre documentary many times.

Notes

10. The original of the second letter of January 22, 1945, with my father's filing note, resides in the literary estate of Wilhelm Hausenstein at Deutsches Literaturarchiv, Marbach am Neckar, Germany.

11. Wilhelm Hausenstein, *Licht unter dem Horizont—Tagebücher von 1942 bis 1946* (Light under the Horizon—Diaries from 1942 to 1946) (Munich: Bruckmann Verlag, 1967), 308, 310–11. My translation.

12. My father knew the director of the Meisterschule für Mode through his past contacts as editor of *Die Frau*, the Woman's Supplement of the old *Frankfurter Zeitung*, of which he was still the editor, albeit under the name of his assistant to keep out of Goebbels's eyes.

13. Georg Graf von Hertling, born in Darmstadt in 1843, was for many years a member of the Reichstag. From 1909 he was chairman of the Center Party (Zentrumsfraktion), and Bavarian minister president in 1912. From October 1917 to October 1918, he was chancellor of Germany (Reichskanzler), and minister president of Prussia. In 1882 he became a philosophy professor at Munich University and made valuable contributions to the history of philosophy. He translated, and wrote the introduction to, *The Confessions of St. Augustine* (Freiburg im Breisgau: Herder and Co., 1905).

14. Erwin Rosenthal, our great friend and former neighbor in Munich, was a prominent antiquarian of rare books and manuscripts, as had been his father, Jacques Rosenthal. He eventually moved to Berkeley, California, before settling in Switzerland, where he owned L'art Ancien in Zürich.

15. Wilhelm Hausenstein, "Vom Vater Gemalt," *Die Frau, supplement of Frankfurther Zeitung*, December 28, 1942; "Portrait by a Father," by Domingos Antonio de Segueira, Portuguese School of the XVIII and XIX Century, Lisbon, Museu das Janelas Verdes.

Hertha Spier, Introduction

1. James E. Young, *Writing and Rewriting the Holocaust* (Bloomington: Indiana University Press, 1988), 38.

2. Israel Gutman, ed., *Encyclopedia of the Holocaust* (New York: Macmillan, 1990), vol. 3, 1141.

3. Esther Katz and Joan Miriam Ringelheim, eds., *Proceedings of the Conference on Women Surviving the Holocaust* (New York: Institute for Research in History, 1983), 17–18.

4. Marlene E. Heinemann, *Gender and Destiny: Women Writers and the Holocaust* (New York: Greenwood Press, 1986), 17. See also Sybil Milton, "Women and the Holocaust: The Case of German and German-Jewish Women," in *When Biology Became Destiny*, ed. Renate Bridenthal, Atina Grossman, and Marion Kaplan (New York: Monthly Review Press, 1984), 297–333.

5. Heinemann, *Gender and Destiny*, 29.

6. Milton, "Women and the Holocaust," 313.

7. Gutman, *Encyclopedia of the Holocaust*, vol. 1, 188.

8. Raul Hilberg, *The Destruction of the European Jews* (New York: Holmes and Meier, 1985), vol. 3, 971.

9. Terrence Des Pres, *The Survivor: An Anatomy of Life in the Death Camps* (New York: Oxford University Press, 1976), 192.

10. Gitta Sereny, *Into That Darkness* (New York: McGraw-Hill, 1974), 183. See also, Des Pres, *Survivor*, 191–92.

Hertha Spier, Essay

1. Die Juden ziehen daher?
   Sie ziehen durchs rote Meer.
   Die Wellen schlagen zu.
   Die Welt hat Ruh.
2. Amon Goeth's official title was *SS Hauptsturmführer* (captain).
3. Presumably *Untersturmführer* (second lieutenant) Leo John.
4. Prisoners streamed in from January to March 1945, the camp administration made no attempt to house them, and a typhus epidemic raged. In the month of March 1945, 18,168 prisoners died. The British army liberated Bergen-Belsen on April 15, 1945. Israel Gutman, ed., *Encyclopedia of the Holocaust* (New York: Macmillan, 1990), vol. 1, 189.
5. After liberation, Bergen-Belsen became a displaced persons' camp. The "formerly occupied SS camp" probably had the best facilities in Bergen-Belsen. The headquarters of the camp commandant and SS camp were separate from the various prisoners' camps.

Eva Hirschberg, Introduction

1. Israel Gutman, ed., *Encyclopedia of the Holocaust* (New York: Macmillan, 1990), vol. 1, 281.
2. Ibid, 282. See also Alfred Hirschberg, "Der Centralverein deutscher Staatsbürger jüdischen Glaubens," in *Festschrift für Leo Baeck* (Berlin, 1970).
3. Karl A. Schleunes, *The Twisted Road to Auschwitz* (Chicago: University of Illinois Press, 1990), 126.
4. Claudia Koonz, *Mothers in the Fatherland* (New York: St. Martin's Press, 1987), 349.
5. Esther Katz and Joan Miriam Ringelheim, eds., *Proceedings of the Conference on Women Surviving the Holocaust* (New York: Institute for Research in History, 1983), 11.
6. Ibid., 12.
7. Ibid.

Eva Hirschberg, Essay

1. Ernst vom Rath was the secretary of the German embassy in Paris. Herschel Grynszpan, a seventeen-year-old Jew who was living in Paris, attacked him after hearing that the Reich government had deported at least 15,000 Jews with Polish passports on October 28, 1938. The National Socialists used this as an excuse for the *Kristallnacht* of November 9–10, 1938.
2. The *Polizeihauptquartier* (police headquarters) was located at the Alexanderplatz. The Jews were taken here and detained.
3. The author remembers this decree to have been in late 1938.

Olga Benario, Introduction

1. Fernando Morais, *Olga*, trans. Ellen Watson (New York: Grove Press, 1990), 241–42.

Notes

Hilde Wiedemann, Introduction

1. Thomas E. Skidmore and Peter H. Smith, *Modern Latin America* (New York: Oxford University Press, 1984), 167.
2. Ibid., 166–68.
3. Ibid., 168–69.
4. Jeffrey H. Lesser, "Pawns of the Powerful: Jewish Immigration to Brazil, 1904–1945," (Ph.D. diss., New York University, 1989), 219.
5. Wolfgang Frühwald and Wolfgang Schieder, eds., *Leben im Exil* (Hamburg: Hoffmann, 1981); Wolfgang Kießling, *Exil in Lateinamerika* (Leipzig: Reclam, 1981); Herbert Strauss and Werner Röder, eds., *International Biographical Dictionary of Central European Emigrés 1933–45* Munich: K. G. Saur, 1983), vol. 2, 22, 34.
6. Robert M. Levine, "Brazil's Jews During the Vargas Era and After," *Luso-Brazilian Review* 5, no. 1 (1968): 53.

Hilde Wiedemann, Essay

1. The problem was that if there was a tap running downstairs, there would be no water upstairs due to lack of water pressure.

Alice Brill Czapski, Introduction

1. Israel Gutman, ed., *Encyclopedia of the Holocaust* (New York: Macmillan, 1990), vol. 3, 984.
2. David Bridger, ed., *The New Jewish Encyclopedia* (New York: Behrman House, 1962), 191.

Alice Brill Czapski, Essay

All notes in this essay are the author's.

1. "Permanent residence" as opposed to "temporary residence" for tourists; permanent residence meant that one could become a resident and stay in the country.

Annelise Strauss, Introduction

1. Annelise Strauss, "A Story of My Life" (manuscript, private collection, São Paulo, Brazil, 1991).
2. *Enyclopaedia Judaica* (Jerusalem: McMillan, 1971), vol. 15, 1539.
3. Israel Gutman, ed., *Encyclopedia of the Holocaust* (New York: Macmillan, 1990), vol. 2, 657, 752; *Encyclopaedia Judaica*, 1539.
4. Robert M. Levine, "Brazil's Jews During the Vargas Era and After," *Luso-Brazilian Review* 5, no. 1 (1968): 53.
5. Jeffrey Lesser, *Welcoming the Undesirables: Brazil and the Jewish Question* (Berkeley: University of California Press, 1994), 118–19. See also Alfred Hirschberg, "The Economic Adjustment of Jewish Refugees in São Paulo," *Jewish Social Studies* 7 (January, 1945): 37.
6. Lesser, *Welcoming the Undesirables*, 100–102.
7. Ibid., 117–19.
8. Ibid., 100–103, 120.
9. Robert M. Levine, *The Vargas Regime* (New York: Columbia University Press, 1970), 154.

10. Lesser, *Welcoming the Undesirables*, 121.
11. Levine, "Brazil's Jews," 55.

Annelise Strauss, Essay

1. "Sons of the Covenant." This was an independent Jewish fraternal order, founded in New York in 1843. By the 1930s there were over 100 lodges in Germany. The basic functions of the B'nai B'rith included charity, education, and social events.

2. Dr. Gärtner was the rabbi in Braunschweig during Annelise Herzberg's last years in Germany. According to the author, he emigrated to the United States and settled in New York.

Käte Kaphan, Introduction

1. For further information, see Mathilde Maier, *Alle Gärten meines Lebens* (Frankfurt: Josef Knecht Verlag, 1978) and Max Hermann Maier, *Ein Frankfurter Rechtsanwalt wird Kaffeepflanzer im Urwald Brasiliens: Bericht eines Emigranten 1938–1975* (Frankfurt: Josef Knecht Verlag, 1975).

Renée-Marie Croose Parry, Introduction

1. Robert M. Levine, "Brazil's Jews during the Vargas Era," *Luso-Brazilian Review* 5, no. 1 (1968): 54.
2. Levine, "Brazil's Jews," 54.
3. Thomas E. Skidmore and Peter H. Smith, *Modern Latin America* (New York: Oxford University Press, 1984), 171.
4. Robert M. Levine, *The Vargas Regime* (New York: Columbia University Press, 1970), 172.
5. Levine, *The Vargas Regime*, 167.
6. Ibid., 177; Skidmore and Smith, *Modern Latin America*, 170.

Renée-Marie Croose Parry, Essay

All notes in this essay are the author's.

1. GOVERNESS—Young lady recently arrived from Europe, requires position in family of good standing, taking care of children. Would teach French. Please reply by tel. 42-4708.

2. *Carióca* is used to describe the inhabitants of Rio, and is derived from an expression in the Tupi Indian language, meaning "house of the white man."

3. Susanne Bach, née Eisenberg, describes her escape from Germany to France in 1933, and to Brazil in 1941, in an autobiographic account, *Karussell—Von München nach München*. Frauen in der Einen Welt, Sonderband 2 (Nürnberg: Zentrum für interkulturelle Frauenalltagsforschung und internationalen Austausch, 1991). A seasoned antiquarian, she was to found the first professional export business of Brazilian literature to Europe, the United States, Canada, and Japan. In the seventies she added to her catalogue literature written by German exiles in Brazil. She now resides in Munich, but spends three months each year in Rio de Janeiro, working with her business.

4. Alberto Dines, *Morte no Paraíso—A tragédia de Stefan Zweig* (Death in Paradise—The Tragedy of Stefan Zweig) (Rio de Janeiro: Editora Nova Fronteira, 1981), 449.

5. "Perspectives of Brazil," an *Atlantic Monthly* supplement, edited by Carleton Sprague Smith (Intercultural Publications, Inc., 1956), 7.

6. Unbeknownst to me at the time, Hans G. Pauls was the correspondent for the *Frankfurter Zeitung* in Switzerland.

7. [. . .] several very moving speeches celebrated his sixty years. An atmosphere of affection and respect made him aware of how much he is loved and appreciated.

8. Fernando Morais, *Olga—Das Leben einer mutigen Frau*, (Olga—The Life of a Courageous Woman) (Köln: Volksblatt Verlag, 1989), 339; originally published as *Olga* (São Paulo: Editora Alfa-Omega, 1985). The author became minister of culture for the State of São Paulo in 1988.

9. Wilhelm Hausenstein, *Kairuan oder die Geschichte vom Maler Klee und von der Kunst dieses Zeitalters* (Munich: Kurt Wolff Verlag, 1921).

10. Dines, *Morte no Paraíso*, 52, 218, 219, 221, 252.

11. Morais, *Olga*, 99, 163–97, 247, 322, 347.

12. Ibid., 328–37.

13. Georg Wassermann as distinguished from Jakob Wassermann who died in Altaussee in 1934.

14. *The Prose of Oscar Wilde*, edited by Albert and Charles Boni (Bonibooks Series, 1935), 757, 756, 749, 762, 755, and 788 respectively all from "De Profundis."

15. For further details surrounding these circumstances see Günther Gillessen, *Auf verlorenem Posten—Die Frankfurter Zeitung im Dritten Reich* (Berlin: Wolf Jobst Siedler Verlag, 1986), 481.

16. Pantheon Books, Inc., founded in 1942. See Michael Ermath, ed., *Kurt Wolff— A Portrait in Essays and Letters* (Chicago: University of Chicago Press, 1991), xxv–xxvii.

17. Wilhelm Hausenstein, *Zwiegespräch über den Don Quichote*, (Dialogue about Don Quixote) (Munich: Kösel Verlag, 1948). Quelho Benton was to assemble a German speaking audience of some 200 people for an evening in appreciation of my father's oeuvre, with readings from this book.

Trudi Landau, Introduction

1. Israel Gutman, ed., *Encyclopedia of the Holocaust* (New York: Macmillan, 1990), vol. 4, 1256.

2. Ibid.

3. Ibid, 1255–59. See also Nana Sagi, *German Reparations: A History of the Negotiations* (New York: St. Martin's Press), 1986.

4. Gutman, *Encyclopedia of the Holocaust*, 1256.

5. Ibid., 1257.

6. Ibid., 1258.

7. Ibid., 1259.

BIBLIOGRAPHY

Primary Sources

Croose Parry, Renée-Marie. "Escape, Hope, and Disillusionment." Manuscript. Gainesville, Florida, 1992.

Czapska, Ilza. "Unser Weg von Obra nach Brasilien, 25 Jahre in Brasilien." Manuscript. Private collection of Alice Brill Czapski. São Paulo, Brazil, 1982.

Czapski, Alice Brill. "Memories from 1933–1945." Manuscript. Private collection. São Paulo, Brazil, 1991.

Hirschberg, Eva. "Als die Männer im Lager waren." Manuscript. Private collection. São Paulo, Brazil, 1975.

Kaphan, Käte. "Das kleine Judenmädchen." "Immigration into the Brazilian Jungle." Manuscripts. Private collection. Rolândia, Brazil, 1956.

Landau, Trudi. "My Life Story." Manuscript. Private collection. São Paulo, Brazil, 1990.

Morais, Fernando. *Olga.* Trans. Ellen Watson. New York: Grove Press, 1990. Originally published as *Olga* (São Paulo: Editora Alfa-Omega, 1985).

Spier, Hertha. "Das Leben in Auschwitz und Bergen-Belsen." Manuscript. Private collection. Porto Alegre, Brazil, 1957.

Strauss, Annelise. "A Story of My Life." Manuscript. Private collection. São Paulo, Brazil, 1991.

Wiedemann, Hilde. "Der Weg ist das Ziel." Manuscript EB autogr. 328, Deutsche Bibliothek, Deutsches Exilarchiv, 1933–45, Frankfurt am Main.

Autobiographical Sources

Bach, Susanne. *Karussell: von München nach München.* Frauen in der Einen Welt. Sonderband 2. Nürnberg: Zentrum für interkulturelle Frauenalltagsforschung und internationalen Austausch, 1991.

Brill, Marthe. "Der Schmelztiegel." Manuscript #318. Institut für Zeitgeschichte, Munich, 1966. Book-length manuscript of life in Brazil.

Eisenberg-Bach, Susi. *Im Schatten von Notre Dame.* London: World of Books, 1986.

Feder, Ernst. *Heute sprach ich mit . . .* Stuttgart: Deutsche Verlags-Anstalt, 1971.

Bibliography

Gruenbaum, Irene. *Escape through the Balkans.* Translated and edited by Katherine Morris. Lincoln: University of Nebraska Press, 1996.

Landau, Trudi. *Crônicas do meu Tempo.* São Paulo: Massao Ohono-Roswitha Kempf, 1981.

Ludwig, Paula. *Gedichte: Gesamtausgabe.* Ebenhausen bei München: Langewiesche-Brandt, 1986.

———. *Träume.* Ebenhausen bei München: Langewiesche-Brandt, 1962.

Maier, Mathilde. *Alle Gärten meines Lebens.* Frankfurt: Josef Knecht Verlag, 1978.

Maier, Max-Hermann. *Ein Frankfurter Rechtsanwalt wird Kaffeepflanzer im Urwald Brasiliens: Bericht eines Emigranten 1938–1975.* Frankfurt: Josef Knecht Verlag, 1975.

Manasse, Ernst M. "The Jewish Graveyard." *Southern Review* 22 (1986): 296–307.

Patai, Daphne. *Brazilian Women Speak.* New Brunswick: Rutgers University Press, 1988.

Rosenblatt, Sônia. *Lembranças Enevoadas.* Recife: Editora de Pernambuco, 1984.

Rosenthal, Inge. "The Kindertransport, Das Leben auf dem Fazenda." Manuscript. Private collection. Rolândia, Brazil, 1989.

Salmoni, Anita. *Você voltaria?* São Paulo: Editora Shalom, 1979.

Schauff, Karin. *Brasilianischer Garten.* Pfullingen: Neske Verlag, 1970.

———. *Schreib mir alles Mutter.* Pfullingen: Neske Verlag, 1987.

Critical Studies

Basseches, Bruno. *Bibliografia dos livros, folhetos e artigos referente a história dos judeus no Brasil, incluindo as obras sobre judaismo publicadas no Brasil.* Rio de Janeiro, 1961.

Benstock, Shari, ed. *The Private Self: Theory and Practice of Women's Autobiographical Writings.* Chapel Hill, North Carolina: University of North Carolina Press, 1988.

Bentes, Abraham Ramiro. *As ruínas de Jerusalem a verdejante Amazonia.* Rio de Janeiro: Editora Bloch, 1987.

Billson, Marcus. "The Memoir: New Perspectives on a Forgotten Genre." *Genre* 2, no. 2 (1977): 259–82.

Breunig, Bernd. *Die deutsche Rolandwanderung* [1932–80]. Munich: Nymphenburger Verlag, 1983.

Bridenthal, Renate, Atina Grossmann, and Marion Kaplan. *When Biology Became Destiny.* New York: Monthly Review Press, 1984.

Brodzki, Bella, and Celeste Schenck, eds. *Life/Lines: Theorizing Women's Autobiography.* Ithaca, Cornell University Press, 1988.

Carneiro, Maria Luiza Tucci. *O anti-semitismo na era Vargas.* São Paulo: Editora Brasiliense, 1988.

Cernyak-Spatz, Susan E. *German Holocaust Literature.* New York: Peter Lang, 1985.

Critchfield, Richard. "Einige Überlegungen zur Problematik der Exilautobiographik" in *Exilforschung, ein internationales Jahrbuch,* ed. Thomas Koebner, Wulf Köpke, and Joachim Radkau. Munich: Gesellschaft für Exilforschung, 1984, vol. 2, 41–55.

Des Pres, Terrence. *The Survivor: An Anatomy of Life in the Death Camps.* New York: Oxford University Press, 1976.

Encyclopaedia Judaica. Jerusalem: McMillan, 1971.

Falbel, Nachman. *Estudos sobre a comunidade judaica no Brasil.* São Paulo: Federação Israelita do Estado de São Paulo, 1984.

Foley, Barbara. "Fact, Fiction, Fascism: Testimony and Mimesis in Holocaust Narratives." *Comparative Literature* 34 (1982): 330–65.

Fouquet, Karl. *Kulturelle Vereinigungen im brasilianisch- deutschen Bereich.Vortrag 1969 in Rolandia.* São Paulo: Instituto Hans Staden, n.d.

Frankenstein, Herbert. *Brasilien als Aufnahmeland der jüdischen Auswanderung aus Deutsch- land*. Berlin: Joseph Jastrow Verlagsbuchhandlung, 1936.
Frühwald, Wolfgang, and Schieder, Wolfgang, eds. *Leben im Exil*. Hamburg: Hoffmann und Campe Verlag, 1981.
Gilbert, Martin. *Atlas of the Holocaust*. New York: Pergamon Press, 1988.
Gordan, Paulus, ed. *Um der Freiheit Willen. Festschrift Johannes und Karin Schauff*. Pfullin- gen: Neske Verlag, 1983.
Gutman, Israel, ed. *Encyclopedia of the Holocaust*. 4 vols. New York: Macmillan, 1990.
Heilbrun, Carolyn G. *Writing a Woman's Life*. New York: Ballantine Books, 1988.
Heinemann, Marlene E. *Gender and Destiny: Women Writers and the Holocaust*. New York: Greenwood Press, 1986.
Hilberg, Raul. *The Destruction of the European Jews*. 3 vols. New York: Holmes and Meier, 1985.
Hirschberg, Alfred. "Report from Brazil." *Dispersion and Resettlement: The Story of the Jews from Central Europe*. London: Association of Jewish Refugees in Great Britain, 1955.
Hirschberg, Alice Irene. *Desafio e resposta: A história da Congregação Israelita Paulista*. São Paulo: Congregação Israelita Paulista, 1976.
Kaplan, Marion A. *The Making of the Jewish Middle Class: Women, Family, and Identity in Imperial Germany*. New York: Oxford University Press, 1991.
Katz, Esther, and Joan Miriam Ringelheim, eds. *Proceedings of the Conference on Women Surviving the Holocaust*. New York: Institute for Research in History, 1983.
Kießling, Wolfgang. *Exil in Lateinamerika*. Leipzig: Reclam, 1981.
Kohut, Karl, and Patrik von zur Mühlen, eds. *Alternative Lateinamerika: Das deutsche Exil in der Zeit des Nationalsozialismus*. Frankfurt am Main: Vervuert Verlag, 1994.
Koonz, Claudia. *Mothers in the Fatherland*. New York: St. Martin's Press, 1987.
Kosminsky, Ethel Volfzon. "Rolândia, a terra prometida: Judeus refugiados do nazismo no norte do Paraná." São Paulo: Faculdade de Filosofia, Letras, e Ciências Humanas/Centro de Estudos Judaicos-USP, 1985.
Kreis, Gabriele. *Frauen im Exil: Dichtung und Wirklichkeit*. Düsseldorf: Claasen, 1984.
Lesser, Jeffrey. "Continuity and Change within an Immigrant Community: The Jews of São Paulo, 1924–1945." *Luso- Brazilian Review* 25, no. 2 (1988): 45–58.
———. *Welcoming the Undesirables: Brazil and the Jewish Question*. Berkeley: University of California Press, 1994.
Levine, Robert M. "Brazil's Jews during the Vargas Era and After." *Luso-Brazilian Review* 5, no. 1 (1968): 45- 58.
———. *The Vargas Regime*. New York: Columbia University Press, 1970.
Lixl-Purcell, Andreas, ed. *Women of Exile*. New York: Greenwood Press, 1988.
Martin, Elaine, ed. *Gender, Patriarchy, and Fascism in the Third Reich: The Response of Women Writers*. Detroit: Wayne State University Press, 1993.
Miller, Judith. *One by One by One: The Landmark Exploration of the Holocaust and the Uses of Memory*. New York: Simon and Schuster, 1990.
Moeller, Hans-Bernhard, ed. *Latin America and the Literature of Exile*. Heidelberg: Win- ter, 1983.
Mühlen, Patrick von zur. *Deutsches Exil in Lateinamerika*. Bonn: Friedrich Ebert-Stiftung, 1985.
———. *Fluchtziel Lateinamerika. Die deutsche Emigration 1933–45: Politische Aktivitäten und soziokulturelle Integration*. Bonn: Neve Gesellschaft, 1988.
Personal Narratives Group, ed. *Interpreting Women's Lives*. Bloomington: Indiana Uni- versity Press, 1989.
Pohle, Fritz. *Das mexikanische Exil*. Stuttgart: Metzler, 1986.

Bibliography

Quack, Sibylle, ed. *Between Sorrow and Strength: Women Refugees of the Nazi Period.* New York: Cambridge University Press, 1995.

Richarz, Monika, ed. *Jewish Life in Germany: Memoirs from Three Centuries.* Bloomington: Indiana University Press, 1991.

Rupp, Leila. *Mobilizing Women for War.* Princeton: Princeton University Press, 1978.

Schleunes, Karl A. *The Twisted Road to Auschwitz.* Chicago: University of Illinois Press, 1990.

Skidmore, Thomas E. *The Politics of Military Rule in Brazil, 1964–85.* New York: Oxford University Press, 1988.

Skidmore, Thomas E., and Peter H. Smith. *Modern Latin America.* New York: Oxford University Press, 1984.

Smith, Sidonie. *A Poetics of Women's Autobiography.* Bloomington: Indiana University Press, 1988.

Strauss, Herbert, and Werner Röder, eds. *International Biographical Dictionary of Central European Emigrés 1933–45.* 3 vols. Munich: K. G. Saar, 1983.

Walter, Hans-Albert. *Deutsche Exilliteratur 1933–1950.* Darmstadt: Luchterhand, 1973.

Young, James E. *Writing and Rewriting the Holocaust.* Bloomington: Indiana University Press, 1988.

Zentner, Christian and Friedemann Bedürftig, eds. *The Encyclopedia of the Third Reich.* New York: Macmillan, 1991.

Zimmer, Rainer. "Zur Autobiographik des Exils 1933–1945." In *Faschismus, Kritik, und Deutschland,* ed. Christian Fritsch, 214–27. Berlin: Argument, 1981.

INDEX

Academia Goetheana, São Paulo (Goethe Academy), 230
Adenauer, Konrad, 239
Alexanderplatz, 119, 122, 124, 250n. 2
American Jewish Joint Distribution Committee, 164
Anti-Semitism, 15–16, 24–25, 32, 35, 68–69, 117–18; in the eighteenth and nineteenth centuries, 24–25; in the German educational system, 68–69, 79–80, 147; in government policy, 25–26; in the 1920s, 116; propaganda, 15–16, 31
Aranha, Oswaldo, 13, 164; and anti-communism, 164; and anti-Semitism, 164; as Brazilian ambassador, 164, 171, 172; and philo-Semitism, 164
Art, degenerate, 75, 84
Auschwitz, 15, 31,104, 105, 109
Auschwitz-Birkenau (women's camp), 105
Autobiography, theory of, 12–14, 24

Bach, Susanne, 189, 191, 220, 252n. 3
Balkan campaign, 91
Benario, Olga, 10, 164, 201, 209–10, 211
Ben-Gurion, David, 20
Benton, José António Quelho, 230
Bergen-Belsen, 104, 105, 112; and liberation, 113, 250n. 4; and SS camp, 113, 250n. 5
Bernburg, 126, 127, 210

Bertina, Martha, 84
Braun, Otto, 126
Brazil: and the Allies, 19, 131, 139, 164, 180, 190, 192, 200; and American cultural influence, 144; and anti-communism, 95, 126, 164, 200; and anti-Semitism, 95, 131–32, 164, 165, 179–80; and the Catholic Church, 19, 181, 194, 227, 232; and dictatorship, 19, 131, 179; and the Estado Nôvo, 131–32, 159, 164, 179–80; and European women, 10; and exile, 10–11; and German immigrants, 94, 131–32, 142–44, 160, 180, 186; and immigration 13–14, 131–32, 164, 171, 179–80; map of, 18; in the 1940s, 20–22; and politics, 130–32, 164, 180; port of Santos, 20, 130, 175; and relations with Nazi Germany, 75, 97, 130–32, 138–39, 179–80; and treatment of women, 19, 126, 139–40, 178–80, 187–88, 213–14, 232; and U.S. Intelligence, 204, 220, 226
Brendel, Georg, 86
Brendel, Günther, 86
Brill, Erich, 14, 146, 147, 159, 161
Brill, Marthe, 14, 146, 148, 154
Brill, Sophie, 148, 161
Buber, Martin, 147
Bühler, Ellen, 91–92, 202

Index

Warthegau (territorial administrative unit), 37–38
Wawel Castle (Krakow), 107
Weizmann, Chaim, 238
Wertheimer, Stefan, 205–6, 218, 220
Wiedemann, Dorothea, 133
Wiedemann, Elisabeth, 138
Wiedemann, Ursula, 138
Wiedemann, Wilhelm, 133, 136
Wiedergutmachung. See Restitution
Wise, Stephan, 166
Wolff, Helen, 226
Wolff, Kurt, 195, 197, 226

Women: in the Brazilian women's prison of Bangú, 212–16; and concentration camps, 104–6; and dependence on other women, 15, 105, 117, 125; and emigration, 14, 125; and gender-related skills, 14, 105, 111-13; as victims of sexism, 10, 180

Yishuv, 239

Ziegler, Adolf, 75
Zweig, Stefan, 191, 230, 252n. 4

www.ingramcontent.com/pod-product-compliance
Lightning Source LLC
Chambersburg PA
CBHW050647270326
41927CB00012B/2905